# HIDDEN
# POSSIBILITIES

# HIDDEN POSSIBILITIES

## Essays in Honor of Muriel Spark

*Edited by*

ROBERT E. HOSMER JR.

*University of Notre Dame Press*

*Notre Dame, Indiana*

Manufactured in the United States of America

Robert E. Hosmer Jr., "'Fascinated by Suspense': An Interview with Muriel Spark," originally appeared in a slightly different version in *Salmagundi* (Spring–Summer 2005). Copyright © Robert E. Hosmer Jr.

John Lanchester, "In Sparkworld," originally appeared in the *New York Review of Books*, November 18, 2004. Reprinted by permission of *The New York Review of Books*.

Doris Lessing, "Now You See Her, Now You Don't," originally appeared in *Time Bites: Views and Reviews* (London: Fourth Estate, 2004). Copyright © 2004 by Doris Lessing. Reprinted by kind permission of Jonathan Clowes Ltd., London, on behalf of Doris Lessing.

Frank Kermode, "Unrivalled Deftness: The Novels of Muriel Spark," originally appeared as the introduction to Muriel Spark, *The Prime of Miss Jean Brodie; The Girls of Slender Means; The Driver's Seat; The Only Problem* (New York: Everyman's Library, Random House, 2004). Reprinted by permission of Everyman's Library, Random House, 2004.

John Mortimer, "The Culture of an Anarchist: An Interview with Muriel Spark," originally appeared in the *Telegraph Sunday Magazine*, March 20, 1988. Reprinted by permission of the *Sunday Telegraph*, The Telegraph Group Ltd., 1 Canada Square, Canary Wharf, London E14 5DT.

Muriel Spark, "What," "Elegy in a Kensington Churchyard," and excerpt from "The Grave That Time Dug," reprinted by permission of Muriel Spark, Penelope Jardine, and Georges Borchardt, Inc.

John Updike, "Stonewalling Toffs," originally appeared in *The New Yorker*, February 12, 2001, copyright © 2001 John Updike. It has also appeared in John Updike, *Due Considerations: Essays and Criticisms* (New York: Alfred A. Knopf, 2007). Copyright © 2007 by John Updike. Used by permission of Alfred A. Knopf, a division of Random House, Inc.

*Library of Congress Cataloging-in-Publication Data*

Hosmer, Robert E.
Hidden Possibilities : Essays in Honor of Muriel Spark / Robert Ellis Hosmer.
    pages   cm
Includes bibliographical references and index.
ISBN-13: 978-0-268-03099-5 (paperback)
ISBN-10: 0-268-03099-5 (paper)
1. Spark, Muriel—Criticism and interpretation.   I. Title.
PR6037.P29Z68   2014
823'.914—dc23

2013044542

# CONTENTS

## THE LIFE

## ACKNOWLEDGMENTS

This book would never have seen the light of print without the support of a number of people, and I take this opportunity to acknowledge them and express my gratitude:

To Dame Muriel Spark, D. B. E., and Penelope Jardine, for patient and generous support at every stage of work;

To Susan C. Bourque, Esther Booth Wiley Professor of Government and Provost/Dean of the Faculty at Smith College, for granting me a sabbatical to begin this project; and to her successor, Marilyn R. Schuster, Andrew W. Mellon Professor in the Humanities, for granting me another sabbatical and her generous support and encouragement;

To Charles P. Staelin, professor of economics and dean for Academic Development, for research, printing, and permissions funding; and to his successor, John Davis, professor of art, for his assistance;

To the reference staff of the William Allan Neilson Library, Smith College, for patient, professional assistance with research;

To Christina Lovely, for meticulous copyediting of the manuscript; and to Wendy McMillen in production;

To five Smith women—Joanna Patterson '03, Candi Deschamps '05, Amanda Houpt '05, Sally Reede '08, and Julia Whiting '14—whose skills at research and text preparation proved indispensable, time and again;

To all fourteen contributors to this volume, for meticulous scholarship, generosity, and patience;

To my late father, Robert Ellis Hosmer, and my late mother, Eileen M. Ryan Hosmer, for unwavering support and affection: this book is for them.

# Introduction

ROBERT E. HOSMER JR.

Scanning the long shelf of my bookcase packed with copies
of all of Muriel Spark's books, then turning to my files of research
materials on her work, I think back, remembering how it all began.
First, while in graduate school writing a dissertation about Anglo-
Saxon poetry, I sought some diversion by reading novels by a number of contemporary British women writers—Bainbridge, Brookner,
Carter, Figes, Fitzgerald, and Lively impressed me, but none as much
as Muriel Spark, with her sly wit, absolute control of plot and often
outrageous characters, inimitable voice, and meditation on great
themes. In a professional literary career that extended from the late
1940s until her death, Dame Muriel wrote poems, stories, plays, novels, and essays that have given immense and varied pleasure. A glance
at the extensive bibliography of her works reveals the astonishing output of a powerful and sustained creative spirit pitched at a high note
until the end.

Riffling through my Spark volumes, I am almost certain that *Not
to Disturb* (1971), that audaciously divine fable of plots and plot-
makers, with time past, present, and future collapsed into an eternal
now and presided over by a Prospero-like butler, introduced me to

the fictional world of Muriel Spark. Without agenda or system, I made my way through what had already been published (*The Comforters* [1957] through *Loitering with Intent* [1981]). When *The Only Problem* appeared (1984), its preoccupation with the problem of suffering and the Book of Job, a focus of my graduate work in religion, prompted me to write what would be my first published article. When *A Far Cry from Kensington* came along (1988), I reviewed it for *Commonweal*; shortly afterward, the literary editor, Rev. David Toolan S.J., commissioned a long essay for a series on Catholic writers: "Muriel Spark: Writing with Intent" (1989) was the result. Thereafter I read each new book and occasionally included one or two in my teaching.

Little did I know that Muriel Spark read what I had written. Penelope Jardine, her extraordinary secretary, saw to it that every word published about Spark's work came to her attention and became part of an extensive file of clippings. I do not know who wrote first. I expect I did, likely in connection with the essay for *Commonweal*; but a frequent correspondence ensued, first by air mail letter, then by fax, and continued until just several weeks before her death on April 13, 2006. In her correspondence she was very much the writer of her fiction—precise, economical, and witty.

The first of several visits took place in March 1999 in connection with an interview commissioned by the *Paris Review* for its famous series, "Writers at Work." Miss Jardine met me at the Arezzo train station, south of Florence, and whisked me off into the Tuscan hills to her palatial (twenty-four-room) converted rectory that the two women shared. I was ushered into one of the house's sitting rooms to wait. Dame Muriel promptly appeared: elegantly coiffed, wearing a designer suit with silk scarf and stunning jewels, she made her way into the room aided by two walking sticks. We exchanged greetings and she sat down opposite me on a large, soft settee. I shall never forget her first words to me; with her eyes twinkling, a slightly flirtatious smile on her face, and in a musical voice that retained traces of Morningside, she said, "I want to thank you for your devotion to my work." Who could resist such charm? I could well believe the stories about her dazzling social life in New York in the mid-1960s and later in Rome. The parties she gave at her flat in the Palazzo Taverna, which happened to have a drawing room the size of a cricket pitch, or at another home, which she liked to tell guests had once been a house of ill repute, were legendary, with artists, film directors, writers, countesses, and cardinals from the Curia gliding in and out.

We did our work that snowy March day and had a lovely tea as well. Subsequent visits revealed a woman of great warmth, sophistication, and grace, always ready to talk about books, current events, religious controversies—really anything, since everything interested her. My first trip to Italy after Muriel's death was utterly strange. Penelope met me, as usual; before stopping at their house, we visited the grave site, a moving experience. The graveyard rests on the hill on the way "home" and looks out over the Tuscan hills with a view toward Assisi. Muriel's tomb is as precisely constructed and economically rendered as her fiction, a single verse from one of her poems the only words inscribed ("Nessun foglio si repete, ripettiamo solo la parola," "Not a leaf / Repeats itself, we only repeat the word") other than her name, dates, and the simple designation of "Poet" to mark her place among the Italian people she loved. They had returned that love earlier, making her an honorary citizen of the small village. And she had thanked them, in a way, by choosing to be buried among them on that windswept hill surrounded by olive trees.

This collection of essays was conceived as a way of partially repaying a great debt all readers have to this extraordinary writer, once described by David Lodge as "the most gifted and innovative British writer of her generation." I had hoped that she would live to see it completed so that I might have the pleasure of pressing the volume into her own hands; but such was not to be, though she did know that it was in preparation. Somehow, the woman who believed so deeply in what she called "another world than this" will see it. In some measure, it also represents partial repayment of my own debt, both personal and professional, to Muriel Spark.

I was gratified when my invitations to potential contributors met with enthusiastic, positive response. Fourteen distinguished contributors have joined me in this endeavor, each one of them generous, enthusiastic, and patient. I have chosen a simple arrangement for their contributions, dividing them into two sections: "The Work" and "The Life." Within "The Work" there are two principles of organization: the section begins with a broad intellectual and cultural focus, setting

Spark's work within the larger European traditions of thought and letters. The succeeding essays sharpen the focus and are chronologically ordered according to her publications, beginning with an essay on her poetry and ending with essays on her last two novels. Within "The Life" pieces follow a roughly chronological pattern for Spark's life, beginning with an essay about her early life and ending with one about her afterlife.

In "The Large Testimony of Muriel Spark," Gabriel Josipovici considers a half dozen of Spark's novels and sets her achievement within a rigorously intellectual and literary context (Kierkegaard, Becket, Proust, Sartre, Golding). Josipovici pays special attention to *Memento Mori* (1959), which, in its end-game grounding, serves him as a template for all of Spark's fiction. Each area of discussion moves gracefully and persuasively toward making a larger point as Josipovici argues that "she couches in Christian terms what is essentially a modernist enterprise." Spark emerges as a novelist of singular creativity and distinction.

Harold Pinter's lecture on the occasion of his receiving the Nobel Prize in 2005 prompted Joseph Hynes's reflection, "Muriel Spark's Fiction: A Context." Pinter's address, titled "Art, Truth and Politics," received a great deal of attention for the playwright's condemnation of U.S. foreign policy in Iraq (and elsewhere), but Hynes concerns himself with Pinter's philosophical statements about truth. After a quick summary of Western philosophical thought and its impact on literature, Hynes focuses attention on the work of Beckett, Sartre, and Robbe-Grillet and what he sees as their role in demolishing modernism and constructing postmodernisms. Against them stands Spark, a writer more "in tune with ancient Greece and the Christian Middle Ages," who rejected postmodernist notions of incertitude, relativism, and meaning and expanded the possibilities of fiction.

My own essay, "'A Spirit of Vast Endurance': Muriel Spark, Poet and Novelist," chronicles Muriel Spark's career as poet, beginning at age nine and continuing well into her ninth decade. Though Spark is certainly less well known as a poet and her four books of poetry are indeed outnumbered by her twenty-two novels (and other works), she still regarded herself as a poet and considered her novels to be poems.

At first, this may seem contradictory; but some explanation may lie in the writings of Cardinal Newman, the single greatest influence on Spark's life and thought. Years ago Dame Muriel declared, "it was by way of Newman that I turned Roman Catholic." My argument is that it was also by way of Newman that she turned poet-novelist.

With special concern for a number of the short stories, Regina Barreca ("Breaking Free of the Grave: Muriel Spark's Uses of Humor and the Supernatural") locates Spark's distinctive, even unique, story-telling in her "juxtaposition of the postmodern with the post-mortem," which infuses everything with potent humor. Professor Barreca's keen understanding of the dynamics of storytelling, and of joke-telling in particular, enables her to illuminate Spark's fiction in a fresh way. And her discussion of the ways in which Spark drew upon "Gothic traditions and these pre-Enlightenment beliefs to create an alchemy of her own" contextualizes the work while extending its significance. "Breaking Free of the Grave" appropriately liberates Spark and her fiction from the narrow confines of any ideology and elucidates the mesmerizing pleasures of one writer's timeless achievement.

In "'Fully to Savour Her Position': Muriel Spark and Scottish Identity," Gerard Carruthers affirms with scholarly depth and precision what Spark herself has asserted time and again: rejecting labels such as "English novelist" and "Catholic novelist," she was, she said, if anything, "a Scottish writer." In underscoring Spark's essential Scottish identity, Carruthers makes skillful and convincing use of James Hogg's *Private Memoirs and Confessions of a Justified Sinner* (1824), showing its formative impact on her fiction. Carruthers supports his contentions by directing attention to two infrequently discussed stories, "The Gentile Jewesses" and "The Black Madonna," as well as *The Ballad of Peckham Rye* (1960) and *The Prime of Miss Jean Brodie* (1961). In the end, Carruthers's high praise for Muriel Spark—he calls her "Scotland's most successful writer of the previous one hundred years"—rings true.

Frank Kermode was a long-time Spark partisan; indeed, so fervid was his devotion that Spark once called him "my apologist." Like John Updike, he rarely missed a chance to write about Spark, and one of his last essays, "Unrivalled Deftness: The Novels of Muriel Spark," gives an authoritative overview of four novels: *The Prime of Miss Jean Brodie, The Girls of Slender Means* (1963), *The Driver's Seat* (1970), and *The Only Problem* (1984). Kermode was always sensitive to the spiritual dimensions of Spark's novels but never at the cost of attention to her sharp satire, what he termed "her intelligent and unfailing contempt for stupidity and weakness." His long and deep study of Muriel Spark's writing gives us what is very likely the single most sustained and astute critical insight into her work. His particular focus on matters of creativity and construction yields a brilliant and illuminating analogy as he asserts, "One has the impression that for Spark there somehow exists, in advance of composition, a novel, or more usually a novella, which can be scanned as it were in a satellite's view of it, from above—a map, rather a temporal sequence." For Kermode, as for Anita Brookner, "a novel is a moral puzzle," and his essay conveys a palpable sense of delight in trying to solve the moral puzzles of Dame Muriel's fiction.

In "The Lightness of Muriel Spark's Novels," Dan Gunn directs attention to two of Spark's novels not often written about: *Not to Disturb* (1971) and *Territorial Rights* (1979). Prompted by a moment from a public interview he conducted with Dame Muriel at the American University of Paris in 2005, Gunn illuminates what he calls the "lightness" of Spark's fiction, drawing subtly and suggestively on the work of Barthes, Robbe-Grillet, Calvino, and Kundera. His careful attention to verbal texture and linguistic elements (pun, ellipsis, interruption, repetition) allows us not only to appreciate Spark's paradoxical lightness but to participate in its inimitable pleasures. Certainly, Gunn's locating these novels within the context of Spark's work and within the larger context of European letters is a long-overdue debt now paid.

Taking as his starting point the creative overlap of Iris Murdoch's *A Word Child* (1975) and Spark's *The Hothouse by the East River* (1973), both of which make use of J. M. Barrie's iconic figure of Peter Pan, John Glavin explores the nature and consequences of two great post–World War II writers' use of what Murdoch called a "wonderful dramatic myth." Differences between their deployment of the myth serve to isolate and illuminate Spark's extraordinary achievement. Glavin describes Spark as "exploring a virtual dynamic that counters and contests a hegemony of the actual." Enriched and amplified by drawing upon the work of Henri Bergson and Anne Friedberg, "Muriel Spark and the Peters Pan" constructs Spark as a master of invention and reinvention, in both art and life.

David Malcolm's "Elliptical and Inconsequential Ladies: Muriel Spark, Jane Bowles, Penelope Fitzgerald, and the *texte contestant*" constructs a dual argument. The first sets Spark's work within what he calls "an honorable tradition of European letters that is as old as Cervantes, Fielding, Sterne, Austen, and Balzac." The second associates her, by way of ellipsis and inconsequentiality, with two apparently disparate writers, Jane Bowles and Penelope Fitzgerald. Malcolm pays particular attention to three of Spark's novels—*Territorial Rights* (1979), *The Only Problem* (1984), and *A Far Cry From Kensington* (1988). His use of theory (Bal, Kristeva, Sturgess, and the lesser-known Esudie and Sandauer) enriches and supports the argument without ever deflecting attention away from Spark's work. In the end, Malcolm sees Spark as "not quite the hippogriff many critics make her out to be."

John Updike long championed Muriel Spark's fiction; indeed, he was one of the first American critics to praise her work, beginning with his review of *The Bachelors* (1960) and ending with the essay reprinted here, "Stonewalling Toffs," originally published in *The New Yorker*. Updike always saw Spark as a moralist with a caustic pen, and here, in reviewing *Aiding and Abetting* (2000), he found her true to form, lacerating the aristocratically pretentious Lord Lucan and his protectors—their moral blindness, class-based contempt, and genetic stupidity viciously exposed. Updike delineates that critical edge of Spark's fiction, certainly honed to razor-sharp intensity in *Aiding and Abetting*, but an element of nearly all her novels (one thinks especially of *Not to Disturb*, *The Takeover* [1976], and *Symposium* [1990]). A poet himself, Updike draws appropriate attention to Spark's language, which he aptly characterizes as "never ornate, it grows simpler . . . with Euclidean precision."

John Lanchester's perceptive essay, "In Sparkworld," focuses on her last novel, *The Finishing School* (2004), and on Spark herself, whom he sees as "a sort of proto-postmodernist, a writer with a sharp and lasting interest in the arbitrariness of fictional conventions . . .

accompanied by a wish to toy with, to subvert, parody, and undermine them." Using *The Comforters* and *The Girls of Slender Means*
as scaffolding, Lanchester deftly reveals the structural mechanics of
Spark's fiction; yet he never reduces the work to mere technical performance, for he is keenly appreciative of Spark's ultimately spiritual
vantage point, noting, "In Spark's fiction, we are never allowed to forget that the author, and indeed the reader, is subordinate to the final
Author: our fictions must not ever seem to compete with His." "In
Sparkworld" is one contemporary writer's homage to another.

"The Life" opens with a piece by Alan Taylor, who brings his own
particular perspective as a Scotsman to the life and career of Muriel
Spark. After visiting her in Arezzo in July 1990, Taylor became a close
friend and confidant. Their friendship flourished as he occasionally
accompanied her on travels abroad (Muriel disliked traveling alone
and Penelope disliked flying anywhere). In "Muriel Spark: Scottish
by Formation" (the characterization is her own), Taylor enriches our
understanding of the deep and lasting impact of Spark's first nineteen years in Edinburgh. The cultural traditions of Edinburgh, particularly the literary heritage of the Border Ballads with what she
called their "steel and bite," permeated the spirit and outlook of this
writer in whose speech one could always detect the lilt and rhythms
of Morningside.

From one of the giants of contemporary letters, Doris Lessing,
comes a poignant memoir, "Now You See Her, Now You Don't,"
written especially for this volume. Lessing draws upon her own life experience in Africa to give us a rich sense of Muriel Spark's life on that
vast continent in the late 1930s and early 1940s. Though the two women
never met while in Africa—Lessing frequented Salisbury and while
Spark spent some time there, most of her time was spent moving about
in Southern Rhodesia (Bulawayo and other more remote places)—
their life stories manifest a number of striking parallels and coincidences. Their African days were days of discontent, isolation, and in-
frequent social pleasures, but most of all, of waiting. Both women went
out of Africa and on to other worlds and literary fame, in Lessing's
telling phrase, "sifting gold from muddy experience." As one great
writer's tribute to another, Lessing's remembrance has unique power.

John Mortimer's "The Culture of an Anarchist: An Interview with Muriel Spark" gives us an insider's view: a close friend, literary colleague, and occasional summer neighbor in Tuscany as well, Mortimer prompted Spark to be particularly candid and personal. Mortimer's offhand wit and informal manner elicited telling responses on art and life. The interview, done in the late 1980s, remains fresh and engaging as the two cover familiar territory with enthusiasm and energy. Like Mortimer's, my own interview, "'Fascinated by Suspense': An Interview with Dame Muriel Spark," conducted over a decade later, covers a range of concerns and questions, all entertained with considerable grace and patience by Dame Muriel. She was never less than frank, forthcoming, and delightful. Both interviews conjure up a sense of a personable, engaging artist, dedicated to her work and eager to set the record straight about her life and accomplishment. Perhaps both give a sense of a rare privilege: an afternoon's civilized conversation with a great writer.

Barbara Epler was Muriel Spark's longtime publisher at New Directions Publishing Corporation. It is thanks to her that we now have so much of Spark's work in print in the United States. "Now I Know They Want Me Back-Stage" is an affectionate memoir chronicling some of her dealings with the author. Epler offers us a vivid panorama of portraits: Muriel in New York, Muriel in Tuscany, and most poignantly, Muriel in a dream vision. With an extraordinary lightness and certainty of touch, Barbara Epler gives us a Muriel Spark only a few were fortunate to know.

The title for this book comes from Spark's most famous novel, *The Prime of Miss Jean Brodie*. Many years after leaving the Marcia Blaine School and Miss Brodie, one of her girls, Jenny, fell in love with a stranger who had also taken shelter from the rain beneath the entrance to a building in Rome. Nothing would come of it, nonetheless, "the . . . happening filled her with astonishment whenever it came to her in later days, with a sense of the hidden possibilities in all things" (79).

It is my hope, as well as that of my contributors, that readers of this volume will gain a keen sense of Muriel Spark as a person, derived in good measure from reading her own words, unfiltered and uncensored, and a considerable critical appreciation of her work as articulated by some of her best readers. And perhaps some pleasure as well. Pleasure always figured large in Muriel's artistic scheme of things; she wanted very much to offer her readers the pleasures of the text, some measure of what she experienced as the creator. Once asked to characterize her life as novelist, she responded, with typical under-statement and irony, "Shall we say I had fun with my imagination?" Perhaps readers of this volume, prompted to turn—or return—to Muriel Spark's novels, will share in that fun.

## WORKS CITED

Lodge, David. "Marvels and Nasty Surprises." *New York Times Book Review* 20 October 1985.

Spark, Muriel. *The Prime of Miss Jean Brodie, The Girls of Slender Means, The Driver's Seat, and The Only Problem.* New York: Alfred A. Knopf/ Everyman Library, 2004.

# Biographical Note

*Muriel Camberg Spark (1918–2006)*

With the publication of her first novel, *The Comforters*, in 1957, Muriel Spark attracted the attention and support of Evelyn Waugh and Graham Greene, and a brilliant literary career was launched. Spark soon settled into a schedule of regular publication: between 1957 and 2004 she published twenty-two novels as well as critical studies, plays, poems, an autobiography, and dozens of essays on topics as diverse as Shelley's residence in Venice, the desegregation of art, the frescoes of Piero della Francesca, the Book of Job, and Marcel Proust. She established herself as one of the preeminent writers of her generation.

Born in Edinburgh on the first of February 1918 to a Jewish father and an Anglican mother, Muriel Sarah Camberg attended one of Edinburgh's distinguished secondary schools, James Gillespie's High School for Girls, where she received a solid foundation in the liberal arts. It became the Marcia Blaine School in *The Prime of Miss Jean Brodie*, and one of its teachers, Miss Christina Kay, became the model for the mythic Jean Brodie. Muriel never attended university; instead she took courses in précis writing and stenography at Heriot Watt College, then went to work as a secretary in an Edinburgh department store before emigrating at the age of nineteen to Southern Rhodesia (now Zimbabwe) to marry Sydney Oswald Spark, a man thirteen years her senior. They had one child, a son named Robin, but the marriage was rocky: Sydney Spark was a manic depressive, given to wandering about the house and randomly firing off a revolver. As Muriel noted in her autobiography, *Curriculum Vitae* (1991), he was "a borderline case and I didn't like what I found on either side of the border" (130).

During World War II Muriel booked passage on a liner bound for Liverpool, leaving husband and child behind. Eventually the marriage would be annulled and Robin entrusted to the care of her parents in Edinburgh. In England she found a job working for MI6, British counterintelligence, writing disinformation, so-called black propaganda. After the war Muriel became secretary of the Poetry Society and editor of its *Poetry Review*, where she made a name for herself by bringing in new poets and actually paying them for their contributions to the journal. Muriel herself had long been a poet, writing verse as a child and once revising Robert Browning's "The Pied Piper of Hamlin" at age nine, "to give it a happy ending," she said. She went on to win the Sir Walter Scott Prize for her poem "Out of a Book" in 1932, and soon became known as the school's poet. Her first publications were poems. She continued to write and publish verse while living in Africa and later during her London years. She was first known as a poet, and she never relinquished her identity as a poet. Though it sometimes seems to be lost in the attention paid to her prose, Muriel never stopped writing poetry; her poems appeared in the *Spectator* and *The New Yorker* frequently. She published four volumes of verse, including *All the Poems of Muriel Spark* (2004).

Spark came to greater literary prominence in 1951 for her short story "The Seraph and the Zambesi," selected as the winner from nearly seven thousand entries submitted in a contest sponsored by the *Observer* newspaper. She continued to write stories, publishing five collections, including *All the Stories of Muriel Spark* (2001) and *The Ghost Stories of Muriel Spark* (2004). But Spark is certainly best known for her novels, in particular *The Prime of Miss Jean Brodie* (1961), first published in its entirety in *The New Yorker* and later adapted for film, stage, and television. These projects attracted the talents of Judi Dench, Maggie Smith, Glenda Jackson, Vanessa Redgrave, Elizabeth Taylor, and Joseph Losey.

Received into the Roman Catholic Church on May 1, 1954, Spark was a woman of profound spiritual depth and religious conviction, if not always of doctrinal orthodoxy. She practiced her faith on her own terms; it was said that she arrived at Sunday Mass after the sermon, considering the sermons an occasion of sin. And she did not hesitate to express her opinions, having once said of the late Pope John Paul II, "I wouldn't take the Pope too seriously. He's a Pole first, a Pope second, and a Christian third."

Spark once described herself as a "constitutional exile." She left Edinburgh in 1937 and returned only for short-term visits, usually for family emergencies. Indeed, she led a rather nomadic existence, moving from London to New York (1962), then on to Rome (1967), and finally settling in the Tuscan village of San Giovanni d'Oliveto (1979), where she lived with her friend and collaborator, Penelope Jardine.

After enduring a number of illnesses and botched surgeries with characteristic courage and resilience, Muriel Spark died on April 13, 2006, in Florence. Always at work on a project (several years earlier, she had told one interviewer, "I do feel guilty at the age of 85 if I haven't done a day's work"), Muriel Spark left behind notes and plans for a twenty-third novel.

Spark was the recipient of many honors and awards, among them the James Tait Black Prize, the Ingersoll T. S. Eliot Award, and the David Cohen Prize for Literature. Made a Dame Commander of the British Empire in 1993, she received an honorary degree from the University of Oxford in 1999, to complement those already bestowed by the universities of Strathclyde, Aberdeen, St Andrew's, and Edinburgh.

Muriel Spark's work has been immensely popular; in Britain a number of the novels and stories remain in print, and more are scheduled for republication. In the United States, under the direction of its esteemed publisher Barbara Epler, New Directions Press has begun an ambitious campaign to make all of Spark's work available; so far, two volumes of stories and one of poems as well as the autobiography and twelve novels are in print. Though it has attracted legions of readers, both in the English-speaking world and beyond (the work has been translated into seventeen languages), and favorable critical reception from readers such as W. H. Auden, Anita Brookner, Frank Kermode, David Lodge, John Mortimer, Lorna Sage, and John Updike, Spark's achievement has not yet received the extended critical attention it deserves.

# THE WORK

CHAPTER ONE

# The Large Testimony of Muriel Spark

GABRIEL JOSIPOVICI

Muriel Spark has always had great fun introducing parodies of novels into her own works. "I have just been re-reading *The Seventh Child*," an old flame of the once-famous and recently rediscovered lady novelist Charmian Piper tells her in *Memento Mori*. "I love particularly that scene at the end with Edna in her mackintosh standing at the cliff's edge on that Hebridean coast being drenched by the spray, and her hair blown about her face. And then turning to find Karl by her side. One thing about your lovers, Charmian, they never required any preliminary discussions. They simply looked at each other and *knew*" (186). Her son Eric, though, at fifty-six himself starting to publish fiction, dismisses his mother's books as consisting entirely "of people saying 'touché' to each other" (97). His father Godfrey, while jealous of his wife's success, is dismissive of his son's latest offering: "I simply could not go on with it. A motor salesman in Leeds and his wife spending a night in a hotel with that communist librarian . . . Where does it all lead you?" (12). In *The Prime of Miss Jean Brodie*, the young Sandy Stranger—of whom Miss Brodie is to say "Sandy will make a great spy"—is busy writing a novel with her friend Jenny:

This was a story, still in the process of composition, about Miss Brodie's lover, Hugh Carruthers. He had not been killed in the war; that was a mistake in the telegram. He had come back from the war and called to inquire for Miss Brodie at school, where the first person whom he encountered was Miss Mackay, the head-mistress. She had informed him that Miss Brodie did not desire to see him, she loved another. With a bitter, harsh laugh, Hugh went and made his abode in a mountain eyrie, where, wrapped in a leather jacket, he had been discovered one day by Sandy and Jenny. (18)

In a later novel, *Territorial Rights*, the hero's mother watches the news on television while she eats her supper.

Then she took up her library book, a novel comfortingly like the last novel she had read: "Matt and Joyce finished their supper in semi-silence. Somehow she couldn't bring herself to ask the vital question: had he got the job? Was it so vital, was anything so vital anyway?

If he had got the job he would have said so without her asking.

Matt got up and stacked the dishes. She followed him into the kitchen and ran the hot tap. What had there ever been be-tween them? Had it all been an illusion? The rain poured out-side . . . "

Anthea's eyes drooped. And so to bed. (50–51)

It would be quite wrong, however, to imagine that Muriel Spark is simply laughing at inept writing, or at the extremes of romantic and realist fiction. There is that, of course, but her real quarry is not bad novels but the novel as such, and one clue to why that might be so lies in a later part of the conversation between Charmian and her former lover Guy Leet, from which I have already quoted. Though Charmian is in some respects senile, in others she is still sturdily commonsensical, helped in this by her Catholic faith. Guy has been praising the way she plotted her novels, and as she responds she seems to metamorphose into Muriel Spark herself:

"And yet," said Charmian smiling up at the sky through the window, "when I was half-way through writing a novel I always got into a muddle and didn't know where it was leading me."

Guy thought: She is going to say—dear Charmian—she is going to say "The characters seemed to take on a life of their own."

"The characters," said Charmian, "seemed to take control of my pen after a while. But at first I always got into a tangle. I used to say to myself,

Oh what a tangled web we weave

When first we practise to deceive!

Because," she said, "the art of fiction is very like the practice of deception."

"And in life," he said, "is the practice of deception in life an art too?"

"In life," she said, "everything is different. Everything is in the Providence of God." (187–88)

The villains in Muriel Spark's novels are those who cannot see the difference between fiction and reality. Or rather, they are those who seek to manipulate the lives of others for their own ends as the novelist manipulates his or her plot: Georgina Hogg in *The Comforters*; Patrick Seaton, the spiritualist in *The Bachelors*; Mrs. Pettigrew, the ladies' companion in *Memento Mori*; Sandy Stranger and Miss Brodie herself in *The Prime of Miss Jean Brodie*; Miss Rickward in *The Mandelbaum Gate*. What happens in the novels of Muriel Spark is that we are gradually made to recognize that the plots of men and women who think life can be manipulated as a novelist manipulates her novels usually backfire, for we are all of us in the Providence of God. More interestingly, it is often *through* the machinations of the blackmailers and plotters, but in direct contradiction to their aims, that God's plot is brought to completion.

Is this the project of a religious, and specifically a Catholic, novelist? But in that case why does it make so much sense to a non-Christian like myself?

The answer is that she couches in Christian terms what is essentially a modernist enterprise, on which such diverse artists and philosophers as the Protestant Kierkegaard, the militant atheist Nietz-sche, Jews without affiliation like Kafka and Paul Celan, and writers in whose lives religion does not seem to have figured at all, such as Proust, Valéry, and Robbe-Grillet, have all been engaged. To under-stand why this should be the case we need to stand back a little and think about the historical provenance of the novel.

From its origins in the Renaissance the novel has dealt with individuals—at first with individuals, such as Robinson Crusoe, who triumph over the odds by a mixture of luck and skill in controlling their environment, and later with tragic individuals, often women, like Anna Karenina and Emma Bovary, who are destroyed by their environment. It is also important to understand that the novel is not a genre but a form that emerges precisely when the notion of genre starts to become suspect. Genre, in its heyday, provided artists with a cushion, with a way of working that did not require them to go back to first principles every time and liberated even as it constrained them. But when genre began to be seen as a barrier to expression rather than as the natural conduit for expression, as it did when Dr. John-son sneered at Milton's exploration of his feelings on the death of his friend Henry King through the genre of Christian pastoral elegy, a new era had dawned, the era Hegel called "the age of prose."

The novel becomes the place where these issues are most clearly explored because, having shed the formal pointers that guided earlier readers to an awareness of what genre they were confronted with, the novel looks transparent, looks like a piece of pure reporting, while at the same time being as much the result of human decisions as any other artifact. Kierkegaard understood this better than anyone. His book *On Authority and Revelation* turns on the question of authority: What authority do I have for what I say and write? What authority do authors have in general and in the present age in particular? Artists are fond of referring to their "calling," but in what sense have they been called? In the same sense as the prophets were called by God or the Apostles by Jesus? And, if not, are they justified in using such a term? He develops the problem by turning to the question of endings in the novel: "It is not improbable," he says, "that the lives of many men go on in such a way that they have indeed premises for living but reach no conclusions . . . For it is one thing that a life is over, and a different thing that a life is finished by reaching a conclusion." The ordinary man, he goes on, the one whose life has no conclusion, may, if he finds he has talent, decide to become an author. But, says Kierkegaard,

> he may have extraordinary talents and remarkable learning, but an author he is not, in spite of the fact that he produces books . . . No, in spite of the fact that the man writes, he is not essentially an author; he will be capable of writing the first . . . and also the second part, but he cannot write the third part—the last part he cannot write. If he goes ahead naively (led astray by the reflection that every book must have a last part) and so writes the last part, he will make it thoroughly clear by writing the last part that he makes a written renunciation to all claim to be an author. For though it is indeed by writing that one justifies the claim to be an author, it is also, strangely enough, by writing that one virtually renounces this claim. If he had been thoroughly aware of the inappropriateness of the third part—well, one may say, *si tacuisset, philosophus mansisset* [if he had kept quiet he would have remained a philosopher]. (3–4)

And he ends with a pregnant aphorism: "To find the conclusion, it is necessary first of all to observe that it is lacking, and then to feel quite vividly the lack of it" (4).

It is not too much to say that those who have felt the full force of Kierkegaard's argument will be forever separated from those—the bulk of writers, readers, and reviewers of fiction in Kierkegaard's day and our own—who have not. And I hasten to add that one does not need to have read Kierkegaard to feel it; one only needs to be aware of the possibilities of art in the post-Romantic age. For Kierkegaard is merely articulating, with great humour and also great power and acumen, what has been felt and struggled with by Hölderlin and Mallarmé, Kafka and Virginia Woolf, Eliot and Wallace Stevens: that since the writer has no authority for what he is saying, to go on writing as if he had is the greatest error, for it falsifies the way things are instead of helping us to clarify it.

The argument turns on the question of the difference between endings and conclusions: "For it is one thing that a life is over and a different thing that a life is finished by reaching its conclusion." In the first case a man goes through life and then dies. His life has not had any meaning, it has simply consisted of a series of actions and reactions, and his death does not have any meaning either. His life is like a line that goes along the page for a while and then stops. Even to say that the line goes from A to B implies that there is a shape to it, a certain kind of progression. But the line does not in fact "go" anywhere. It exists for a while and then stops existing. In Beckett's *Endgame* Clov and Hamm wind up an alarm clock and then listen to it ringing. When it stops Clov says: "The end is terrific!" "I prefer the middle," replies Hamm (Beckett 34). This is both funny and disturbing. Funny because Hamm and Clov, by treating or pretending to treat the undifferentiated ringing of an alarm clock as they would a piece of music, make fun of concert-goers and critics. Disturbing because behind the concert-goers stand the recipients of art in general, and its practitioners, and we ourselves, who insist on seeing meaning and value in our lives against all the evidence. As Kierkegaard puts it, all we ever have in life are gossip and rumor; the world of the newspaper and the barbershop is not the world of Jesus and his Apostles. A person seduced by our culture's admiration for art embarks on a more dangerous enterprise than he or she may realize. If they embark on a work of fiction they imagine that they have escaped the world of rumor, that instead of living horizontally, as it were, they live vertically, in touch with some transcendental source of authority. And we who read them do so because we feel that this must indeed be the case. As Sartre put it in *La Nausée*, I walk along the street, carrying my confused and confusing life with me (Sartre 37). But if I open a novel and read that the protagonist walks down the street, I am filled with excitement. Though his life seems open I know that an adventure awaits him, something that will give meaning to his life. The comforting sense of the pages still to come enclosed by my right hand reassure me. This is why, after all, I have picked up the novel in the first place. But it is a lie. The only way for some semblance of truth and clarity to emerge is for the author to recognize that the conclusion, that which would give authority to the book, is lacking, and to feel this quite vividly and make us feel it as well.

Let us go back to *Memento Mori.* At first sight it appears to be a
novel about what it means to be old, but a longer acquaintance with
it brings us to understand that it is a novel about what it means to be
human. All the characters are losing their faculties, some, like Charmian, in blissful ignorance of the fact, others painfully aware of it,
while yet others try to pretend that nothing has changed. For Dame
Lettie Colston, seventy-nine, lifelong committee woman and orga-
nizer of good causes, there is no such thing as old age. When the man
(for all are agreed at least on this, that it is a man) rings up and tells her
"Remember you must die," she immediately informs the police that
he has called again and chivvies them on their lack of progress in tracking him down. Nevertheless, she is shaken and accepts her brother's
invitation to spend the night with them. Charmian, her sister-in-law,
on the other hand, lives in a twilit world: " 'That was a pleasant young
man who called the other day,' " she says to her husband. " 'Which
young man?' 'From the paper. The one who wrote—' 'That was five
years and two months ago,' said Godfrey" (10–11). Godfrey himself is
convinced that he alone shows no signs of ageing, but Muriel Spark at
once and brilliantly shows us how things really are. He drives out to
fetch his sister from her home in Hampstead and of course on the return journey there is only one topic of conversation:

"Nonsense," said Lettie, "I have no enemies."

"*Think,*" said Godfrey. "Think hard."

"The red lights," said Lettie. "And don't talk to me as if I
were Charmian."

"Lettie, if you please, I do not need to be told how to drive.
I observed the lights." He had braked hard, and Dame Lettie was
jerked forward.

She gave a meaningful sigh which, when the green lights came
on, made him drive all the faster.

"You know, Godfrey," she said, "you are wonderful for
your age."

"So everyone says." His driving pace became moderate; her
sigh of relief was inaudible, her patting herself on the back, in-
visible. (11)

The problems of old age are not just mental. At the funeral tea after the burial of one of their friends a short while later, Godfrey finds himself with his friend's housekeeper/companion, Mrs. Pettigrew, and the eighty-year-old poet Percy Mannering:

> To Godfrey's relief Mrs. Pettigrew refilled his cup. She also poured one for herself, but when Percy passed his shaking cup she ignored it. Percy said: "Hah! That was strong meat for you ladies, wasn't it?" He reached for the teapot. "I hope it wasn't me made Lisa's sister cry," he said solemnly. "I'd be sorry to have made her cry." The teapot was too heavy for his quivering fingers and fell from them on to its side, while a leafy brown sea spread from the open lid over the tablecloth and on to Godfrey's trousers. (29)

The resemblance of this to a children's tea party is not coincidental. We take time to learn to manipulate the objects around us and eventually, with age, they once again become intractable. "Being over seventy is like being engaged in a war," remarks Jean Taylor, once Charmian's maid and now confined to a geriatric ward. "All our friends are going or gone and we survive amongst the dead and the dying as on a battlefield" (37).

> A year ago, when Miss Taylor had been admitted to the ward, she had suffered misery when addressed as Granny Taylor, and she thought she would rather die in a ditch than be kept alive under such conditions. But she was a woman practised in restraint; she never displayed her resentment. The lacerating familiarity of the nurses' treatment merged in with her arthritis, and she bore them both as long as she could without complaint. Then she was forced to cry out with pain during a long haunted night when the dim ward lamp made the beds into grey-white lumps like terrible bundles of laundry which muttered and snored occasionally.

A nurse administers an injection and the physical pain subsides, "leaving the pain of desolate humiliation," so that she wishes the physical pain were back.

After the first year she resolved to make her suffering a voluntary affair. If this is God's will then it is mine. She gained from this state of mind a decided and visible dignity, at the same time as she lost her stoical resistance to pain. She complained more, called often for the bed-pan, and did not hesitate, on one occasion when the nurse was dilatory, to wet the bed as the other grannies did so frequently. (16–17)

But she has regained that wisdom which, we gradually realize, had always been a central feature of her character. When her scientifically minded one-time lover, Alec Warner, who is making a study of old age, says to her on one of his visits, "I always like to know whether a death is a good one or bad one. Do keep a look-out," she snaps: "A good death doesn't reside in the dignity of bearing but in the disposition of the soul" (167).

Jean Taylor understands what practically none of the others do, that we are never in full control of our own lives and that it would be as well to recognize this sooner rather than later. It is she who deciphers the enigma of the phone calls, though the others are not willing to listen. "What should I do about the phone calls?" Dame Lettie asks her on one of her visits.

"Can you not ignore it, Dame Lettie?"
"No, I can not. I have tried, but it troubles me deeply. It is a troublesome remark."
"Perhaps you might obey it," said Miss Taylor.
"What's that you say?"
"You might, perhaps, try to remember you must die."
She is wandering again, thought Lettie. "Taylor," she said, "I do not wish to be advised how to think." (38–39)

Surprisingly, the only other person to respond in this way to the telephone calls is Mortimer, the police inspector. When the friends gather at his house to hear his views on who the criminal hoaxer might be he almost preaches them a sermon:

"If I had my life over again I should form the habit of nightly composing myself to thoughts of death. I would practice, as it were, the remembrance of death. There is no other practice which so intensifies life. Death, when it approaches, ought not to take one by surprise. It should be part of the full expectancy of life. Without an ever-present sense of death life is insipid. You might as well live on the whites of eggs." (150)

Yet when one of the company responds with "I consider that what Mr. Mortimer was saying just now about resigning ourselves to death is most uplifting and consoling. The religious point of view is too easily forgotten these days, and I thank you, Mr. Mortimer," he replies: "Why, thank you, Janet. Perhaps 'resigning ourselves to death' doesn't quite convey what I mean. But of course, I don't attempt to express a specifically religious point of view" (150–51).

This is important. Religion, specifically the teachings of the Roman Catholic Church, is vital to Muriel Spark not because it is "religion" but because it makes more sense than other belief systems. Mortimer and Jean Taylor are not religious but wise. They understand that if you don't remember Death, Death will remind you, as Jean Taylor puts it. Lettie Colston is unwilling to listen and is surprised by death in the form of a burglar who has heard that a rich old lady is living alone in a cottage in Hampstead. Alec Warner's files, which will form the basis of his magnum opus on old age, disappear in an instant when his house is engulfed by fire. We came naked into the world and naked we will leave it. We may try to ignore our frailty, our dependence, but sooner or later it will be driven home to us, and if we go on denying it the marks of repression will show on our faces and bodies. Mrs. Pettigrew, beautifully groomed and still sexually attractive to elderly gentlemen like Gerald because she "looks after herself," passes for sixty-five but is in fact well over seventy. Like Dame Lettie she imagines she is in charge, though for someone of her station that requires a more active pursuit of worldly goals than for Lettie. She is determined to get her hands on the money of her old employer and if possible to become Gerald's mistress. In typical Sparkian fashion there is a story of wills and unexpected discoveries that reveals that even a Pettigrew cannot manipulate the world to her will. Yet by a further twist she does in the end inherit, though no amount of grooming will keep the ravages of Time at bay:

> Mrs Pettigrew had her reward. Lisa's will was proved in her favour and she inherited all her fortune. After her first stroke Mrs Pettigrew went to live in a hotel at South Kensington. She is still to be seen at eleven in the morning at Harrod's Bank where she regularly meets some of the other elderly residents to discuss the shortcomings of the hotel management, and to plan various campaigns against the staff. She can still be seen in the evening jostling for a place by the door of the hotel lounge before the dinner gong sounds. (218)

As in Dante, so here: a person suffers the pains of hell not in some mythical afterlife but here and now, in the very quality of life she has chosen for herself. Her evil is not just an instrument she turns against the world but both the core of her being and an instrument that is turned against herself. Thus Sandy Stranger, the betrayer of Miss Jean Brodie, remains what she always was, although she is a nun now, and famous, and has a new name, Sister Helena of the Transfiguration: "What was your biggest influence, then, Sister Helena?" the journalists ask. "Was it political, personal? Was it Calvinism?"

> "Oh no," said Sandy. "But there was a Miss Jean Brodie in her prime." She clutched the bars of the grille as if she wanted to escape from the dim parlour beyond, for she was not composed like the other nuns who sat, when they received their rare visitors, well back in the darkness with folded hands. But Sandy always leaned forward and peered, clutching the bars with both hands, and the other sisters remarked it and said that Sister Helena had too much to bear from the world since she had published her psychological book which was so unexpectedly famed. (*The Prime of Miss Jean Brodie* 35)

The compassion of the sisters is not just foolish innocence. Jean Taylor no doubt speaks for them when she says: "We all appear to ourselves frustrated in our old age, Alec, because we cling to everything so much. But in reality we are still fulfilling our lives" (*Memento Mori* 218). But most readers will feel that both Mrs. Pettigrew and Sandy have got what they deserve (though one of the reasons why *The Prime of Miss Jean Brodie* is such a great book is, of course, that Miss Brodie is hardly an innocent victim, is indeed herself a prime manipulator of others, but in a mysteriously innocent way).

They, like the other manipulators, spies, and blackmailers who throng the pages of Muriel Spark, are living examples of pure selfishness, which in effect means being unable to imagine anyone other than oneself. The ultimate form this selfishness takes is the desire to control your own death. Muriel Spark only once treats the subject head-on, but it forms the theme of the book she often said was her favourite, *The Driver's Seat*. Lise, the protagonist, cannot bear her boring life in London any more and flies to Rome (the city is not named), determined to find a man to kill her there. "Tie my hands first," she says, when she has at last found him. "Tie them with the scarf."

> He ties her hands, and she tells him in a sharp, quick voice to take off his necktie and bind her ankles.
> "No," he says, kneeling over her, "not your ankles."
> "I don't want any sex," she shouts. "You can have it afterwards. Tie my feet and kill, that's all. They will come and sweep it up in the morning."

But even Lise cannot retain total control over her own death:

> All the same, he plunges into her, with the knife poised high.
> "Kill me," she says, and repeats it in four languages.
> As the knife descends to her throat she screams, evidently perceiving how final is finality. (158–59)

It is interesting that two English novelists, William Golding and Muriel Spark (all right, Spark is Scottish, but "British novelists" sounds wrong) should, at about the same time (the nineteen sixties), write books every bit as radical as those of the *nouveau romanciers* on the other side of the Channel, and for the same reasons: their sense that the traditional form of the novel was itself complicit in a false and radically impoverished form of life. Yet they do so in order to stress (in a very English way) moral and religious concerns that one cannot imagine a Nathalie Sarraute or an Alain Robbe-Grillet ever expressing. Both William Golding's *Pincher Martin* and Muriel Spark's *The Hothouse by the East River* are novels that take place in the instant of death, and the plots they develop are gradually understood to be nothing other than the plots devised by the fevered imagination of the dying in order to stave off the finality of death. For those who put themselves and only themselves at the center of their lives, there can be no greater disaster than the disappearance of their self. But if you try to blot death out, death will remind you soon enough, and both Pincher Martin and the protagonists of *The Hothouse* eventually have to give in—at which point the novel ends. Thus at one and the same time we are made to understand the effort of will and control that drives the making of novels (the novelist is always in the driver's seat) *and* the place of such will and control in the larger vision of our lives as human, fallible, mortal beings. For both Golding and Spark the refusal to acknowledge death is but a manifestation of what psychologically and ethically can be seen as selfishness and philosophically as solipsism or the inability to grasp the fact that other people exist. That the novelist is so like Pincher Martin and Lise and the protagonists of *The Hothouse* is of course the paradox that drives these novels (we have to call them that).

Jean Taylor, receiving a visit from Alec Warner in the Maud Long Ward, recalls a conversation with him on a country walk almost fifty years before. "Do you think, Jean," he had asked, "that other people exist?" Their walk has led them to the edge of a graveyard.

> She stopped and leaned over the low stone wall looking at the gravestones.
>
> "This graveyard is a kind of evidence," she said, "that other people exist."
>
> "How do you mean?" he said.
>
> She was not sure. Having said it, she was not sure why. The more she wondered what she had meant the less she knew.

They enter and walk among the graves, stooping to read the names on the stones.

> "They are, I quite see, they are," he said, "an indication of the existence of others, for there are the names and times carved in stone. Not a proof, but at least a large testimony."
>
> "Of course," she said, "the gravestones might be hallucinations. But I think not."
>
> "There is that to be considered," he said, so courteously that she became angry.
>
> "But the graves are at least reassuring," she said, "for why bother to bury people if they don't exist."
>
> "Yes, oh precisely," he said. (70–71)

Why is a graveyard, if not a proof, at least a testimony, "a large testimony," says Alec, of the existence of others? Perhaps because the selfish person thinks of those who are alive as obstacles to achieving his or her desires, whereas the dead make no claims on us. They lie in the earth and the tombstones erected over them attest to the fact that they meant something, when they were alive, to their family and their friends. In time the members of the family who saw to it that the tombstone should be put up will themselves die and in turn be buried by their loved ones. There is no reason to do this in the calculus of loss and gain, tombstones are only erected out of piety, that is, out of the desire to have a tangible reminder, a memorial, of a life that is no more, out of nothing but respect for that life and grief that it is gone. The very lack of practical advantage to anyone makes of these memorials the most unanswerable of rebukes to the person who puts self at the center of their being, as each tombstone opens onto another world and another and another. Wordsworth, who understood this profoundly, wrote an essay on epitaphs that stands at the hinge of the old world and the new in much the same way as Johnson's essay on Milton, discussed above. "A sepulchral monument," he says,

> is a tribute to a man as a human being; and . . . , an epitaph [. . .] includes this general feeling and something more; and is a record to preserve the memory of the dead, as a tribute due to his indi-

vidual worth, for a satisfaction to the sorrowing heart of the survivors, and for the common benefit of the living: which record is
to be accomplished, not in a general manner, but, where it can, in
close connection with the bodily remains of the deceased; and
these, it may be added, among the modern nations of Europe, are
deposited within, or contiguous to, their places of worship. (730)

In the place of plot, that is, intrigue, which is the realm of the novelist and the blackmailer, the cemetery confronts us with tombstones,
names, and dates. The novelist who recognizes the temptations of the
novel and counters them by placing within his or her novels a traitor
and blackmailer, or else someone absolutely determined to hold on to
their self forever if necessary, has, perhaps, other possible strategies.
Can one make a novel like a graveyard?

*Memento Mori* concludes with Alec, now in a nursing home and
his filing system destroyed in the fire, searching through his mind "as
through a card-index, for the case histories of his friends, both dead
and dying." But what follows is a paragraph that feels less like the
transcript of case-histories than like a litany:

> Lettie Colston, he recited to himself, comminuted fractures of the
> skull; Godfrey Colston, hypostatic pneumonia; Charmian Col-
> ston, uraemia; Jean Taylor, myocardial degeneration; Tempest
> Sidebottome, carcinoma of the cervix; Ronald Sidebottome, car-
> cinoma of the bronchus; Guy Leet, arteriosclerosis; Henry Mor-
> timer, coronary thrombosis. (219–20)

This is taken up by the narrator in the final paragraph of the book,
speaking of and for all the "grannies" of the Maud Long Ward who
have no one to remember them: "Miss Valvona went to her rest. Many
of the grannies followed her. Jean Taylor lingered for a time, employing her pain to magnify the Lord, and meditating sometimes confid-
ingly upon Death, the first of the four last things to be ever remembered" (220). This is not the normal tone of the novel, and someone
turning to the end without having read the rest of the book might
dismiss it as mere Catholic piety. That would be a serious mistake.
What it is doing is reasserting what Homer, Shakespeare, and Spark's

beloved border ballads knew instinctively, indeed what every person before the onset of the Enlightenment knew in his or her bones: that life and death are one and that to deny the one is to deny the other. By the same token, to affirm the fact of death is not to rob life of its meaning; on the contrary it reminds us of its richness and complexity. "Thou mett'st with things dying," says the old shepherd to his son in *The Winter's Tale*, "I with things new-born." (Interestingly, *The Winter's Tale* is the only work I can think of outside the novels of Muriel Spark where the machinations of a character in order to gain advantage for himself result in the working out of the plot to the benefit of the protagonists, who remain blissfully ignorant of what has led to this.) In book 3 of the *Iliad*, Helen, looking from the walls of Troy at the Greek army assembled below, searches in vain for the sight of her two brothers, Castor and Pollux. "But the two marshallers of the host can I not see," she says,

> Castor, tamer of horses, and the goodly boxer Polydeuces, even mine own brethren, whom the same mother bare. Either they followed not with the host from lovely Lacedaemon, or though they followed hither in their seafaring ships, they have now no heart to enter into the battle of warriors for fear of the words of shame and the many revilings that are mine.

"So she said," says the narrator. "But," he adds, explaining to us the real reason why she cannot see them, "they ere now were fast holden of the life-giving earth there in Lacedaemon, in their dear native land." That is, they are dead. But the poet does not simply say that; instead he says that the earth, which gives life, now holds them in its embrace, and not anywhere but in the one place everyone wants to be buried in, their dear native land. The effect of this is curiously sooth-ing, both immensely sad and yet deeply satisfying. The same effect is achieved by slightly different means in the ballad of *Sir Patrick Spens*:

> "Mak hast, mak haste, my mirry men all,
> Our guid schip sails the morne";
> 'O say na sae, my master deir,
> For I feir a deadlie storme.

"Late late yestreen I saw the new moone,
Wi the auld moone in hir arme,
And I feir, I feir, my deir master,
That we will cum to harme."

O our Scot nobles wer right laith
To weet their cork-heild schoone:
But lang owre a' the play wer playd
Thair hats they swam aboone.

O lang, lang may their ladies sit,
Wi thair fans into their hand,
Or eir they se Sir Patrick Spens
Cum sailing to the land.

Two stanzas of dialogue are followed by a stanza that recounts the
feared outcome but does it by quite wonderful indirection. The first
two lines convey the fastidious Scottish nobles high-stepping to keep
their shoes dry as the sea starts to cover the decks, and the next two
doom-laden lines, commenting from some position outside the realm
of men (as do the two lines in the *Iliad* telling us about the fate of
Helen's brothers), describe the whole expedition and the storm as a
play or game (with all the characters from the King down to the messenger imagining that they are the players when we sense that they
are only the pawns) and then present us with the stark image of the
noblemen's hats afloat on the water, the only sign left of the fate of
the ship and its occupants. Finally, in the next stanza, as in the Song
of Deborah, we cut to the wives and mothers, sitting and waiting for
the men to return, "their fans in their hands"; but they are waiting, of
course, in vain.

Prolepsis—the narrator moving forward beyond the immediate
moment to the eventual outcome—is a notable feature of the border ballads and a powerful contributor to the sense of doom and inevitability they convey. It is not normally a feature of the novel, but
Muriel Spark has from the start of her career used it to good effect. It
contributes to the mood of both *The Prime of Miss Jean Brodie* and
*The Girls of Slender Means*, but it of course has a special role to play

in *The Driver's Seat*, where, as far as Lise is concerned, she is in a sense dead already. Its most startling use is in *Not to Disturb*, where the servants sit and wait for the master and mistress and the lover they share to shoot each other, but they have already written their accounts of the occurrence and warned the papers of what will, by the morning, have happened. "But what's done is about to be done and the future has come to pass," as Lister, the master manipulator in the servants' quarters, puts it (12). (What is peculiarly unsettling in this novel is that Lister is somehow both an aspect of the God of the earlier books and of the blackmailer/manipulator.) It may be that Muriel Spark discovered the possibilities of prolepsis by reading the border ballads, but the essential point is that in both prolepsis is the sign of a vision that extends beyond the perspective of individual, mortal men, which has tended to be the vision of the novel.

There are other striking features of her work that are the result of her need to take the novel away from its normal ground and into realms occupied by earlier literature. Take the communal aspect of some of her titles (*The Ballad of Peckham Rye, The Bachelors, The Girls of Slender Means*), and the curious choric quality of so many of her novels. Think of what Brian Moore would have done with *The Prime of Miss Jean Brodie*—a study of plucky spinsterhood and muted despair—and recall what Muriel Spark does with it: Miss Jean Brodie is in a sense only the sum of the memories of her of "the Brodie set," and she emerges from this, in the novel, as mysterious, imperative, life-affirming, even if slightly dotty, in contrast to the mean and desperate Sandy Stranger. Think of the end toward which *The Girls of Slender Means* drives: Nicholas Farringdon's vision of pure evil on the night of the fire propelling him to a lonely martyrdom far from London, a destiny that makes perfect sense as it comes to us out of the chorus of the voices of the girls and the fragments of English poetry recited by Joanna and her pupils but that could not be conveyed in the traditional form of the novel. These are books that dance and sing, and they do so because they understand evil in a way a secular novelist like Angus Wilson, for all his concern with the *idea* of evil, never does. Having looked evil in the eye, having meditated on death, the first of the Four Last Things, Muriel Spark can celebrate the wondrous nature of the life we have been given: "And so, having entered the fullness of my years, from there by the grace of God I go on my way rejoicing" (222), as the heroine of *Loitering with Intent* ends her account of an episode of her youth.

My aunt, an avid though undiscriminating reader, with a passion for the sprawling novels of John Cowper Powys, called Muriel Spark a girl of slender means. She could not have been more wrong. Only her novels are slender; her arsenal was better stocked than that of probably any novelist since Dickens. But equally wrong was the Penguin blurb writer who commented: "For comic observation and spicy dialogue it is impossible to outclass Muriel Spark." That may be a way of selling books, but it sells this author very short indeed. For Muriel Spark is not the cosy English lady novelist the Penguin blurb implies; in fact, she has the broad and humane vision of a Sophocles or a Shakespeare, and it is our great good fortune that she had the means and the determination to convey that vision in novels of incomparable lightness and brilliance.

WORKS CITED

Beckett, Samuel. *Endgame*. London: Faber and Faber, 1964.

Kierkegaard, Søren. *On Authority and Revelation*. Trans. Walter Lowrie. New York: Harper Torchbook, 1966.

Sartre, Jean-Paul. *La Nausée*. Paris: Gallimard, 1958.

Spark, Muriel. *The Driver's Seat*. London: Macmillan, 1970.

———. *Loitering with Intent*. London: Macmillan, 1981.

———. *Memento Mori*. Harmondsworth: Penguin, 1961.

———. *Not to Disturb*. London: Penguin, 1961.

———. *The Prime of Miss Jean Brodie*. Harmondsworth: Penguin, 1965.

———. *Territorial Rights*. London: Panther Books, 1980.

Wordsworth, William. "On Epitaphs." *The Poetical Works of William Wordsworth*. Ed. Thomas Hutchinson. Rev. Ernest de Selincourt. Oxford: Oxford University Press, 1936.

# CHAPTER TWO

# Muriel Spark's Fiction

## A Context

JOSEPH HYNES

"What is truth?" asked Pontius Pilate of the one who had
on another occasion spoken of himself as "the way, the truth, and the
life." Earlier and subsequent attempts to answer, interpret, deflect,
dodge, or rephrase Pilate's probably rhetorical and either skeptical or
cynical query are of course innumerable. In these pages I want to look
at some such attempts over the centuries, at least in the Western world,
as a way of zeroing in upon Muriel Spark's own notions of truth. My
assumption, not surprisingly, is that we cannot expect to deal significantly with her novels (the area of my investigation here) unless our
literary criticism—our reading—copes with what her novels (as aug-
mented by some of her extranovelistic remarks) explicitly and implicitly make of this large, slippery, and fundamental topic.

I

Let us start with the Greeks, as so much does. Philosophically, their
method was deduction. More specifically, Plato and Aristotle operated

on the premise that whatever is—whatever happens—must be understood as an effect, and that any effect has to have a cause. Reason followed the causal chain back and back to the point where that same reason compelled inquirers to acknowledge that some uncaused cause, or prime mover (capital letters optional), is rationally required to account for the existence of anything but that uncaused cause. Deduction thus logically required the existence of an uncaused cause apart from all effects. Such a cause was seen as objectively existent—real—and necessary to the existence of all else. Ironically, Lucretius's subsequent insistence that deduction won't do and that only materialism makes sense famously posited that "nothing can come from nothing." Lucretius apparently meant that first-cause advocates demanded "somethinghood" of a prime mover, whereas he demanded—proceeding inductively—that "something" had to be materially intelligible; that is, creation *ex nihilo* is materially, rationally, a contradiction in terms. For me the irony of such a premise as his lies in its being a confirmation or rephrasing of the very Greek idea that Lucretius deplores. That is, the Greeks in question would seem to agree with Lucretius that whatever is (that is, something) cannot have been caused by what is not (that is, nothing). Thus Lucretius's move to eliminate the (nonmaterial) cause can be understood to support the necessity of such an entity. Theologically or religiously speaking, scholastic thinking obviously follows Aristotle's first-cause deducing, wherein the Prime Mover is eventually named God.

Renaissance (early modern/Enlightenment) thinking gradually but definitely rejected deduction and embraced induction—the scientific method—as alone, in Lucretian terms, capable of delivering truth or reality; in other words, matter alone can be known, and human study and knowledge must focus on what can be known. All else is airy speculation and confined to that intellectually insignificant attic reserved for outworn notions such as fantasy, dreams, belief, wishful thinking, and all else nonmaterially approachable. The inductive reasoner tells us, often, that some day, in some unforeseeable way, the contents of this attic may prove materially, inductively, approachable and analyzable—in which case they could come to be seen as serious, real, and important to adult human beings. In the meantime we are advised to grow up and wax inductive.

As we work our way toward Spark, I think it is useful to remark on some consequences of induction's reign. One highly familiar term is *humanism*, which of course focuses our attention on that which induction searches out. Thus for the typical post-Enlightenment mind such qualifiers of *humanism* as *Christian, Judaic,* or *Islamic* are simply self-contradictory attempts to have things both ways. For the terminal humanist—that is, for one who regards the term *secular humanism* as the redundant equivalent of "wet rain"—such modifiers are merely back stair climbs to that dusty attic filled with adolescent illusions. Best to make do with Lucretius, love one another, and trust the scientists to build on the only possible body of truths.

But then, when this materialist emphasis left much for many to desire, the term "modernism" was born. Darwin, Marx, and Freud, all no less secular than their humanistic predecessors, strove biologically, economically, and psychologically to find, explore, explain, and doctor the roots of our human discontent. Writers like Pound and Eliot famously worked to "make it new"—literally to recombine chunks of the literary past so that the resulting literary fragments would both connect readers with our human past and merge that past with now. We can see today that Eliot of the quilted *Waste Land* was the perfect reviewer of Joyce's *Ulysses*, a tome designed to merge one twentieth-century character's single day with Homer's *Odyssey* and the whole of Western literature and history.

Modernism, from a slightly different angle, may be seen as concerted efforts to nail down meaning. If the skies are empty and the grave is the end, what is our human purpose? Wallace Stevens urges us to see value in the very beauty that assaults our senses and our psyches precisely because it and we cannot last. His "Sunday Morning" tells us to be glad that life ends, that seasons change; eternity would be a bore in its ceaseless harp-twanging. Life matters as process, not product; in the quest we each decide upon, not in achieving any specifiable overall goal. This theme is wonderfully established, for example, in Beckett's plays. Vladimir and Estragon wait, stay alive and together, and deliberately decline suicide, only because they seem to recall Godot's eventual arrival as having been promised to them sometime in the past. Who Godot may be, and what exactly hinges on his showing up, are unknown to these characters and hence to us. But Godot is, or promises, purpose and meaning. Similarly, Win and Will, of *Happy Days*, push Beckett's same point. "I can't go on; I'll go on" establishes the thesis that "to be" supersedes "not to be." The two characters' names must be taken both ironically and straight on.

Modernism thus, as I see it in literature, accepts the inductive operations of science but still looks for overall meaning in human life. Then along came Jean-Paul Sartre with his existentialism to blow up any such hope. Sartre's basic premise is that, since we cannot know anything of where we came from or where we're headed, we simply waste our time discussing the human "essence" and its generic worth. All we know is that each of us exists. Our lives, then, are defined by the choices we make. The totality of these choices will eventually define our own essence (elected by us rather than generically imposed from without), and who we have become, by virtue of these acts of will. Forget about lawgiver, judge, forgiver, rewarder, or punisher: each of us makes choices and there's no one to whom we can appeal for a second chance. We just are. So universal human purpose (*sans* purpose-maker) is impossible. Indeed, Sartre sets his *No Exit* in a hell that he clearly deems nonsensical, simply to make his point that there exist no afterlife and nobody save ourselves to judge us. His positing of eternity merely emphasizes his point that choices cannot be unmade and must add up to who we are. Similarly, in *The Flies* Sartre creates the foolish character of Zeus only to show us how silly it is for anyone to imagine the existence of god(s) for us to appeal to or fear. Gods, purpose, meaning, significance are bad logic. We have no choice but to be, or end our lives. There's no Godot to wait for. Clearly such a term as *Christian existentialism* is for Sartre as self-contradictory as others find *theistic humanism*.

For our present purposes, the importance of Sartre is that his existentialism assaulted modernism. The modernists may very well have conceded much to science and the inductive method. The modernists may very well have granted that acceptance of an objective reality and of a belief system based thereon could not be, would not do. What they attempted, however, was to root humanism in the value attached to searching for something—anything—else that would take the place of such a metaphysical, theological entity. The old system might be gone, but since there *ought* to be something to supply end or purpose, humanists would find that something in wedding past to present; history to philosophy or literature; human imagination to human need; the abstract purity of mathematics or of nonrepresentational painting or music or sculpture to our sense of beauty virtually transcendent. As we have suggested, Sartre saw such a way of thinking as grounded in an irrational, sentimental conviction that, though God is missing, a human(istic) essence will (should) in the long run become inductively clear to us as our *raison d'etre*. Sartre told us to forget about essence, realize that it is a fable, and bear down instead on the inevitable fact that each of us is alone and forced to effect his/her self as we choose our ways to the extinction that is death.

This prospect Sartre saw as optimistic, as hopeful, because facing it and living in accord with its premises would force us to shed the lie that humanism proffered. In short, Sartre's existentialism is the truth that can set us free to act on the value of our being self-creators condemned to choose and to be responsible for those choices. We and our necessarily free wills are of course headed for permanent burial, but we are to rejoice in jettisoning humanistic soppiness and in confronting our individual dead-end futures in the clear light of who we are making ourselves to be.

As I see things, Sartre's way of thinking is heavily responsible for that loose and baggy monster called *postmodernism*, a vague label that will doubtless sort itself into sublabels in time. But for now it seems to me to include those who accept Sartre's code. Another way to make this point is to see modernists as latter-day humanists working to supply life's missing cosmic significance, to see Sartre as the dynamiter of any such purpose, and then to see postmodernists as antihumanistic Sartreans who have abandoned purpose in favor, literally, of what strikes their fancy.

Much of the fiction emerging from the postmodernist impetus is indeed ingenious and worthy of critical attention. For one example, the "magic realism" of Garcia Marquez demonstrates my point about literary postmodernism. On the one hand, time, place, and appearance of particular characters and environments, as well as attention to states of mind and cravings of body—these are all as carefully rendered as in orthodox realistic books by Austen, Tolstoy, or Updike. But, on the other hand, the tag "magic" covers ground reserved by Hawthorne in his declaration that the label "romance" was a necessary but adequate generic justification for the revelation, to Dimmesdale, of a large *A* in the sky. The term *magic* presumably clarifies (if necessary) any seemingly arbitrary or dreamlike events in *One Hundred Years of Solitude*. The result of this genuine mix, at least in my reading, is appreciation for Garcia Marquez's imagination and simultaneous awareness that appreciation of that imagination may be the real point of his book. Obviously, the quality of any author's imagination emerges from our reading, but the immediate point here is that *Solitude* seems to preclude our fairly asking what the book is *about*, beyond authorial ingenuity.

In something like the same way, we can tackle the so-called metafictionists, prominent especially in the 1960s and 1970s. I think here of writers such as John Barth and Robert Coover, both of them brilliant experimenters with generic teasing, narrative slipperiness, and postmodernist game-playing. *Giles Goat-Boy*, *The Sot-Weed Factor*, and *Sabbatical* all manifest Barth's intimate knowledge of the novel's colorful history, while Coover's *The Universal Baseball Association, Inc., J. Henry Waugh, Prop.* and his short-story collection *Pricksongs and Descants* do a similar job for his reputation. My point about these authors is anything but denigratory. Rather, I remain in awe of their creative fireworks and cite these writers to buttress my comments on postmodernism. As metafictionists Barth and Coover refuse to write *about* anything that can be called objectively real, either past or present. Instead, they turn their fiction in upon itself, so that, notoriously, the author and his imaginative speculations from outside the fiction (the thing made) are seen to be inseparable from whatever contents might be considered to exist inside the fiction. The reader juggles past and present and possibly future, together with multiple voices and with maker and thing made. And because profound skepticism or genuine denial of reality beyond the author's intelligence and imaginative skill govern the product, we are left, however ingeniously, with metafiction, ultimate subjectivity, fiction about itself.

In this vein, let me mention one other instance, that of Nabokov's *Pale Fire*. Here, atypically among Nabokov's works, we have all the qualities discussed as Barth's and Coover's, with the added possibility that the (?) narrator may be lucidly insane. Everything, including a detailed index, contributes to the sort of self-referentiality found among metafictionists. It's a splendid achievement *sui generis*.

Far be it from me to suggest where this historic trail may ultimately lead us. But as a final example of where it has gone to date, I would like to discuss the *nouveau roman* of Alain Robbe-Grillet, Sartre's fellow countryman. (Why do such critical theory and practical work so often come from France?) Sowing along in Sartrean furrows, Robbe-Grillet not only rejects humanism as childishly soft on what Sartre treats as the compulsory, dignifying freedom of humans stranded, happily alone, between birth and death, the latter quite terminal. Robbe-Grillet moves on more specifically to literature, which, for him, means necessarily abandoning the novel—by which he means the habit of realism with its assumption of discernible and representable objective truth. In RobbeGrillet's view, objectivity is nonsense. We are left instead with total subjectivity, and that means we must dump the term *novel* with its "out there"–"in here" sophomoric split and instead use a label like *nouveau roman*. Why? Because we need a new term to express the fact that we can no longer kid ourselves with stories—beginnings, middles, ends; instead, we have to acknowledge that, as subjectivists, we can convey phenomena only. Robbe-Grillet is hence a phenomenologist, and a *text* (not a *novel*, for Dickens and Flaubert were profoundly misled) cannot weave a tale taking characters through experiences to outcomes. In a text—a *nouveau roman*, such as *La Maison de rendez-vous*—Robbe-Grillet exhibits extraordinary skill in giving us, literally, vivid sense-impressions of things, stuff. He is elaborately adroit (at least in translation) at offering detailed sights, sounds, scents, and tactile sensations and then re-offering them from no particular points of view (for psychology died with the novel). Thus we experience much of the metafictionists' skepticism, but here Robbe-Grillet has not only ransacked the House of Realistic Humanism but has indeed burned it down. The *nouveau-roman* writer shows us how things and places look, how nameless registers (not *characters*, of course) pick up impressions, and that's precisely and expertly all he means to give us. Such a text, by definition, cannot go anywhere, explain or teach anything to anyone, or come to an end or conclusion. A novel pretends to do such things; the *nouveau-roman* simply shows, to no eventual purpose. It eventually stops, but only arbitrarily; it does not end.


II


Just ahead lie connections between Muriel Spark's novels and observations derived from my cursory bicycle ride through the criticism and practice of fiction, and through concepts and possibilities of truth encountered along the way. First, however, I would like to speak briefly about Harold Pinter's 2005 Nobel Prize Acceptance Lecture, entitled "Art, Truth & Politics" and reprinted in the May 2006 issue of *PMLA*, for this speech has triggered my own essay.

Right up front, Pinter lays out his thesis:

> In 1958 I wrote the following: "There are no hard distinctions between what is real and what is unreal, nor between what is true and what is false. A thing is not necessarily either true or false."
> I believe that these assertions still make sense and do still apply to the exploration of reality through art. So as a writer I stand by them but as a citizen I cannot. As a citizen I must ask: What is true? What is false? (811–18)

Pinter proceeds to specify that some of his plays took shape because a single word, sentence, or image popped into his head. He then followed this or that lead where it took him, until he achieved a full play—*The Homecoming* or *Old Times*—and thus found out what the completed play was (is) about, at least for himself—or what its truth is, in his reading. Then for the remainder (perhaps 90 percent) of his lecture he tells us that that course is all well and good for an artist, but its tentativeness won't do for a citizen. The citizen must seek and demand the truth of political events. Pinter's assertion is that the administrative, political, and military history of the United States (with Britain humbly in tow) since the end of World War II has been nothing but lies about spreading democracy to cover this nation's presumptuous, immoral support of dictators, always to bolster and justify our own power grabs. He offers our Latin American and Iraqi ventures as cases in point. No doubt Pinter's observations on political occurrences have been only intensified by events since his 2005 lecture, and no doubt a great many American voters have come to his conclusions, even when they may have no knowledge of Pinter or his work.

My intent is not to enter the significant fray that is Pinter's focus. Rather I want to look at his split between aesthetic truth and political truth. For what Pinter does here is to separate objective truth from subjective truth. The former can be measured in accord with external standards: things happened in this or that way. The latter may not be namable as truth in anything like the same sense. That is, Pinter's attitude (not clarified, regrettably) is that one of his plays strikes him as "true" at some stage, and this feeling of rightness or of being finished equals "truth." So he doesn't know where the germ for the play came from and he doesn't say why the term *truth* applies to his final reaction. But he does know when this or that work is finished. Wherein "true"? Subjective truth thus sees the writer as maker or creator; objective truth is "out there" to be seen, represented, shared, discussed, evaluated. Pinter's distinction appears to stem from a familiar observation about the philosophical course traced to this point in my essay: that is, the diminishing, or disappearance, of objective reality drives one inevitably deeper into the abyss that is solipsism. But of course no one can *live* solipsism but must sanely acknowledge the (a, some) reality outside of the self. So for Pinter and many (most? all?) others there exist two kinds of truth: inside and outside. I want not to pit these against each other or probe into whether one is better than the other but instead to suggest that this longstanding dichotomous peak is a convenient site from which to take on Muriel Spark's novels.


III


Because the same sensibility is on display, however variously, throughout Spark's fifty years of novel writing, I shall focus on her first novel,

*The Comforters* (1957), with occasional glances at some of her other writings. "There are more things in heaven and earth . . . than are dreamt of in your philosophy," Hamlet remarks to Horatio. This comment at once points to the two possible realms of awareness with which we have volleyed. In *The Comforters*—a title that appears to refer to the Holy Spirit (God as Third Person of the Trinity) as the true Comforter, as well as to those uncomprehending if well-intentioned friends who try to alleviate Job's sufferings—the book's central figure, Caroline Rose, worries about her sanity. Caroline—who, like Spark at the time, is a half-Jewish convert to Catholicism—hears a tapping typewriter and a voice or several voices saying/singing some of the exact words we have just read in this novel, or that we shall encounter in a page or two. These narrated words thus repeat past narrative or project to future narrative, and they can refer to Caroline or to others in *The Comforters*. Because a tape-recorder cannot detect tapping or voices, Caroline and others wonder about her mind. On the one hand she shares their concern for phenomena that are not scientifically verifiable; on the other hand, however, she is convinced of the truth of her own experiences. She knows what she knows; she was there.

Where we are, then, is in the midst of a standard Spark situation: mystery of one sort plus mystery of a second sort. *The Comforters* gives us the plot-expanding issue of whether, how, and why seventy-eight-year-old Louisa Jepp, nice old grandmother of Laurence Manders—the young BBC sportscaster and ex-Catholic who shares Caroline's love but no longer, since her conversion, her apartment—heads a "gang" that smuggles jewels from France to England. This is mystery on the police-department level. The other sort of mystery, of course, the police and electric gadgetry cannot resolve or even detect—hence the common assumption, even by Caroline, that she may be dotty. The first kind of mystery is eccentric and funny and likely accounts for Spark's popularity. The second kind appears often to be overlooked, disregarded, or pooh-poohed as distinctly papist, even when it is noticed.

Obviously, one misses the book unless one attends to both strands of the mysterious. When we look more closely, however, we note that Caroline's interests and hence her tracking are several. Like Laurence, science, and the modern world, she is interested in the ratiocinative, inductively trackable, level. But when, as she rightly predicts, machinery fails to record her particular sounds, she doesn't fold. Instead, she uses her newly acquired religious belief to consider events from a philosophical-theological perspective. Moreover, since she is both a novelist and a student of narrative form, she looks at her experience as both practically and theoretically aesthetic.

Crime is one thing; sin another. Jewel-smuggling matters in the area of civil law. Laurence Manders's family, and especially Helena, Lady Manders, old Louisa's daughter, do what they can to stop Louisa's enterprise and to avoid police detection and publicity. The plot involves them with the occult (regarded as false religion by the Catholic Manders family) but mainly with Louisa, one of Spark's true delights. The plot also involves them with Mrs. Georgina Hogg, a Catholic grotesque embodying a view that recurs in Spark's fiction: "the True Church was awful, though unfortunately, one couldn't deny, true" (81). Aside from the fact that Georgina physically resembles her surname, she persists in regarding her blackmailing endeavors as her Catholic duty. Georgina is developed as a moral crook, even a "witch" properly disposed of by drowning.

Conversely, genuine Catholicism for Caroline and Helena Manders calls for charity, perhaps to arguably counterproductive lengths. Primarily, Caroline thinks, it requires all-inclusive "love," the practice of which may be as impossible as it is essential. As in all Spark books, and perhaps as in all books and in anyone's living of life, what stand out comically, tragically, ironically, or in any other adverbial sense are deviations from such a lofty goal. Still, however, we must try. More pointedly, we must respect others in their uniqueness (for example, homosexuality), and we must not violate their privacy, even as we must pray for what we regard as their moral welfare. Trying to girdle such requirements goes a long way toward clarifying Caroline's converted awareness of what may be impossible expectations.

By now, the subjective-objective, inside-outside splits previously discussed should be seen as featured elements in *The Comforters*. Moving now to the specifically aesthetic level (obviously not separable for Caroline from the strictly constabulary and the religious levels), we note Spark's penchant for the third-person narrator (only *Robinson*

and *Loitering with Intent* are first-person books) and for narratives—
letters, telegrams, phone calls, notebooks, voices—reportable in the
third person. The effect, of course, is to render events and character
depiction as reliable and objectively real for the reader—and to keep
under control what could easily be read by us as it is read by her ac-
quaintances as severely unreliable subjective recording. That Caroline should be "having difficulty with the chapter on realism" (57) in
her study of *Form in the Modern Novel* should hardly surprise us, especially in view of our discussion of modern literature's steady movement toward the acceptance of the sensibly perceivable, the scientifically explainable, as the sole march to reality.

In the final few pages of *The Comforters* Spark pulls off what
seems to me a marvel of narrative complexity. At Caroline's invitation, while she is out of London writing a novel (by now she has
completed *Form in the Modern Novel*), Laurence goes to her London flat to get some books she wants sent to her. Snoop that he is,
and that she fondly knows him to be ("fondly" because Laurence, unlike Mrs. Hogg, never uses his findings to violate one's privacy or one's
self; he's said to be endearingly nosy), Laurence goes through everything meticulously and collects the books. He then writes Caroline a
long letter in which he tells her that he loves her and what's wrong
with her reading of himself and others in their lives. He tells her that
he's read the bundle of notes for the novel she's writing and he can't
figure out why she's left them behind (these constitute her writing
down what her voices said) unless she *wanted* him to read them. In
the letter he also confirms Caroline's belief that the characters in the
book we are now finishing are all being novelized by the typing and
voices she has jotted down. "How is it all going to end?" (203) he asks
her. On his walk home he becomes dissatisfied with the letter he has
just written, tears it into pieces, and tosses them to the wind. They
are said to land, "some on the scrubby ground, some among the deep
marsh weeds, and one piece on a thorn-bush; and he did not then fore-
see his later wonder, with a curious rejoicing, how the letter had got
into the book" (204).

The reason I see these final pages as a marvel is that they place
Spark so clearly in relation to the mindsets discussed earlier, and they
do so in a way that, for me, sets off literary-philosophical-theological

fireworks brilliantly, whether for the grizzled academic or for the general reader of novels. Let me explain.

Plainly, this book, like all Spark novels, loves particular details of the here and now as fervently as does Robbe-Grillet, though Spark generally writes economically and most decidedly in full consciousness of what *The Ballad of Peckham Rye* calls "another world than this" (143). She is, I think, never preachy, but she leaves no doubt that her sensibility is in tune with ancient Greece and the Christian Middle Ages rather than with the strictly skeptical inductive premises of science and Enlightenment, or with modernists' efforts to construct significance out of yesterday's whole cloth, or with Sartrean and postmodernist insistence that we must first despair of achieving meaning before we can maturely will our separate ways *en route* to pointless demise, or with Pinter's eloquent relativism. Caroline's voices and the typewriter tapping away are, for her, solid signs of "another world than this," just as are all those phone calls in *Memento Mori*, delivered in different voices to separate characters and as untraceable by Scotland Yard as are the sources of Caroline's experiences.

What burgeons in these final pages of *The Comforters* is a beautifully controlled manifestation of Spark's ties to what she sees as real, as true. And here I despair of attempting finally to separate literary, philosophical, religious, commonsensical strands from one another. But I think that my inability to do so is Spark's profound point and a measure of the size and scope of what are customarily brief works. Specifically, Caroline's theory is that she, "the character called Laurence Manders" (202), and all of their friends are characters in a novel dictated by her voices and whacked out on that audible typewriter. Caroline is not only one of the characters in the novel we are just finishing, but she is the author of that book, which is inspired by the Muses (*sic*) that no one else thinks real. Spark in turn is the creator of the third-person narrator of *The Comforters*, which is her character Caroline's third-person narrative about this whole gang of characters, whose appearances and activities Spark's inspiration invents. These layers within layers make a kind of sense of the slippery use of tenses: "was," "is," "will be" can both confuse us and alert us to narrative layers and sequences being discussed. Because, for example, Laurence is a dictated character, Caroline's (eventually Spark's) narrator can speak assuredly of his writing and shredding that letter to Caroline and can then tell us just as confidently of Laurence's subsequently reading that "same" letter in Caroline's eventual novel (compare this to tense-play in *Not to Disturb*).

Thus *The Comforters*, like all of Spark's novels—I think in particular of *Memento Mori, The Public Image, Not to Disturb, The Girls of Slender Means, The Prime of Miss Jean Brodie, Reality and Dreams*—is grounded in mystery, if I may speak oxymoronically. As I have said, I refer only in passing to mystery presented by Louisa Jepp's activities, but I emphasize mystery that can be so overpowering as to call for comforters. Psychiatrists, occultists, and friends prove as ineffectual as Job's companions. Only her religious faith in the larger reality—Comforter as Holy Spirit—steadies Caroline in her thinking and writing. On one occasion, for example, she and Laurence discuss determinism and free will. As devil's advocate he pushes for the former. Her faith predictably insists on the reality of God's omniscience and of human freedom of choice. Neither Caroline nor Spark nor anyone else can explicate this orthodox belief, but it remains necessarily true just the same.

Caroline, like some other Spark protagonists, experiences an intense, nearly undiscussable, awareness that God as Maker, Creator, is to creation as artists are to what they make. And the link between these two clearly vast declarations is that God creates the artist. Hence the problem about determinism versus free will, which belief alone juggles satisfactorily. Knowledge is not belief, but each is real and true (for the believer), however difficult it may be for knower and believer to speak with each other. Spark remarked on one occasion that she became a Catholic not because the church offered her a way of seeing and thinking but because she discovered her mind and imagination were those of the church.

Asked what her novel will be about, Caroline answers, "characters in a novel" (202). In his destroyed-preserved letter, Laurence asks, "How is it all going to end?" (203). The big answer would seem to be well beyond any novel or the characters within it. Spark and Caroline are involved with God, with Being, with that "truth" facing Pilate, which can have neither beginning nor end but simply *is*. In saying that her fiction is "a pack of lies" concerned to convey "absolute truth" (Kermode 80), Spark clearly sets herself apart from the Pinters who simply stop when the creative oven dings "done." And of course none of what I have been saying will strike home unless the scriptural mustard seeds, like the scattered bits of Laurence's letter, land on fertile ground. So "it," the subject of Laurence's question, cannot "end." The mystery abides—as it must, to account for the reality of all other beings. We can hardly expect this ultimate mystery to be resolved, of course; but that it can be accommodated by belief and artfully intimated in witty novels are important measures of Muriel Spark's gift to us.

## WORKS CITED

Kermode, Frank. "The House of Fiction." *Partisan Review* 30 (1963): 63–82.
Pinter, Harold. "Art, Truth and Lies." *PMLA* (May 2006): 811–18.
Spark, Muriel. *The Ballad of Peckham Rye*. New York: New Directions Press, 1999.
———. *The Comforters*. New York: New Directions Press, 1994.

# CHAPTER THREE

# "A Spirit of Vast Endurance"

## Muriel Spark, Poet and Novelist

ROBERT E. HOSMER JR.

*I have been writing since the age of 9, when, on a corner of the kitchen table, I wrote an "improved" version of Robert Browning's "The Pied Piper." (I called him "the Piper Pied" to rhyme with "he cried.") I gave my poem a happy ending, not being at all satisfied with the children of Hamelin disappearing into a mountainside forever, as Browning made them do.*

　　　　　　　—Muriel Spark ("The Writing Life")

Muriel Spark's late-in-life recollection (2001) reveals not only her early interest in poetry but her daring revisionist spirit. As she told one interviewer, "I didn't hesitate to improve on Browning" (Glavin 221). The sheer bravado of going the great Victorian poet one better distinguished this young girl who would never lack the courage of her artistic convictions in a career that would span nine decades.

Muriel Sarah Camberg spent twelve years at one of Edinburgh's great educational institutions, James Gillespie's High School for Girls, endowed in the eighteenth century by a wealthy snuff merchant. Edinburgh is a city rich in traditions, none perhaps more esteemed than its dedication to the instruction of the young. In her autobiography, *Curriculum Vitae* (1992, hereafter abbreviated to *CV*), Spark noted that "the Scottish idea was that nobody should be denied this privilege" (49), girls as well as boys. Within the confines of a rigorous academic regimen designed on classical models (Greek, Latin, history, science, math, with Scripture as well, for Edinburgh was the city of John Knox, after all), young Muriel flourished, excelling to such an extent that her later years at Gillespie's were completed on full scholarship.

But it was literature, poetry in particular, that held pride of place for young Muriel. The great influence of her schooldays was, of course, Miss Christina Kay, who would later become the mythic, unforgettable Miss Jean Brodie. As Spark told it, "I fell into Miss Kay's hands at the age of eleven. It might well be said that she fell into my hands. Little did she know, little did I know, that she bore within her the seeds of the future Miss Jean Brodie, the main character in my novel, in a play on the West End of London and on Broadway, in a film and television series" (*CV* 56). Miss Kay was a charismatic teacher of extraordinary impact, as Spark details in her autobiography: "She entered my imagination immediately. I started to write about her even then. Her accounts of her travels were gripping, fantastic. Besides turning in my usual essays about how I spent my holidays I wrote poems about how she had spent her various holidays (in Rome, for example, or Egypt, or Switzerland)" (57). In Miss Kay's classroom the eleven-year-old girl acquired a sense of the richness and variety of biblical verse and read the major poets of the English literary tradition as well as the Border Ballads collected by Sir Walter Scott, a staple of Scottish literary tradition ("very sweet, very harsh, very lyrical" she once called these ballads [Ivry 56]), whose "steel and bite . . . so remorseless and yet so lyrical, entered my literary bloodstream never to depart" (*CV* 98).

Muriel could not get enough poetry in school. She once recalled, "I read exclusively poetry. I used to go to the public libraries [another great Edinburgh institution] and borrow poetry" (Frankel 444). Her whole life Spark acknowledged her deep indebtedness to those public libraries, as she noted in 1992, "without those public libraries of Edinburgh I really don't know how I could have developed or matured" (unpublished notes, archives of the National Library of Scotland). One has a mental picture of this young schoolgirl trudging home to #160 Bruntsfield Place weighed down with volumes by the writers she loved most—some poets of older generations such as Burns, Wordsworth, Tennyson, Scott, Swinburne; others more recent poets such as Blunden, Brooke, de la Mare, Yeats, Masefield, Bridges, and Meynell. The formative influence of these poets is often palpable in Spark's own verse, particularly early on.

Muriel Camberg did more than just read poetry and compose verse of her own, though. She haunted the literary precincts of the city; a favorite excursion was visiting the house where Robert Louis Stevenson once lived ("he had a huge influence on me, as he had on all Scottish writers" [Robson D9]). And she went to hear poets; a reading by John Masefield left an indelible impression: "I was taken to hear him read his poems. He was an exceptionally good reader. He gave every vowel, every syllable, full value" ("Personal History" 63). Muriel soon moved beyond merely revising Browning into crafting more of her own verse. Gillespie's, for all its rigor and structure, gave her creative space, as she observed many years later: "I was allowed to get on with my writing, and was under no pressure to play hockey" (Wilson 4).

Get on with her writing she did, soon establishing herself as what she called "the school's poet and dreamer" (Gilham 411–12), with frequent publication in *Gillespie's School Magazine*. Yet she was more than the in-house poet, as her description of an event in 1930 reveals:

I had a batch of five poems published in an anthology of young people's poems called *The Door of Youth*. I was one of the youngest contributors. This fact, and the number of poems, drew some attention to them. They had a certain lyrical quality. There was a poem about time (in which I noted that "as I write this verse on Time / that self-same Time is flying."); one about a stag hunt (in

which the stag gets away); a poem about the sea, in which it features as a ravenous lion preying on ships and, in another mood,
as a horse; a poem against the snaring of rabbits and against fox
hunting; and a poem "To Everybody," which was used as the dedi-
catory poem in the book. (*CV* 65–66)

Further, Muriel achieved the great distinction of winning first prize
at the age of fourteen for her poem "Out of a Book" in a contest held
to commemorate the centenary of Scott's death in 1932. While the
praise and the parcel of books that accompanied the title of "Queen
of Poetry" were welcome, the public crowning was not: "I felt like
the Dairy Queen of Dumfries," she later recalled (*CV* 68).

Muriel left Gillespie's School in 1937, well educated and sure of
her vocation as a writer. *Vocation* is the correct term, too, since, "Miss
Kay predicted my future as a writer in the most emphatic terms. I felt
I hardly had a choice in the matter" (*CV* 66). In 1938 she traveled to
Rhodesia and embarked on what would turn out to be a disastrous
marriage to the emotionally unstable Sydney O. Spark. The years in
Africa were largely unhappy in personal terms ("a waste," she noted in
an interview [Wachtel]), relieved by the birth of her only child, Robin;
but the people and landscape of the great continent made a deep and
lasting impact on her writer's sensibility. Connections can and have
been made between Spark's African life and her fiction: stories like
"The Seraph and the Zambesi," "The Curtain Blown by the Breeze,"
"The Portobello Road," and "Bang! Bang! You're Dead" dramatically
conjure up the world of Africa. Not so often linked are Spark's African
years and her poetry, but place and vocation intersect here as well. Several poems not published until the late 1940s—"The Victoria Falls,"
"Three Thoughts in Africa," "Like Africa" (the first and last among
her best)—demonstrate the deep impress of the African ethos. Verse
composition remained important to Spark; in her own words: "All
this time [that is, 1938–43], I had never stopped writing poetry. I entered twice for the Rhodesian annual poetry competition and won
twice. I published in local magazines" (*CV* 135).

That chapter of her life ended with her departure for England in
early 1944 on board a troop ship that made its way through U-boat

infested waters from Cape Town to Liverpool. In transit, Spark read a packet of poetry books purchased before sailing, including T.S. Eliot's *The Dry Salvages* (*CV* 140). Once there, she went to work for the Foreign Office, crafting black propaganda (psychological warfare) at a post near Woburn. With the war over, Muriel Spark's involvement with poetry and the lives of poets quickened. In 1946 she became general secretary of the fractious Poetry Society and at the age of twenty-nine she became editor of its *Poetry Review*. Though her tenure would be brief (1947–49), she did much to encourage younger poets; Spark recounted these days vividly in *Loitering with Intent,* with the author's lightly disguised fictional alter ego, Fleur Talbot, leading a bohemian existence on the fringes of post–World War II literary life, and in *Curriculum Vitae.*

Simultaneously these London years mark a watershed in Spark's own writing of poetry, as dozens of poems appeared, some published in *Poetry Review*, but many in other journals such as *Poetry Quarterly*, *World Review*, and the *Fortnightly Review*. Her notebooks from the period, now kept in the Spark archives at the National Library of Scotland, Edinburgh, show her persistence in sending out poems (at least several dozen are listed) and in carefully recording rejections as well as acceptances. Dismissed from her position, the victim of political infighting and personal attack, Spark founded a short-lived poetry magazine, *Forum* (it lasted just two issues), before taking other work to support herself. Though the next several years proved difficult, she continued to write and publish poems in 1950 and 1951. Other literary projects occupied her as well: with Derek Stanford she published *Tribute to Wordsworth* (1950); on her own, she wrote a study of Mary Shelley, *Child of Light: A Reassessment of Mary Wollstonecraft Shelley* (1951), and began drafting an extended critical consideration of John Masefield's work.

The year 1951 marked a turning point in Spark's literary career. From over 6,700 entries, her short story, "The Seraph and the Zambesi and the Fanfarlo" (later called simply "The Seraph and the Zambesi"), written on a bet, won the *Observer*'s Christmas literary contest. The prize of £250, a handsome sum, rescued her, at least temporarily, from financial distress, enabling her to prepare an edition of letters

by the Brontës and work on another book with Stanford. The greatest
effect came in a request from Alan Maclean, fiction editor at Macmillan: Would she write a novel for the firm? Overcoming her very
considerable qualms about novel writing, Spark produced *The Comforters*, which was published to great acclaim in 1957 and became the
first of twenty-two novels. That she is known foremost as a "novelist" always troubled her: in 2005 she told an interviewer, "when I
started writing novels and began getting a name for novelwriting, I still
thought of myself as a poet and I still do . . . because I have a poetic
way of seeing things" (Hosmer 8).

That extraordinary run of novels, so often praised with phrases
like "one of the most trenchant and accomplished bodies of literary
work since the Second World War" (Schiff 37), earned Spark a reputation as "the most gifted and innovative British novelist of her generation" (Lodge 38) and "our only woman satirist and postmodernist of
real stature" (Craig 26). It is not my purpose here to focus on Spark's
fiction; rather I would like to concern myself henceforth with her
poetry in two ways: first, by giving some attention to her considerable output as poet, work which, as we have seen, predates her work
as fiction writer and continued throughout her career, alongside her
novels; second, by exploring ways in which Spark's oft-repeated assertion that she thinks of herself as a poet who writes novels might
have meaning.

Nor is it my primary purpose to defend Spark's reputation as
poet, though I would certainly take issue with critical verdicts like that
rendered anonymously in the *Times Literary Supplement* (*TLS*) concerning the *Collected Poems I*: "in general these are the marginal and
not really very accomplished accumulations of a writing career that
has not always been as successful as it is now" ("Verse and Versatility"
155). The difficulties in assessing the poetry (*The Fanfarlo and Other
Verse* [1952]; *Collected Poems I* [1967]; *Going Up to Sotheby's* [1982];
and *All the Poems of Muriel Spark* [2004]) fairly are abundant, the
most vexing likely being the long shadow cast by her acclaimed reputation as novelist.

*The Fanfarlo and Other Verse* included fourteen poems, three of
them translations from the Latin; *Collected Poems I* printed forty-
four poems, including all fourteen from *The Fanfarlo*, though in dif-

ferent order; *Going Up to Sotheby's* reprinted those forty-four poems, in identical order, prefaced by five other poems, including the title poem. Finally, *All the Poems of Muriel Spark* prints some seventy-three poems, chosen by the poet herself, and arranged by Barbara Epler at New Directions Press. For present purposes, two things need be said concerning *All the Poems*: (1) like the previous two collections, it reprints the entire contents of *The Fanfarlo and Other Verse*—those fourteen poems have remained the heart of Spark's poetic corpus; and (2) eighteen of the poems are "new," that is, written after the publication of *Going Up to Sotheby's* (indeed, thirteen are dated 2000 or later), clearly indicating that Dame Muriel persevered in her dedication to the poet's craft.

Critical reception and attention paid to the work varies. *The Fanfarlo and Other Verse*, published by the Hand and Flower Press, an enterprise run by a generous woman who printed the work of poets whose work she admired in lovely but limited editions, attracted scant attention, not surprisingly. The *Collected Poems I*, published after a string of successful novels including *Memento Mori* (1959) and *The Prime of Miss Jean Brodie* (1961), earned notice in places like the *Spectator* and *TLS* and from distinguished critics such as Frank Kermode and A. S. Byatt. Yet *Going Up to Sotheby's* passed virtually unnoticed (perhaps because it offered so few new poems), and *All the Poems of Muriel Spark* has been largely ignored, suffering the same unfortunate fate as so many volumes of poetry today.

*All the Poems of Muriel Spark* offers a fairly comprehensive look at her poetic achievement of six decades, affording some insight into the characteristics that have distinguished her verse. In truth, the volume does not comprise "all the poems," only those chosen by Spark herself from an output that easily runs to at least twice as many. It does, however, offer poems from each decade of her work in the genre. That the collection is not organized in chronological fashion is significant and telling, for it thereby illuminates a point of central and crucial importance about Muriel Spark as poet: to borrow a phrase from Howard Moss's characterization of Elizabeth Bishop, "she was herself from the beginning" (Moss 303).

And by that I mean at least two things. First, Spark's poetic voice is uniquely hers, unmistakable for its wit, sly eccentricity, verbal punch, timing, sense of throwaway lines as well as "the steel and bite" she admired so much in the Border Ballads. Take, for example, an early poem like "The Grave That Time Dug," a deceptively simple exercise that might at first appear to be nothing more than a nursery-room entertainment ("This is the grave that time dug. This is the box that lay in the grave that time dug. This is the hand that rapped on the box. . . ."); yet its hypnotic, insistent rhythm and cumulative, repetitive phrasing culminate in an unexpected tragic note, almost before the reader apprehends Spark's design. The poem achieves its impact in a manner reminiscent of what Spark had praised in a poem by Andrew Young, "with a kind of riddle-imagery which makes its impact a fraction later than the literal meaning" ("What You Say, and How You Say It" 235).

Playful consideration of serious ideas and themes, often laced with irony, satire, and ambiguity, is, perhaps, the single most distinctive feature of Muriel Spark's verse, qualifying it as metaphysical. Again and again, around a serious idea—often death ("Four People in a Neglected Garden," "Elegy in a Kensington Churchyard," "The Card Party") but perhaps sin and grace ("The Fall") or the diminishments of aging ("Dimmed-Up") or just plain loss ("The Empty Space")—a poem takes shape. And likely not the same shape, for Spark is master of multiple forms, using the diverse disciplines of sonnet, ballad, ode, villanelle, rondel, and acrostic to make her point. Describing her self-imposed training, she once noted, "I'd also had an apprenticeship in the use of words because I was always very interested in formal poetry. I used to try every type of meter and rhyme" (Ross 455). *All the Poems of Muriel Spark* demonstrates the benefits of that training.

From the first, Muriel Spark reveled in the play of language, with that peculiar blend of wit and audacity that gives zest to so much of her verse. What she said about one of her late novels, *Aiding and Abetting*, applies equally to her poetry: "Shall we say I had fun with my imagination?" (Robson D9). Writing a poem *is* fun, and it is meant to give pleasure to its creator as well as its readers. Late poems like "That Bad Cold" (2003); "Holidays" (2002); "Facts" (2003); "Letters" (2003); and "The Creative Writing Class" (2003) make the point with characteristic subtlety and undiminished impact.

But the presence of wit and humor does not mean that the poems lack seriousness. What she asserted in 1999, she had said many times: "comedy isn't necessarily frivolity" (Wachtel), and in her case, it never was. Those who have faulted Spark's verse for an absence of profound statement would seem to transpose to the poetry expectations derived from the fiction, where such expectations are perhaps more often, if subversively, fulfilled. This is part of the game. Many of the poems have a serious, even sly, point, to be taken or not: "if you don't want to take my point, then don't; but it's there, nevertheless," she seems to say. A late poem comes to mind:

> What?
> A black velvet embroidered handbag full of medium-sized carrots
> All of which said 'Good morning' in one voice.
> What does the dream mean?
>
> The black velvet is death; and the embroidery?
> Oh, I daresay, a fancy funeral.
> The carrots are sex, plenty of them.
>
> Why did they say 'Good morning'?
>
> Well, I said 'Good morning' back to them,
> This in my dream being the right thing to do.
> (All the Poems of Muriel Spark 8)

A few poems are indeed difficult, dense, perhaps even obscure; seen from another angle, they are puzzles with solutions perhaps never to be worked out but engaging and stimulating nonetheless. Perhaps Harvey Gotham, the protagonist in Spark's novel *The Only Problem* (1984), spoke for his creator when he asserted, "The *Book of Job* will never come clear. It doesn't matter; it's a poem" (127). Several longer poems fall into this category ("The Nativity," "The Pearl Miners," "Canaan"), and, most prominently, "The Ballad of the Fanfarlo," a twenty-page sequence, is arguably the most difficult poem in the corpus. Complicated in structure, drawing upon the Border Ballads, and with colloquial verse alternating with stanzas that echo Burns,

Yeats, and Coleridge, Spark's poem is a twentieth-century rescripting of Baudelaire's novella, *The Fanfarlo*, into a surrealist-symbolist meditation on the search for identity. Some have thought it nonsense verse in the tradition of Lewis Carroll (or just nonsense); others have thought it a parody of Eliot's poetic strategies, while still others have deemed it nothing more than a *jeu d'esprit*. Whatever else it might be, "The Ballad of the Fanfarlo" is a puzzle challenging the reader. It is a long exercise, marking the last time Spark wrote a long poem, so far as we know, since nearly every poem written afterwards is no longer than a page, and many are shorter. Perhaps like *The Mandelbaum Gate*, a novel considerably longer that anything before or after, the "Fanfarlo" just attempts to do too much.

But such lapses are rare, and poems like "The Rout," a marvelously witty conflation of two disparate historical events into a prickly satire of human foibles; "Four People in a Neglected Garden," a measured meditation on death in a fallen world; and "Against the Transcendentalists," an invigorating argument about poetry and the poet that wittily deflates a number of misconceptions before it asks, "What is Truth true of? And what good's a God's-eye view of anyone to anyone but God?" are major accomplishments by nearly any measure.

Let anyone with any doubts study the brilliantly metaphysical achievement of "Elegy in a Kensington Churchyard":

Lady who lies beneath this stone
Pupil of Time pragmatical,
Though in a lifetime's cultivation
You did not blossom, summer shall.

The fierce activity of grass
Assaults a century's constraint.
Vigour survives the vigorous,
Meek as you were, or proud as paint.

And bares its fist for insurrection
Clenched in the bud; lady who lies
Those leaves will spend in disaffection
Your fond estate and purposes.

Death's a contagion: spring's a bright
Green fit; the blight will overcome
The plagues that overcame the blight
That laid this lady low and dumb,

And laid a parish on its back
So soon amazed, so long enticed
Into an earthy almanack,
And musters now the spring attack;
Which render passive, latent Christ.
                (*All the Poems of Muriel Spark* 65)

Any fair estimate of Muriel Spark's poetry acknowledges its considerable excellences (metaphysical depth and seriousness, wit, technical facility) and admits its occasional difficulties (obscurity, vagueness, length, cerebral density), which do not diminish its accomplishment. Hers is not the poetry of Eliot or Auden or Brontë or Masefield; nor should it be read as though it were. It is hers. It is neither copied nor capable of being copied; as one reviewer has recently noted in an essay on the poetry of Paul Muldoon, "Poets are writers who can't be copied" (Phillips 65). Spark's poetry simply does not fit neatly into any standard category, and that is no surprise, coming from the pen of one who many years ago had the creative audacity to take on Robert Browning. It is, rather, a singularly distinctive verse, highly original, carefully set in perspective, mood, and time, nearly always enveloped in a richness of ambiguity occasionally sufficient to create its own cloud of unknowing, always inviting readers into the dynamics of the serious play that is fine poetry.

Perhaps the jury will always be out, wrangling and failing to reach a summary verdict. While those deliberations continue, we can consider something more important for present concerns: the relationship between Dame Muriel's poetry and her fiction. The provocation for such consideration comes from the writer herself: "I always tell students of my work, and interviewers, that I think of myself as predominantly a poet" (CV 206); and again, "The way I conceive a novel as a work, the way I conceive life, I think I'm a poet first of all" (Blume 16). What are we to make of such an assertion, that one of the greatest contemporary novelists thinks of herself not as a novelist but as a poet and considers her novels poetry? With twenty-two novels published in contrast to four books of poetry, the contention might seem absurd—perhaps Dame Muriel, in customary fashion, is merely having us on?

Certainly, the full meaning of such an assertion does not lie in the "poetic" quality of the prose that graces her fiction, though it is lyrical, spare, and economical and threaded with many poetic devices and figures. Indeed, she has dismissed such a notion; once asked what she meant by saying that a novel is a poem, she responded, "That doesn't mean that there has to be poetic speech and that it has to be rather lush, like Lawrence Durrell's writing" (Ross 455). While she admired Durrell's prose, she rejected anything flowery in her own writing, striving to make her prose "sheer and clean" (Wachtel).

Nor does it lie in the undeniable sound, rhythm, and cadence of her prose, though Spark, like her fictional alter ego in *Loitering with Intent*, Fleur Talbot, has acknowledged a certain precedence of sound over sight: "All poets hear inner voices—words, sentences—rather than seeing visualised scenes. Dramatists visualise scenes. Henry James visualised everything he saw: everything was scenic" (Frankel 450).

Nor is a satisfactory explanation to be derived from the fact that her novels sometimes include a poet, professional or amateur, in the cast of characters (for example, Percy Mannering in *Memento Mori*, Freddy Hamilton in *The Mandelbaum Gate*, Nicholas Farringdon in *The Girls of Slender Means*). Nor in the fact that Spark's novels often include poetic excerpt, reference, or allusion; nor in what one critic has suggested about *The Prime of Miss Jean Brodie*, that Spark uses "quotations from poetry to bind her novel, and to act as refrain and incantation" (Stubbs 24–25), though a valid insight, to be sure.

The answer might lie, at least partially, in the fact that the poems sometimes rehearse the great concerns of the fiction. If we take only the last novel, *The Finishing School*, and its explicit consideration of creativity, publication, and literary afterlife, we discover echoes of those concerns in a cluster of poems written in the several years immediately before the novel ("Created and Abandoned," "While Flicking Over the Pages," "Hats," "Author's Ghosts," "The Creative Writing Class"). A careful, comparative study of the fiction and poetry would test, perhaps prove, such a hypothesis.

Or it might lie, again partially, in the "poetic vision" of the novels; as Spark told Stephen Schiff, "There is also such a thing as poetic vision. It is being aware of words, sometimes in their etymology, in two or three senses, in a very quick flash as one is going along. That I can do quite easily. That is sort of a poetic method" (Schiff 41). Certainly, Spark's sense of herself as a poet meant looking at life as a verbal art, "naming a thing. Naming a thing precisely. And then elaboration on that. And music, the sounds, too, because it's connected to sounds and images, it seems to me" (Blume 16). Yet, there must be something more substantial to this notion of the novel as poem.

An answer of greater meaning and fullness might perhaps be found elsewhere. For some understanding of the real and lasting significance of poetry in Muriel Spark's work, we might turn to the writings of John Henry Cardinal Newman. His influence has often been acknowledged by Spark but not in this particular context. In the months prior to her reception into the Roman Catholic Church on May 1, 1954, Muriel Spark, in a manner recalling her childhood devotion to poetry, read as much of Newman as she could get her hands on, preparing some of the materials for later publication (*The Letters of Cardinal Newman*, a joint project with Derek Stanford, 1957; *The Plain Sermons of Cardinal Newman*, edited by Fr. Vincent Blehl, with a foreword by Spark, 1964).

The impact of Newman's work on Spark was first and foremost spiritual. She herself has put it emphatically, asserting, "It was by way of Newman that I turned Roman Catholic" (*The Plain Sermons* ix). In an interview, later converted into an essay by the interviewer and titled "My Conversion," she noted, "Newman helped me to find a definite location" (59). And when asked fifty years later how she felt about her conversion, she retorted, "The same way I did then. It changed my life" (conversation with author, March 2001).

That change was profoundly spiritual, lasting, and of paramount import. And from that came a correlative event, what might be called Spark's "literary conversion." When asked about formative influences on her own style, she always cited Newman: for her, he is not only "a great man," but "a great writer, a persuasive stylist" ("My Conversion" 59). And she elaborated on that point just a bit: "I didn't get my style until I became a Catholic because you just haven't got to care, and you need security for that" ("My Conversion" 62). It was Newman's prose that prompted this comment, not his poetry. Nevertheless, Newman's formative, abiding, and greatest influence lies beyond stylistics.

Until the mid-1950s, Spark was a poet, essayist, and short story writer, not a novelist. She has long perceived the role of her religious conversion in her literary conversion: "I think there is a connection between my writing and my conversion, but I don't want to be too dogmatic about it. Certainly all my best work has come since then . . . I'm quite sure that my conversion gave me something to work on as a satirist. The Catholic belief is a norm from which one can depart" ("My Conversion" 59–60). What she told an interviewer in 1970 she has often said about her position in the late '40s and early '50s: "I had resisted the novel because I thought it was a lazy way of writing poetry" (Gilham 412). The distance between that position and her lifelong understanding of her artistic self would seem considerable: "I feel I am writing a poem when I am writing a novel," she told an interviewer in 1993 (Schiff 41).

That transformative distance is bridged by her conversion, to be sure, and it has been effectively summarized by the writer herself in an essay, "How I Became a Novelist": "I had been ill . . . I had written nothing for over a year and in the meantime had entered the Roman Catholic Church, an important step for me, because from that time I began to see life as a whole rather than as a series of disconnected happenings. I think it was this combination of circumstances which made it possible for me to attempt my first novel" (683). Implicit within that statement is an acceptance of a profoundly Christian worldview, an understanding of a providential order/design, a structured universe into which all things are integrated *sub specie aeternitatis.* While such a worldview is indeed shared by any number of thinkers, Christian as well as non-Christian, Spark's readings were in the former category, not the latter. The connection becomes even stronger if we turn to one of Newman's early essays, "Poetry with Reference to Aristotle's

*Poetics*" (1829), and discern what is essential to Spark's understanding of her mature literary vocation.

Fundamental to Newman's discussion in the essay is his use of the term "poetry," which is not limited to verse; rather, he uses the term in the comprehensive Aristotelian sense: "poetry" is the making of fiction and is virtually synonymous with "literature." Within his Christian scheme, which owes a great deal to Aristotle by way of Saint Thomas Aquinas, everything has a place and everything belongs in its designated place. The tightly economical, integrated structure of poetry mirrors the providential universe. Like the medieval theologian, Newman had one eye on the hereafter, one eye on the here-and-now; and like Aristotle, his attention was focused consistently on the end of the story, a concern that dovetails neatly with Christian eschatology. For Newman, poetry is ultimately founded on correct moral perception: "where there is not sound moral principle in exercise, there will be no poetry," he declared (*Essays Critical and Historical* 21). The primary end of art is to give pleasure, and the narrowly didactic and moralistic view of poetry set forth here ("A right moral state of heart is the formal and scientific condition of a poetical mind" [21]) disappeared when he returned a number of years later to the subject in *The Idea of a University* (1852). Near the end of section 6 in "Poetry with Reference to Aristotle's *Poetics*" Newman delivers an exhortation: "With Christians, a poetical view of things is a duty" (23). Put another way, for Newman, "the Christian view of the universe is necessarily a poetical one" (Stanford 51). In effect, Newman has subsumed Aristotle's *Poetics* within a Christian view of the universe and human life.

What Newman set forth in "Poetry with Reference to Aristotle's *Poetics*" sounds much like a summation of Spark's artistic credo, principles often noted by critics and acknowledged by the writer herself. Of greatest import for present concerns, however, is the comprehensive sense of *poetry*, something, I would argue, that allowed Muriel Spark to overcome her disdain for the novel as "a lazy way of writing poetry" and allowed her to write *The Comforters*. For her, as for Newman (and Aristotle), "poetry" is literature and so she could, and did, stipulate that a novel is a poem. In *Curriculum Vitae* she recorded her dilemma and its resolution:

I began to think how I could go on about writing a novel, and especially the novel about my hallucinations that I had resolved to write. I didn't feel like 'a novelist' and before I could square it with my literary conscience to write a novel, I had to work out a novel-writing process peculiar to myself, and moreover, perform this act within the very novel I proposed to write. I felt, too, that the novel as an art form was essentially a variation of a poem. I was convinced that any good novel, or indeed any composition which called for a constructional sense, was essentially an extension of poetry. It is always comforting to come across confirmation of one's private feelings in the pronouncements of others who are more qualified to speak. I was particularly delighted when I came across the following piece of dialogue in a book of dialogue-criticism (*Invitation to Learning,* New York, 1942) mainly by the American scholars and writers, Huntington Cairns, Allen Tate (soon to be one of my closest friends) and Mark van Doren.

The magic piece of dialogue (they are discussing Bunyan's *The Pilgrim's Progress*) goes thus:

Van Doren: Why should we not say that this is trying to be a good poem too? Any book that is trying to be good is trying to be a poem.

Tate: It is a poem because it deals with action conveyed through fictions of the imagination.

Van Doren: This would satisfy Aristotle's definition of a poem.

All my hallucinatory experiences, looking back on them, seemed to integrate with this idea. (206)

It is important to note Spark's word choice when she speaks of the "confirmation of one's private feelings." What Spark had long intuited by way of Aristotle, articulated by Newman, found confirmation in Tate's remarks.

Once she discovered formal confirmation of her own understanding, already derived from Aristotle's comprehensive definition of poetry in his *Poetics*, amplified in Newman, Muriel Spark found the freedom and assurance to set to work on a novel. Her self-described project of trying to "square it [novel writing] with [her] literary conscience" could then commence. And when she began what could become *The Comforters*, she proceeded from an orthodox, integrated Christian vision of the world which gave design, order, and stability to the work of art, as to life, employing her own dazzling, economical, precisely *poetic* method to give the vision form, substance, and meaning. In her own words, the accomplishment was the result of "a certain amount of formality and a certain amount of imagination, and a totally different vision from that of what I then thought of as a novel" (Massie 18).

Spark remained emphatic on the point, declaring time and again, "I think I still am a poet" (Gilham 412); "I feel I am writing a poem when I am writing a novel" (Schiff 41); "there has to be a poetic conception. To me, poetry is the first thing, and a novel is, to me, a poem" (Ross 455). And certainly Fleur Talbot speaks for Spark in declaring, "a novel . . . requires a lot of poetic concentration because, you see, I conceive everything poetically" (*Loitering* 28).

In "A Special Message for the First Edition from Muriel Spark," a brief introductory essay written for a 1984 printing of *The Only Problem*, Spark again referred to Tate's comments,

> The American critic, the late Allen Tate, made a claim in a broadcast discussion, to the effect that a good novel should be a poem. He meant this in a very special sense; he was not thinking of ornate language or of the prose-poem; he meant the intrinsic construction, the conception, the vision. I would wish all my novels . . . to be judged under this deep and haunting light. (n.p.)

Muriel Spark was a poet in the customary, received sense of the word to be sure. Crafting verse was a sort of verbal gymnastics for her, disciplined imaginative and technical exercises in precision, economy, and wit. And it was sometimes the place where she rehearsed the concerns to be elaborated upon in her fiction. But she was also a poet in Tate's sense: a novelist whose work illuminates the "intrinsic construction, the conception, the vision" of poetry. "Poetic insight is what I think I have," she once said, asserting that her novels had "a certain lyricism of meaning and recurrence of themes in one's view of life. One can see images returning, as Eliot said, 'what images return'" (Wachtel). That lyricism and recurrence of themes fused all of Spark's creative work, no matter the genre, into one integrated poetic vision.

Yet no one, not even Dame Muriel herself, I believe, would have argued that her poetry overshadows her prose. And that leads, again and finally, to Newman. The peculiar paradox of Newman's principles of poetry is that they find full expression not in his poetry. With the exception of "Lead, Kindly Light" (1833), assured lasting life because of its having been set to music and become a liturgical staple, and "The Dream of Gerontius" (1845), a skillful composition of nearly one thousand lines described by its creator as "the grand Requiem," Newman's poetry is neither well known nor highly praised. One critic put it crisply, simultaneously directing our attention for present concerns in an appropriate direction: "He was a poet who did not write poetry. His real poetry is to be found, not in his metrical compositions . . . but in his prose . . . in that prose which, even when it deals with things within the range of ordinary, familiar experience, invests them with a strange, unearthly light, as with the glow of some mystic dawn" (May 279, 286).

Perhaps, without denying the quality of Spark's poetry and acknowledging that her verse is indeed vastly superior to Newman's, this may be so for her as well. For her, Newman's understanding of *poetry* and the principles by which it lives found powerful, lasting expression in prose fiction. Newman led Muriel Spark to a place and role she never expected. Without Newman, she would never have become the poet who wrote twenty-two extraordinary novels. And what rare pleasure the experience has been, both for the writer and for her myriad readers. Time and again, she achieved an objective emphatically stated years ago, "My whole aim, and I think the whole aim of art, is to give pleasure in one way or another" (Gilham 413). And we are all in debt to Muriel Spark, "a spirit of vast endurance" herself, for the great pleasure her work will continue to give so long as such achievement is valued.

NOTE

"A spirit of vast endurance" is a line from "The Dark Music of the Rue du Cherche-Midi," by Muriel Spark, used by permission of the author and her agent, Georges Borchardt, Inc. All subsequent excerpts are likewise used by permission of the author and her agent. I am greatly indebted to Dame Muriel for her kindness in granting me permission to quote so extensively from her poetry throughout this essay and for her patient attention in commenting on a draft of this essay shortly before her death.

WORKS CITED

Anonyomous. "Verse and Versatility." *Times Literary Supplement* 15 February 1968: 155.

Blume, Mary. "The Infinitely Mysterious." *International Herald Tribune* 29 May 1989: 16.

Craig, Amanda. "Applause, Please." *Literary Review* (July 1992): 26–28.

Frankel, Sara. "An Interview with Muriel Spark." *Partisan Review* 54.3 (1987): 443–57.

Gilham, Ian. "Keeping It Short: Muriel Spark Talks about Her Books." *Listener* 24 September 1970: 411–13.

Glavin, John. "Muriel Spark's Unknowing Fiction." *Women's Studies: An Inter-Disciplinary Journal* 15.1–3 (1988): 221–41.

Hosmer, Robert E., Jr. "A Certain Plausibility: Muriel Spark in Conversation with Robert Hosmer." *London Magazine* (August/September 2005): 22–48.

Ivry, Benjamin. "Knowing at Second Hand: An Interview with Muriel Spark." *Newsweek* 24 August 1992: 56.

Lodge, David. "Marvels and Nasty Surprises: *The Stories of Muriel Spark*." *New York Times Book Review* 20 October 1985: 1, 38–39.

Massie, Allan. "Spark of Inspiration" *Times* [London] 1 August 1987: 18.

May, J. Lewis. *Cardinal Newman.* New York: Dial Press, 1930.

Moss, Howard. "The Poet's Voice." *Minor Monuments: Selected Essays.* New York: Ecco Press, 1986. 293–303.

Newman, John Henry Cardinal. *Essays Critical and Historical.* New ed. Vol. 1. London: 1897.

———. *The Idea of a University.* Ed. Frank M. Turner. New Haven, CT: Yale University Press, 1996.

———. *The Plain Sermons.* Ed. Vincent Ferrer Blehl, S.J. Foreword by Muriel Spark. New York: Herder and Herder, 1964.

Phillips, Adam. "Someone Else" (Review of *The End of the Poem: Oxford Lectures on Poetry* and *Horse Latitudes* by Paul Muldoon). *London Review of Books* 4 January 2007: 35–36.

Robson, David. "Spark Still Burning Bright." *Toronto Globe* 7 October 2000: D8, D9.

Ross, Jean W. "Interview with Muriel Spark." *Contemporary Authors, New Revision Series, Volume 12.* Farmington Hills, MI: Gale, 1984. 455–57.

Schiff, Stephen. "Muriel Spark: Reading Between the Lines." *New Yorker* 24 May 1993: 36–43.

Spark, Muriel. *Curriculum Vitae*. London: Constable, 1992.

———. "How I Became a Novelist." *John O'London's Magazine* 1 December 1960: 683.

———. *Loitering with Intent*. New York: Coward, McCann and Geoghegan, 1981.

———. "My Conversion." *Twentieth Century* 170 (Autumn 1961): 58–63.

———. *The Only Problem.* Illustrated by Vivienne Flesher. 1st ed. Franklin Center, PA: Franklin Library, 1984.

———. "Personal History: Visiting the Laureate." *New Yorker* 26 August 1991: 63–67.

———. "What You Say, and How You Say It." *Poetry Quarterly* 2.4 (Winter 1950): 234–37.

———. "The Writing Life." *Washington Post Book World* (11 March 2001): T06.

Stanford, Derek. "The Early Days of Miss Muriel Spark: Some Prime Recollections." *The Critic* 20.5 (April–May 1962): 49–53.

Stubbs, Patricia. *Muriel Spark*. London: Longman Group, 1963.

Wachtel, Eleanor. "Eleanor Wachtel Interviews Dame Muriel Spark." Writers and Company, CBC Radio. 1999.

Wilson, Conrad. "Muriel Spark Prefers to Hide in the South." *Scotsman* (20 August 1962): 4.

# CHAPTER FOUR

# Breaking Free of the Grave

## Muriel Spark's Uses of Humor and the Supernatural

REGINA BARRECA

*[Spark] turned to writing novels, which are remarkable for their success in combining two things which regularly do not go together, but which she contrives to make apparently natural companions: on the one hand the accurate evocation of ordinary life, including the speech and thought patterns of industrial workers, or of girls of slender means, or of comfortable bachelors, all depicted with a most feline touch; and on the other hand something altogether higher and less mundane, indications of the activity of the supernatural, sometimes providential, but sometimes—it cannot be denied that Dame Muriel's mind has its dark and sinister aspects—apparently malign. . . . She is a mistress of the spoken word, and an expert in depicting the interplay of the living and the dead.*

—Chancellor's Speech on the Conferment of Muriel Spark's
Honorary Degree, Oxford University, 1999
(*Oxford University Gazette: Encaenia 1999* [supplement],
June 25, 1999, paraphrase from the Latin)

> *Spark underscores the irreparable duplicity of the universe,*
> *where ordinary things coexist with supernatural ones in hideous*
> *harmony. . . . Spark makes use of the imagery of hell and all of its*
> *attributes (spirits, ghosts, fire), and yet she pretends to take them as*
> *literary references while hell gapes beneath her transparent language.*
> —Helene Cixous, "Grimacing Catholicism: Muriel Spark's
> Macabre Fiction," 1968 (translated by Christine Irizzary)

Muriel Spark has no shame when it comes to trafficking in the uncanny. Born into a half-Jewish and half-Protestant family in Edinburgh, Spark repeatedly recited the story of her conversion to Roman Catholicism as unhesitatingly and ritualistically as one might recite the Nicene Creed. Yet despite—or perhaps because of—her deep faith, Spark's work is thoroughly informed by the supernatural. Spark's novels and stories practically rattle with deftly wrought versions and visions of the spectral, the weird, and the occult.

Spark both astonishes and fascinates with her stories of the supernatural; her biographer, Martin Stannard, announces in his discussion of Spark's first published story "The Seraph and the Zambesi" that "The story represents a formal and stylistic revolution which arguably makes it the first 'postmodern,' 'magic realist' text by a British author" (103). I would add that, to a great extent, it is the incandescent humor in Spark's supernatural stories that juxtaposes the postmodern with the postmortem. Breaking free of the grave in all senses, Spark unapologetically twins death with humor. Stannard goes on to argue that Spark "is careful about her writing, but not about the world. The world fascinates her, but she is somehow distant from it, as though listening to voices through a wall or watching the figures act out their pantomime behind plate glass" (104). It is the apparent lack of passionate entanglement between Spark and her creations that provides the distance necessary for the construction of a convincingly comic perspective, and, as the primary ghost from the story "The Executor" explains, perspective cannot be overestimated:

He once said that if you could imagine modern literature as a painting, perhaps by Brueghel the Elder, the people and the action were in the foreground, full of color, eating, stealing, copulating, laughing, courting each other, excreting, and stabbing each other, selling things, climbing trees. Then in the distance at the far end of a vast plain, there he would be, a speck on the horizon, always receding and always there, and always a necessary and mysterious component of the picture; always there and never to be taken away, essential to the picture—a speck in the distance, which if you were to blow up the detail would simply be a vague figure, plodding on the other way. (*All the Stories of Muriel Spark* [*AS*] 289)

Indeed, Stannard's words also conjure up the explanation given by the narrator of Spark's short story "The Fortune Teller," who offers the following perspective on her own entertaining and indefatigable talents: "You mustn't think that because I take my gifts seriously, I take them solemnly. It is all an airy dream of mine, unsinkable because it is light" (*AS* 299). Spark makes light and, as a result, illuminates the uncanny, removing it from the shadows and brushing off the cobwebs. In a 2004 interview with James Brooker and Margarita Estévez Saá, Spark explains that "My books often deal with the supernatural. . . . I treat the supernatural as if it was part of natural history. If I write a ghost story it wouldn't come under the heading of ghost story necessarily because I treat it as if it was a natural thing. This is in fiction. In private life, I have never met a ghost, ever, but in fiction I have imagined a lot of psychic situations" (1036).

One could hardly disagree. Of her novels, *The Hothouse by the East River* concerns a group of English people who find themselves dead and living in New York (even though "One should live first, then die, not die then live" [123]), while *The Ballad of Peckham Rye* produces characters that virtually dance around the maypole of a once double-horned figure self-described as "one of the wicked spirits that wander through the world for the ruin of souls" (106). Spark's fascination with the sibylline can be found even in her first novel, *The Comforters*, which is structured by a narrator who cannot escape the sound of a ghostly typewriter that insists on anticipating and tapping out her destiny ("'it is as if a writer on another plane of existence was writing a story about us.' As soon as she had said these words, Caroline knew that she had hit on the truth" [63]).

And of Spark's forty-one collected short stories, twelve deal with the uncanny. Not surprisingly, then, this number of examples lead Spark's readers to ask the same question posed by Virginia Woolf when approaching the ghost stories of Henry James (a writer with whom Spark is often compared in term of their use of the uncanny): "Shouldn't so much evidence of the delight which human nature takes in stories of the supernatural . . . inevitably lead one to ask what this interest implies both in the writer and in the reader?" (61).

What it most certainly does not imply in Spark's work is the misty, dreary shadow-world where ordinary tales of the extraordinary too often find themselves congealing into a sort of gelatinous goo. Instead, Spark's precise prose places her lapsed characters in a lapidary setting; her words work like a sharpened blade striking an adamantine seam in order to release the precious from the inert. Uncluttered and unclouded as the writing of her supernatural tales remains, Spark does not recoil from the excesses available only within the framework of the unreal. Spark unveils and acknowledges the fantastic in order to move briskly toward her real business, which is to see how the characters (whether of this earth or not) manage the tasks they've been assigned.

Whether they are ghosts or some other sort of Other—an angel in "The Seraph and the Zambesi," an infant in "The First Year of My Life," a UFO sighter in "Miss Pinkerton's Apocalypse," to name a few—they are treated with respect. Spark handles her narrative elements in a manner similar to the way the narrator of "The Fortune Teller" deals her deck of cards: "I shuffle and deal and see what comes up, and in the meantime my ideas take form as if the cards were a sort of sacrament, 'an outward and visible sign of an inwards and spiritual grace' as the traditional definition goes" (*AS* 304). And yet, somehow, Spark manages to infuse her supernatural stories with this sense of spiritual grace while never dipping into her religious capital; her writing is never dogmatic and includes only the rare mention of religion per se.

We are much more likely to get our legs pulled by the comic than our heads bowed by the tragic or our spines tingled by the scary when we encounter the uncanny in Spark. One need only to look at "The Young Man Who Discovered the Secret of Life" to learn that Spark places her emphasis on the "natural" in supernatural:

> The main fact was, he was haunted by a ghost about five feet high when unfurled and standing upright. For the ghost unfurled itself from the top drawer of a piece of furniture that stood in the young man's bed-sitting room every night, or failing that, every morning. The young man was a plasterer's apprentice, or so he claimed.
>
> But I have been told on good authority that this is absolutely absurd. There is no such thing: plasterers do not have apprentices. (*AS* 384)

The joke works because it flips our expectation like a pancake. What is bizarre is *not* that a ghost lives in a dresser-drawer but that a plasterer should have an apprentice. The laugh, in other words, is on us. Spark's humor lies in the initial misperception on the part of the reader who believes in the ridiculousness of ghosts. In fact, this particular spirit is out of step with the spirit of the age as embodied by Ben. The top-drawer ghost is less effective than most of his spectral brethren, in part because he exhibits a snobbishness that is incompatible with his residence in the bureau of an underemployed young man. "The ghost is a terrible snob," according to Ben, as well as being manipulative: "He makes me feel great and terrible—" (386). Ben, however, is nobody's fool: "I can't think of any more mindless occupation than to be a ghost . . . [S]o very unnecessary. I could have you psychoanalyzed away" (386). And although Ben exhibits very little patience for the ghost's effete tastes—"Curl up and return to your drawer," Ben bade him, "And mind you don't crush my pyjamas"—the ghost can't help but betray his own imperious class prejudice: "'Your pyjamas,' said the ghost, 'have no place in the top drawer where I come from. They are not even pure silk; they are Marks & Spencer's'" (385). In contrast to "The Portobello Road," the living in this story have the last laugh. "'This quenching of the ghost,' Ben wrote, 'is to me the secret of life.'

He said 'quenching' for he felt the ghost had been thirsty for his soul, and had in fact drunk his fill," explains the narrator, as she tells us about Ben's contented and successful life (386).

## WITH APOLOGIES TO SPARK, THE HEADING FOR THIS SECTION IS "GHOSTS"

Unlike the ghost of Jacob Marley, "dead as a doornail," who appears to Scrooge in *A Christmas Carol*, the ghosts created by Muriel Spark tend not to walk the Earth for penance. They do not wander around "wearing the chains they forged in life," as is the case with Scrooge's former partner. Instead, Spark's spirits seem to sense that something has escaped them during their lifetimes. They come back not to frighten those left behind but to monitor them ("The Young Man Who Discovered the Secret of Life") or, with a certain amount of spite, to thwart them ("The Executor"; "The Portobello Road"). Occasionally they return to help with the housework ("Another Pair of Hands"). And while Emily Dickinson pointed out that one need not be a house to be haunted, Muriel Spark points out that one need not be actually dead ("The Leaf Sweeper")—or, at least, not be aware of being dead (*Hothouse*; "The Girl I Left Behind Me"; "The House of the Famous Poet")—to haunt.

It is as if the wall between the living and dead thins and becomes permeable. In their article " 'Releasing Spirit from Matter': Comic Alchemy in Spark's *The Ballad of Peckham Rye*, Updike's *The Witches of Eastwick* and Mantel's *Fludd*," Horner and Zlosnik argue that not only do all three writers "seem to be in touch with arcane knowledge beyond the reach of mere mortals" (136) but that this particular brace of modernists embrace "older forms of belief and writing which blur the boundary between the world of the everyday senses and the realm that lies beyond it. We might argue that these late twentieth-century texts draw both upon Gothic traditions and these pre-enlightenment beliefs to create an alchemy of their own: one that is creative rather than destructive, liberating rather than redemptive and comic rather than terrifying" (137). And so, in revisiting her work, we cite the significance of ghosts in Spark even if she did not have a sighting herself.

Ghosts most often appear as the result of a promise broken or as a result of a character misunderstanding the terms of an agreement. Whereas one character might have thought that a promise was merely a ritual reassurance to be given lightly and without consideration of the currency behind the words, for example, another will have conferred upon the words a different value. Such is the case in "The Portobello Road." George, an infuriatingly weak villain, kills his childhood friend, Needle, because she insisted on keeping her word to inform George's fiancée (another old friend) about George's already-existing marriage to a woman in the Congo. George has trouble imagining that Needle will make good on her threat of disclosure and prefers to believe—at least initially—that he can wheedle her into indulging his moral and spiritual laxity. Convincing himself that because he had "married Matilda in the Congo" the marriage contract was not binding ("'I'm not sure that the Congo marriage was valid,' he continued. 'Anyway, as far as I'm concerned, it isn't'"), George relieves himself of both responsibility and guilt for what he regards as an act of folly (*AS* 16). Needle, however, defines it differently: "'It would still be bigamy,' I said. He was furious when I used that word bigamy. He lifted a handful of hay as if he would throw it in my face, but controlling himself meanwhile he fanned it at me playfully" (16).

For George, promises, vows, and perhaps language itself is disembodied, set free from meaning. For Needle, in contrast, the wedding vows exchanged during a Roman Catholic ceremony in Africa when George married his native mistress constitute not a meaningless bartering of sex for security but a sacrament. It is an event of considerable significance, not merely a transaction whereby the currency of the event loses value if converted into another country's vocabulary. Needle employs language quite differently from the way George uses it; she has an undying relationship to the word. When the wedding vow he made to his first wife, Matilda, proves to be bankrupt, Needle responds with a spiritual blow that inverts the power dynamic. She refuses to pretend that the marriage was invalid, refuses to underwrite George's lie. George, in response, kills her:

> "You'll keep my secret, won't you? You promised." He had released my feet. I edged a little further from him.

I said, "If Kathleen intends to marry you, I shall tell her that you're already married."

"You wouldn't do a dirty trick like that, Needle? You're going to be happy with Skinny, you wouldn't stand in the way of my—"

"I must, Kathleen's my best friend," I said swiftly.

He looked as if he would murder me and he did. (17)

What George cannot anticipate, however, is that Needle refuses to lie down and die. She haunts him even after he admits to his crime of murder (although not of bigamy: "the marriage didn't come out— who would think of looking up registers in the Congo?"), perhaps because the police do not accept George's confession of guilt since "Dozens of poor mad fellows confess to every murder" (19). By the end of the story, however, Needle seems to be more accepting of her state; looking back at a photograph of her friends in their "young youth at high summer" snapped by George's camera, she sees herself as "secure in my difference from the rest" even then (20).

As I have argued elsewhere (Barreca), in Spark's work what is apparently metaphoric becomes devastatingly literal: Needle is found in a haystack after her murder. She sees George "just" before her death. He looks "as if" he would murder her and he does. The reader who dismisses an early line or reference with patient or indulgent skepticism must regroup original ideas and begin to read with renewed attention. Details of first meetings, initial conversations, and deceptively off-handed comments become central to understanding and making sense of the apparently accidental or arbitrary. Spark's fiction breaks the boundaries of what is conventionally regarded as the range of possible meaning; the reader is forced to return, briefly, to the point where clichés or imagery thinned by overuse are once again invested with their heightened, original meanings. Translation of metaphor and literary convention into plot structure is often at the center of her supernatural plots. Part of Spark's art, therefore, is her ability to revitalize the ghost story itself.

The effective and skillful ability to haunt is a power belonging to the vanquished, not the victor. In part this power depends on the subterfuge of the vanquished, the camouflage offered by their perceived insignificance. In Spark, the crafty acknowledgment of a perceived powerlessness by the ghost (or infant, or UFO-sighter, for that matter) permits the most marginalized of characters to have a voice and effect on the ordinary world. It turns out that the uncanny is a marvelously effective tool for those considered ineffective—and who is regarded as more ineffective than a corpse?—within a society bound by convention. Spark's marginal figures, however, are able to use the liminality of their inscription within the larger social order to draw upon forces outside narrow or orthodox belief systems.

Having been denied the chance to fully participate in life, many of Spark's ghostly figures are determined to get their money's worth after they die. It is, therefore, through a combination of spite and compassion, for example, that Needle emerges as a far more powerful spirit than she ever was as a woman. By forcing the reader to rewrite Needle's life after hearing about her experience after death, Spark is also drawing attention to the way tales of the supernatural "call our calendars into question" as Bliss Cua Lim writes in "Spectral Times: The Ghost Film as Historical Allegory" (287). Lim's comments about the use of the ghost in film apply neatly to the disruption of time in Spark's narratives:

> The temporality of haunting, through which events and people return from the limits of time and mortality, differs sharply from the modern concept of a linear, progressive, universal time. The hauntings recounted by ghost narratives are not merely instances of the past reasserting itself in a stable present, as is usually assumed; on the contrary, the ghostly return of traumatic events precisely troubles the boundaries of past, present, and future. (287)

"Linear, progressive, universal time" becomes as twisted as Christmas garland in "The Leaf Sweeper" when we experience a character who is haunted by a more conventional version of himself. His mother refers to a pleasant young man as "Johnnie's ghost" and explains that although he "comes home every Christmas" she doesn't like him, preferring her institutionalized, mad, holiday-hating offspring to his dandy double: "I can't bear him any longer, and I'm going away tomorrow. I don't want Johnnie's ghost, I want Johnnie in flesh and blood," says Johnnie's mother (*AS* 131). When the narrator meets Johnnie's ghost she tells him, point-blank, to go away. She knows that "it sounds hard. But perhaps you don't know how repulsive and loathsome is the ghost of a living man. The ghosts of the dead may be all right, but the ghost of my Johnnie gave me the creeps" (131). Only after introducing ghostly Johnnie to living Johnnie is anyone given peace; like Wendy sewing Peter Pan's shadow back onto him, the narrator of the "The Leaf Sweeper" can offer the central character the solace of having all of himself in one place. And even if Johnnie and his ghost disagree, at least they sweep the leaves in tandem; even if they remain divided, at the very least they are in the same place.

Spark plays with linear time the way she plays with the dividing line between life and death. "Sometimes my predictions are wildly astray as they pertain to the present time and environment, but I have known them to become surprisingly true much later in life, in a different place, and presume that this may happen, too, in some of the cases where I lose sight of the person whose fortune I have told" says the narrator in Spark's "The Fortune Teller" (299). But it is not only in her stories of the supernatural that we find Spark fiddling with sequence. We learn in the early pages of *The Prime of Miss Jean Brodie*, for example, that Mary Macgregor, who is "lumpy, with merely two eyes, a nose and a mouth like a snowman," will later be "famous for being stupid and always to blame" and yet even later will have been discovered "at the age of twenty-three" to have "lost her life in a hotel fire" (22). The seeds of Mary's violent and ignominious demise are nascent even as we encounter her for the first time.

SPARK'S OTHER "OTHERS"

In *The Shape of Fear: Horror and the Fin de Siècle Culture of Decadence*, Susan Navarette offers us a passage that, oddly enough, connects Spark to Shelley through a belief concerning the preternatural knowledge of newborns:

Thomas Jefferson Hogg reminds us of the afternoon stroll in which Shelley sought to prove definitively that infants must retain visions of another world, memories that fall away from us as we grow older. Having caught hold on Magdalen Bridge of a several-weeks-old infant, he insisted on asking its mother, "Will your baby tell us anything about pre-existence, Madam?" When she demurred, Shelley insisted that the baby *could* "speak if he [would], for he is only a few weeks old": "He may fancy perhaps that he cannot, but it is only a silly whim; he cannot have forgotten entirely the use of speech in so short a time; the thing is absolutely impossible." The baby failing to relent, the exasperated poet exclaimed, "How provokingly close are those new-born babes!" (117)

In Spark's "The First Year of My Life," we learn that Shelley was merely anticipating what science would later prove after "long and far-adventuring research and experiment," which is that "all of the young of the human species are born omniscient. Babies, in their waking hours, know everything that is going on everywhere in the world; they can tune in to any conversation they choose, switch on to any scene" (*AS* 274). No wonder Shelley was exasperated by his interaction with the closed-mouth infant. The first-person narrator of Spark's story, feeling a teensy bit oppressed by what seems to be the poor timing in terms of history (being born "on the first day of the second month of the last year of the First World War") is anything but "close" given a willingness to blend history, literary criticism, and political opinion with general autobiography:

> The strongest men on all fronts were dead before I was born. Now the sentries used bodies for barricades and the fighting men were unhealthy from the start. I checked my toes and fingers, knowing I was going to need them. *The Playboy of the Western World* was playing at the Court Theatre in London, but occasionally I beamed over to the House of Commons which made me drop off gently to sleep. Generally, I preferred the Western Front where one got the true state of affairs. It was essential to know the

worst, blood and explosions and all, for one had to be prepared, as the boy scouts said. Virginia Woolf yawned and reached for her diary. Really, I preferred the Western Front. (277)

Before growing into an ordinary "healthy and house-trained person," the narrator spent an entire year unsmiling, to dismay of relatives (280). Only at a first-birthday party did the circumstances change— not because the infant was delighted, as all the guests claimed, by the celebration ("The cake be damned" says the baby)—but because of an overheard remark about the value of war that is so absurd as to be hilarious. Repeated by a "stout gentleman with his backside to the fire" at the party, we hear "words uttered in the House of Commons after the First World War by the distinguished, the immaculately dressed and the late Mr. Asquith": "'All things have become new. In this great cleansing and purging it has been the privilege of our country to play her part'" (279–80).

"That did it," explains the baby; "I broke into a decided smile and everyone noticed it, convinced that it was provoked by the fact that my brother had blown out the candle on the cake" (279). The truth is more complex: "when I really mean a smile, deeply felt from the core, then to all intents and purposes it comes in response to [those] words uttered in the House of Commons" (279). The absurdity, the hypocrisy, the smug, self-satisfied and self-congratulatory words concerning what even a babe-in-arms knows was the slaughter of a generation— "On all the world's fighting fronts the men killed in action or dead of wounds numbered 8,538,315 and the warriors wounded and maimed were 21,219,452" (278)—uttered by a man whom the baby has seen drunk and groping women in the backseat of car, is simply too much to bear without a laugh.

In "Miss Pinkerton's Apocalypse" Spark introduces her readers to an entirely different brand of the extraordinary: the extraterrestrial. Laura Pinkerton and her companion George Lake see a "small round flattish object" flying around their drawing room. It's interesting that the narrator refers to the female character exclusively by her surname, where the male character is referred to by the narrator as "George" throughout; we learn Miss Pinkerton's first name and George's last name only because the characters themselves use those appellations.

Clearly the narrator is on Miss Pinkerton's side, as we discover at the end of the tale: "Personally, I believe the story, with a preference for Miss Pinkerton's original version. She is a neighbor of mine" (*AS*, 120).

In fact, the story has far more to do with a struggle for power between Miss Pinkerton and George than it does with any conflict between the earth and outer space; George wants to tell his version of the story, Miss Pinkerton wants to tell hers. The space ship is, in terms of the narrative trajectory, incidental. In other words, Spark's story about a flying saucer focuses on the type of saucer—in this case Spode—not the unexpected and inexplicable appearance of a vehicle from another planet. George and Miss Pinkerton get into a heated argument about the discrepancies between their two versions of what actually happened.

What brings the crisis to a head is that Miss Pinkerton knows her china whereas George thinks he knows everything else. When they call in newspaper reporters, George explains that although he is "extremely sceptical as a rule," he can attest to the veracity of the U.F.O. sighting (118). Miss Pinkerton, in contrast, explains to the press that the experience is not new for her because "'Personally, I've been in china for twenty-three years. I recognised the thing immediately.' The reporter scribbled and enquired, 'These flying discs appear frequently in China?' 'It was a saucer. I've never seen one flying before,' Miss Pinkerton explained" (118).

More certain than George is concerning the object's identity— "'It's a saucer,' said Miss Pinkerton, keen and loud, 'an antique piece. You can tell by the shape'"—Miss Pinkerton draws on the fact that she has "been in 'antique china for twenty-three years in the autumn'" (115). George, in a lapse of diplomacy, counters with his own authoritative statement: "It can't be antique, that's absolutely certain" (115). And, with an almost visible shaking of the head, the narrative then tells us "He ought to have been more tactful, and would have been, but for the stress of the moment. Of course it set Miss Pinkerton off, she being in the right" (115). When George declares that the space ship was aiming directly for him, Miss Pinkerton disagrees: "'Mr. Lake was not attacked . . . There was no danger at all. I saw the expression on the pilot's face. He was having a game with Mr. Lake, grinning all over his face.'" The pilot, as Miss Pinkerton saw him, was "a tiny man half the size of my finger" who "sat on a tiny stool. He held the little tiny steering-wheel with one hand and waved with the other. Because, there was something like a sewing-machine fixed near the rim, and he worked the tiny treadle with his foot. Mr. Lake was not attacked." And when George counters with "Don't be so damn silly," the story takes a sharp turn (119).

Miss Pinkerton will have the last laugh. She decides she will pretend to the reporters that she and George were drinking heavily and made up the whole story: "Oh, what a mess! What an evening! We aren't accustomed to drink, you see, and now oh dear, oh dear!" (119). The newspaper photographer and journalist leave the premises, convinced by the lie Miss Pinkerton tells in order not to have her version of reality overwritten by George's, and Miss Pinkerton is left in control of the tale. When, in the final paragraph, the narrator tells us "I have reason to believe this version because, not long afterwards, I too received a flying visitation from a saucer. The little pilot, in my case, was shy and inquisitive. He pedaled with all his might. My saucer was Royal Worcester, fake or not I can't say" (120), the weight of narrative rests, like a cup, on the saucer. Visitations, whether from other planets or other lifetimes, are domesticated and confiscated by the humorous authority of Spark's voice.

Like the narrator of "The Fortune Teller," Spark seems to follow her "own secret rules" when writing her short stories of the supernatural, rules that

> arise from deep conviction. They cannot be formulated, they are not as sincere and indescribable as are the primary colours; they are not of a science but of an art. Very often I make a mistake, but I know it; at such moments I'm thinking my way, talking through a dense fog, shining the torch of my intuition here and there until it hits on some object which may or may not prove to be what I say it is. (299)

The illumination provided by Spark's torch of intuition into otherwise shadowed corners of existence is one of the most provocative and delightful results of her (almost) uncanny brilliance as a writer.

## WORKS CITED

Barreca, Regina. "Metaphor-into-Narrative: Being Very Careful with Words." *Last Laughs: Perspectives on Women and Comedy*. Ed. Regina Barreca. New York: Gordon and Breach, 1988. 243–56.

Brooker, James, and Margarita Estévez Saá. "Interview with Dame Muriel Spark." *Women's Studies* 33 (2004): 1035–46.

Horner, Avril, and Sue Zlosnik. "'Releasing Spirit from Matter': Comic Alchemy in Spark's *The Ballad of Peckham Rye*, Updike's *The Witches of Eastwick* and Mantel's *Fludd*." *Gothic Studies* 2.1 (2000): 136–47.

Lim, Bliss Cua. "Spectral Times: The Ghost Film as Historical Allegory." *Positions* 9.2 (2001): 287–329.

Navarette, Susan. *The Shape of Fear: Horror and the Fin de Siècle Culture of Decadence*. Lexington: University Press of Kentucky, 1998.

Stannard, Martin. "Nativities: Muriel Spark, Baudelaire, and the Quest for Religious Faith." *Review of English Studies* new ser. 55.218 (2004): 91–105.

Spark, Muriel. *All the Stories of Muriel Spark*. New York: New Directions, 2001.

———. *The Ballad of Peckham Rye*. New York: Perigee, 1960.

———. *The Comforters*. New York: New Directions, 1957.

———. *The Hothouse by the East River*. London: Macmillan, 1973.

———. *The Prime of Miss Jean Brodie*. Philadelphia: J. B. Lippincott, 1962.

Woolf, Virginia. *Granite and Rainbow*. London: Hogarth P, 1981.

# CHAPTER FIVE

# "Fully to Savour Her Position"

## Muriel Spark and Scottish Identity

### GERARD CARRUTHERS

In a rather uncharacteristic moment of bad judgment, Robin Jenkins opined that it would be "very difficult to get any real Scottish person accepting [Muriel Spark] as a Scottish writer."[1] Jenkins was at the time Spark's only serious contender for the title of Scotland's "senior" living novelist, but he was not motivated by rivalry. Rather, Jenkins spoke as one entrapped by the predominant impulse of twentieth-century Scottish literary volition. Self-conscious of Scottish literature's supposedly inadequate criticism of its own national context through the nineteenth-century colonial period (both Scotland's alleged colonization by England and Scotland's enthusiastic collaboration in the British imperial project), early twentieth-century Scottish literature expended much inward energy reflecting historically both upon massive shortcomings in itself and in Scottish society. The outcome of this new scrutiny included the promulgation of a vigorous nativism in expression, of which a Scots language revival was the most obvious exemplar, and a muscular corpus of Scottish fiction of historical and social critique, both of which were, at the time, creatively "modern." It certainly could not be argued, then (as it could be for the nineteenth century), that the nation indulged any longer in a frivolous, escapist, anachronistic, literary product designed to evade the contemporary realities of national behavior at home and abroad.[2] However this might be, a negative counter-effect of this understandable aspiration to engage with and, indeed, recreate Scottish national circumstance through literary expression has led to long-lingering attitudes concerned in overwrought ways with "realism" and the priority of alighting upon "Scottish" subject-matter.[3] While the construction of "English" literature (at least in university, college, and school courses) has tended to be historically rather unreflective and loose in its consideration of national parameters, the construction of "Scottish" literature (one of the most prominent cultural projects of twentieth-century Scotland) has leaned toward being too discriminating, and the ghost of essentialist cultural nationalism continues to haunt it. As the twentieth century ended, Robin Jenkins sincerely voiced the opinion that Scotland's most successful writer of the previous one hundred years (no one else of her national origin in this time comes close to combining the international critical and popular regard that Spark garners) is a cosmopolitan misfit who does not, at least in too many of her books, have an insistent enough agenda of "being Scottish."[4]

Essentialism in identity is something that consistently, though often obliquely, concerns the fiction of Muriel Spark. Spark's own origins are problematically heterogeneous, as she herself indicates in her most revealing semiautobiographical short story, "The Gentile Jewesses" (1967). Here we find the recurrent Sparkian motif of oxymoronic identity where the title alludes to the fact that the narrator is the third woman in a direct family line to be progeny through mixed Jewish and "non-Jewish" blood.[5] What we have, then, is both recognition of the orthodox matrilineal means of Jewish succession and a brazen acknowledgment of the collapsing of this mechanism. This simultaneous invoking and ironicizing of tradition is a hallmark of Spark's fiction, indicating her view that stories, or history, ought to be replayed and even sometimes reworked rather than simply accepted as givens. Narratives for Spark are potentially both wonderful imaginative acts of transformation and, at other times, lazily and even nefariously designed, and in this ambiguous nature of story telling, Spark recognizes both the human aspiration toward transcendence over everyday materialist reality and the faulty, fallen human propensity toward selfishly motivated articulations. In "The Gentile Jewesses" the narrator refuses to be denied her Jewish heritage simply because of Talmudic law and defiantly embraces and gently mocks this law as a person who is possessed of enough imaginative empathy for her Jewish forbears for them and their origins to matter to her. In this unwillingness by the narrator to be shut out by the tradition on this matter, we witness an important maneuver in Spark's Judaeo-Christian anagogic practice, where the word is rendered precisely nonstatic and instead comes alive or, in a sense, is mischievously made awkward flesh.

The febrile imaginative capacity of the narrator in "The Gentile Jewesses" is such that she has consciously to remind herself of the distinction between the very little that she has actually witnessed in life and those big historical events she has merely heard about: "Was I present at the Red Sea crossing? No, it had happened before I was born. My head was full of stories, of Greeks and Trojans, Picts and Romans, Jacobites and Redcoats, but these were definitely outside of my lifetime" (312). Here "Scottish" Picts and Jacobites are part of a much wider pattern of struggling, antagonistic identity when set against the longer view of history encompassing the stories of the Old Testament and ancient Mediterranean civilization, both cradle-experiences of Western civilization. It is precisely because such instances of strife in identity are so rife, or normative even, that the narrator is licensed to not be perplexed by, and, indeed, exuberantly creative with, such fissures. As well as the coinage "gentile Jewesses," she has fun grafting together unrelated identities in response to the stereotypical expectations of her aunts who remark upon her Scottish father's seemingly un-Jewish career as an engineer. In response, she asserts, "all Jews [are] engineers" (313). At this point Spark has very mischievously had her narrator transpose one of the most stereotypical occupations of the Scot onto her Scottish Jewish father. A key Sparkian technique is here revealed. Lazy, or stereotypical, versions of the world license a certain amount of "poetic justice," or payment in kind (which the narrator slyly visits upon her aunts). This is a story, clearly, that, to use a key Sparkian word, "rejoices" in the actual plurality of the human world as we see again in the death of the narrator's beloved grandmother: "She was buried as a Jewess since she died in my father's house, and notices were put in the Jewish press. Simultaneously my great-aunts announced in the Watford papers that she fell asleep in Jesus" (314). Registered here is the fact that the truth is beyond any one human narrative, especially any that attempts to be unequivocal. The narrator's grandmother is wonderfully evasive in her essence even as, and partly because of the fact that, set identities gather around her. At its conclusion, the story reaches consideration of the one unitary reality that is beyond the comprehension of humanity:

> My mother carries everywhere in her handbag a small locket containing a picture of Christ crowned with thorns. She keeps on one table a rather fine Buddha on a lotus leaf and on another a horrible replica of the Venus de Milo. One way and another all the gods are served in my mother's household although she holds only one belief and that is in the Almighty. My father, when questioned as to what he believes, will say, "I believe in the Blessed Almighty who made heaven and earth," and will say no more, returning to his racing papers which contain problems proper to innocent men. To them, it was no great shock when I turned Catholic, since with Roman Catholics too, it all boils down to the Almighty in the end. (315)

Here we have a tender docketing of a welter of images and stories that extends even to a "horrible" item not to the narrator's taste. All of these aspire to a larger truth that benighted humanity can never actually hope to encapsulate. On the other hand, the narrator's father is an "innocent" man, which carries the connotation of a certain purity shown in his resistance to concrete imagery with which to describe God. The one human universality among the attitudes of the narrator's parents, though (and by extension, the attitudes of many different world faiths), is the belief in something transcendent. In the narrator's comment on her conversion to Catholicism (which, of course, mirrors Spark's own spiritual peregrination) she offers the offhand remark that with her adopted faith, "it all boils down to the Almighty in the end." Drawing upon this clichéd metaphor, the narrator cheerfully concedes the ultimately threadbare nature of human imagery so that the ending represents another oxymoronic moment, where the sublime is dealt with in throwaway language but attested to nonetheless.

"The Gentile Jewesses" is arguably more revealing of Muriel Spark's truly personal thoughts on identity than her autobiography, *Curriculum Vitae* (1992), in which one might sometimes feel that Spark (characteristically) is playing games with and teasing the reader. In her introduction Spark explains that the premise of her surely mockingly flat-titled memoir is utilizing "nothing that cannot be supported by documentary evidence or by eye-witness . . . Truth by itself is neutral and has its own dear beauty."[6] Is it conceivable that the writer of "The Gentile Jewesses" believes that "truth" is so readily, neutrally, and uniformly available as these words taken at face value seem to suggest? (Though whether these words, with their Brodie-esque turn of phrase, are to be taken seriously is another question.) *Curriculum Vitae* documents Spark's early life in Edinburgh in a way that points to its author's lack of belief in autobiography as a practice involving much meaningful precision in itself (something that should little surprise students of her fictional oeuvre). Paradoxically, this is implied in the throwaway cataloguing rubrics such as "Commodities," "Neighbours," and even "The Doorbell" that organize parts of *Curriculum Vitae* and that suggest that Spark's habitual sense of parody is slyly in operation. For Spark the artist and thinker on humanity, the actualities of physical location (as "The Gentile Jewesses" so clearly suggests) are not in themselves the really important things. Rather, for Spark the relationship *between* things, how they are configured, constitutes the realm of importance and of possibility. To clarify, we might turn to a statement by Spark herself on her national origins:

> I am certainly a writer of Scottish formation and of course think of myself as such. I think to describe myself as a "Scottish Writer" might be ambiguous as one wouldn't know if "Scottish" applied to the writer or the writing. Then there is the complicated ques-

tion of whether people of mixed inheritance, like myself, can call themselves Scottish. Some Scots deny it. But Edinburgh where I was born and my father was born has definitely had an effect on my mind, my prose style and my ways of thought.[7]

This is Spark's response to a question about her feelings of national origin posed by the Scottish critic Alan Bold. It is ludicrously symptomatic of the essentialism of the Scottish literary critical mind that it needs to be posed in the first place. Spark's commonsense answer points to the not to be gainsaid interactions that any person must, of necessity, have with the environment in which they exist. Amidst the cool obviousness of Spark's answer here, though, lurks a subtler signal toward her practice of drawing upon Scottish "experience" but never taking this as a straightforward given. It has an "effect" on her; it does not simply define her. Spark is quite clear about the tense relationship she has to the city of her birth: "Edinburgh is the place that I, a constitutional exile, am essentially exiled from. I spent the first 18 years of my life, during the Twenties and Thirties, there. It was Edinburgh that bred within me conditions of exiledom; and what have I been doing since then but moving from exile into exile? It has become a calling."[8] As in "The Gentile Jewesses," we find here Spark's wryness with regard to personal identity as she invokes the notion of the exiled Jew. If Edinburgh is humorously Jerusalem here, it is also, in the same essay, "no mean city" (as Spark is well aware, a label more usually applied to the Scottish capital's great civic rival, Glasgow, after a notorious novel memorializing this title and written in 1935 by Alexander McArthur and H. Kingsley Long).[9] Litotes and other deferrals of material reality are a pronounced part of Spark's stock in trade, and we become aware of this again in another of her descriptions of the Edinburgh location: "The Castle Rock is something, rising up as it does from pre-history between the formal grace of the New Town and the noble network of the Old. To have a great primitive black crag rising up in the middle of populated streets of commerce, stately squares and winding closes, is like the statement of an unmitigated fact preceded by 'nevertheless.'"[10] Even the imagery of this statement is not quite as clear as it might at first appear. Spark's relentless, chiastic wit here has the "black crag" as the "mitigating" element and the seemingly rational activity of the city as that which needs to be re-ordered.

Elusiveness and slippage in identity are characteristics that have allowed Spark's fiction to be appropriated, to some extent, by the Scottish canon. The overworked trope of "crisis in identity" is often applied to either or both manifest subject matter and mode in works of Scottish literature. One cited cause of bifurcated Scottish impulse is the intrusive influence of English culture. More recently, however, it has become fashionable to see the Scottish trauma in consciousness as related to Calvinism. This has attractions for Scottish critics in that it allows an emphasis upon a supposedly indigenous *mentalité*, now very capable of rehabilitation (when "puritanical" Calvinism, as an histori-cally anti-artistic element in Scottish culture, had been for the first part of the twentieth century largely beyond the pale). The growth of this critical tendency in the embryonic postmodern age has its origins with the republication of James Hogg's *Private Memoirs and Confes-sions of a Justified Sinner* (1824) in 1947 with an introduction penned by André Gide. Largely ignored for over a century, Hogg's novel becomes, as Cairns Craig has astutely remarked, "a part, almost, of twentieth-century rather than nineteenth-century Scottish writing."[11] Craig claims that after the republication of *Confessions of a Justified Sinner* Scottish fiction rediscovered something of the old Calvin-ist *mentalité* of the nation in viewing the world as a "fearful" place (since in the logic of the Fall, Earth becomes an outcast place, with even its pleasures often potential traps for those insufficiently mindful of the essentially ruined status of the human environment). Among the very wide list of examples in fiction inspired by Hogg in the re-turn to a Calvinist *weltanschaunng* Craig cites Spark's first novel, *The Comforters* (1957).[12] It is true that the character of Georgina Hogg (probably including the name itself) is inspired by Hogg's novel in re-garding herself as being among the elite members of her faith. Georgina has a resemblance to Hogg's central character of Robert Wringhim, particularly since, as Caroline Rose wisely speculates, "she has no pri-vate life whatsoever."[13] Georgina, then, is indicated to have erased the space of considered conscience in her blind adherence to canonical regulation. The strange typewriter repeating Caroline's thoughts also echoes the multiplicity of voice that is found in James Hogg's novel. Yet, even as *The Comforters* can be said to form part of a Scottish canon during the second half of the twentieth century revitalized by Hogg's work, it is in some ways an obviously problematic choice. The title itself, of course, derives from the Book of Job and Spark's interest in the long Judaeo-Christian problem of the existence of suffering. Georgina Hogg is a Catholic and so speaks of a condition that is universal and not merely to be attributed to the Calvinist outlook. As Catholic convert Sandy Stranger learns in *The Prime of Miss Jean Brodie,* she joins a church "in whose ranks [there are] quite a few Fascists much less agreeable than Miss Brodie," a character who in some ways acts in a very Calvinistic manner.[14] It should also be noted that the odd states of unreality that *Confessions of a Justified Sinner* and *The Comforters* share are ultimately of a different status. Whereas the voices and visions, either demonic or psychological illness, that afflict Wringhim cause him to commit suicide, there is no such apocalypse for the beset Caroline in Spark's novel. For one thing, Caroline's numinous typewriter has its basis in Spark's personal biography as a result of delusions she suffered through overwork and using dexedrine as a dieting aid while living in London. The Jungian therapy that the writer underwent not long after coming off the drug at the hands of the Catholic priest, Father Frank O'Malley, is remembered in Caroline Rose's ministering from the character Father Jerome, who counsels her to accept the intrusive voices as not necessarily worrying with the casual diagnosis, "these things can happen" (63).[15] *The Comforters,* then, in the final analysis is not a novel of Calvinist mistrust in the face of the (demonic) world, but of Catholic acceptance that the numinous might commingle with everyday reality.[16]

It was long an oversight in Spark criticism that the influence of Hogg's *Confessions of a Justified Sinner* did not register. In *Muriel Spark: An Odd Capacity for Vision* (1984), edited by Alan Bold, a concerted effort by critics informed about Scottish literature, including Trevor Royle and Allan Massie (and the guiding hand of Bold himself), put this to rights to some extent.[17] Prior to this, it is little short of extraordinary that excellent studies (all highly aware of Spark's various literary lineages) by Peter Kemp, Ruth Whittaker, and even Massie himself should be essentially oblivious to the importance of Hogg, most especially with regard to *The Ballad of Peckham Rye* (1960).[18] This is probably symptomatic of the fact that, in spite of 1947 marking a watershed for the rediscovery of Hogg, it was only really during the 1970s that academic Hogg studies flourished. Even the Scottish critics who show an awareness of *Confessions of a Justified Sinner* do so rather belatedly when we consider the utilization of this novel by Spark. It would be interesting to know when precisely Spark became interested in Hogg. One might surmise, though, that the new vogue for Hogg initially inspired by Gide, a cosmopolitan, gay French intellectual, represented confirmation of the European kinship within Scottish culture so proudly noted by Jean Brodie. It should also be emphasized that with her interest in Mary Shelley and the Brontës, Spark was likely to be interested in Hogg as a Romantic writer. In editing the Brontë letters, Spark must have been very struck by the remark of Branwell Brontë about Hogg, that "the writings of that man . . . laid a hold on my mind which succeeding years have consecrated into a most sacred feeling."[19] Spark certainly comes to have Hogg in her literary genes, but these are not some set of essentially national genes.

Let us comment more widely than has been done before on the treatment of the "Scottish" materials informing *The Ballad of Peckham Rye*. With regard to Hogg, the character of Dougal Douglas is cleverly made into a döppelganger, a phenomenon by which Robert Wringhim is plagued, through the simple expedient of having Dougal reverse his name to become Douglas Dougal so that he can nefariously enjoy employment at two rival firms. Another feature of Hogg's novel is the apparent collapse of time-sense for its central character, which here, of course, is managed by the sleight-of-hand simultaneity of Dougal's working arrangement. We find, then, a characteristic Spark technique of economically (or artfully) mimicking the supernatural. It is a favored approach of anthologizers of the Scottish short story to include supernatural work by Spark on the basis that her interest in such terrain marks out an inherently Scottish mindset.[20] As *The Ballad of Peckham Rye* shows, however, Spark's highly playful incorporation of supernatural "effects" is altogether more literary than "folk-based" (there exists a prominent idea that Scottish literature is, or ought to be, based much more upon demotic oral traditions in contradistinction to English literature which is taken to be much more *literary per se*).

We see Spark, of course, in *The Ballad of Peckham Rye*, make use precisely of the oral medium of the Scottish border ballad known for its featuring of dramatically bloody deeds and its portrayal of internecine strife (both family and cross-border travail). Dougal Douglas is a visitor of such division upon the dreary, pre-swinging sixties London suburb into which Spark parachutes him. He also represents, to some extent, an English stereotype of the Scot come to life. He is diabolic (and so roughly equivalent to the supposed bleak or "dour" Scottish type, even as this is contradicted by his demonic, shape-changing propensities that involve joyfully madcap mimicking routines). Dougal is, too, the "Jock-on-the-make" stereotype of which James Boswell is the best example. Dougal, a writer of biography among his many activities, is also something of a hypochondriac who fears contact with illness, is sexually licentious, and is a skilful mimic. All of these qualities are associated with Boswell, and Spark is surely consciously drawing upon his character.[21] As a Scottish outsider and someone perceived with his humpback, now in the 1960s interpreted as a "handicap" rather than in folklore as the "mark of the beast," Dougal easily stirs up prejudice. He is sent to traumatize metropolitan modernity with his very deliberated and very Scottish grotesqueness.

Spark's choice of mode in *The Ballad of Peckham Rye* (albeit that it is consonant with the development that her fiction had been undergoing since the start of her career) represents the novelist at her most unfashionable (one suspects willfully so).[22] Flying in the face of the "kitchen-sink" realism of English culture during the late 1950s and early 1960s, Spark chooses to find exactly the opposite of the grimy, suburban, domestic attractiveness that underwrites this mode. Peckham is a location where the imagination is in danger of collapse. Oxymoronic, multifaceted Dougal (with the hallmarks of the imagination therein) is a literary judgment upon the place for its sins of ordinariness. We find a nice example of this as Dougal's employer, Mr Druce, murders his lover Merle Coverdale after Dougal has also become her boyfriend so as to turn an adulterous affair into a *ménage à trois*.

Here the folk rules, as these are to be found also in Hogg's *Confessions,* operate. The devil cannot simply create evil out of nothing (since in the divine economy God is ultimately omnipotent). Rather, he must be allowed in "through the keyhole" of freely chosen human badness but can then exacerbate the situation of moral turpitude to which he has gained admittance. It is a typically Sparkian twist that Druce and Coverdale, like so many characters in the novel, have settled into a very mundane, threadbare kind of sinfulness. We see the pair sharing dull suppers together and Druce very neatly folding his trousers prior to their passionless lovemaking with the implication that they have lost not only a keen sense of goodness, but of badness also. An instrument of the Divine Economy rather than merely of the dark side, Dougal is justified in his claims to be an exorcist and to have "the ability to drive devils out of people."[23] Thus he helps along an all too literal poetic justice as Druce, agitated by Dougal, murders Merle by plunging a corkscrew into her neck. This death is at once horribly violent, after the manner of the ballads, and mockingly reductive given the suburban weapon of homicide.

Dissonantly comic in its collision of the worlds of seemingly workaday London suburb and the ballads, the novel also reflects the fact that such discordance is much more "normal" than the inhabitants of Peckham would care to acknowledge. We see this in the Crewe family (given a typically and rather snootily disdainful unromantic moniker from the English town centered upon the locomotive industry), which is conjoined by actually disparate elements where the father Arthur has not sired his daughter and may not be the father of his son either. The member of this family who most attracts the diabolic attentions of Dougal is seventeen-year-old Dixie, who is working hard to save for her wedding to Humphry Place, whom Dougal befriends. Dixie's efforts involve her not only being employed by one of the firms for whom Dougal works but also taking on an evening job as a cinema usherette. She is, then (albeit more mildly), possessed of the protean propensity manifested by Dougal, and she is also illegitimate so that the folk equation of bastardry and the mark of the devil might be brought to mind. In another Sparkian turn, however, her own mother Mavis observes that Dixie should be out indulging herself in her youth rather than fretting as much as she does over her respectable future (in her loss of the present, Dixie has a resemblance to Robert Wringhim, who loses sense of the temporal sphere). Mavis, it seems, has had an enjoyable time while young, so that she conceives Dixie to an American GI. We see here a pattern that is sometimes found in Spark's fiction where those who stand for the life principle are not, on the face of it, conventionally moral people.[24] Dixie's desire for respectability, presumably in the face of her anxiety over her own origins, leads her into a petty-minded narrowness that Dougal implicitly encourages by representing to her his roguish disrespectability. Dougal is licensed, yet again, to interfere in Dixie's life because of her existing predisposition. He does a skit prior to the wedding for Humphry's entertainment of the groom refusing his marriage vows, which is what Humphry does at the first attempted nuptials. Later, because of freewill (as guaranteed by God; even if Dougal is a real demon he cannot simply take control of someone's destiny in perpetuity), Humphry does indeed marry Dixie:

> Humphry drove off with Dixie. She said, "I feel as if I've been twenty years married instead of two hours."
>
> He thought this a pity for a girl of eighteen. But it was a sunny day for November, and, as he drove swiftly past the Rye, he saw the children playing there and the women coming home from work with their shopping-bags, the Rye for an instant looking like a cloud of green and gold, the people seeming to ride upon it, as you might say there was another world than this. (142)

Dougal has gone but his influence lingers on, and we see that he is almost as much an agent of God as of the devil. The color green, so often an indication of the intrusion of an ambiguous supernatural/ fairyland sphere in the border ballads and other effects, extend the offer of grace to Peckham. As with so many of Spark's endings, a note of lyrical tenderness provides a counterpoint to the preceding human folly, and the possibility of forgiveness is registered. It is up to Humphry in his conjugal state and in his newfound apprehensions how he will attempt to manage his life from now on.

*The Ballad of Peckham Rye* shows Spark managing a hybrid form, the contemporary "English" tendency toward domestic realism and the notion of the "Scottish" supernatural tradition. Both of these things, in fact, are parodied even as they are effectively utilized to provide Spark's polished literary artifact (which is very unballad like). Those critics who wish to see the novel as purveying some essentially different "Scottish" cultural *mentalité* knowingly dissecting the "English" world do not take enough account of Spark's construction of a plane of critique in this novel (as elsewhere) that is about showing the dissonance and fissures in universal human nature through wielding (and, indeed, welding) those materials she has most conveniently to hand. It is not a question, particularly, of any kind of national cultural inherence or partisanship on the part of Spark. Spark as author here, as so often, might be thought to be very much like Dougal himself as an outsider, making elegant oxymoronic patterns she is in full control of but from which she stands in comprehensive ironic detachment.

As with Dougal Douglas, Jean Brodie, Spark's most exuberant character creation, is constructed amidst somewhat well-trod Scottish materials. *The Prime of Miss Jean Brodie* (1961) takes as a theme education, in which Scottish fiction has been very interested, prompted by the supposedly prodigious success of Scotland in this sphere. It is a nice coincidence that Spark's novel should appear in the same year as the work that has become the most celebrated study of Scottish intellectual history, George Davie's *The Democratic Intellect* (1961), which expounds the idea that Scottish "generalism" represented the historic Scottish socioeducational ethic as opposed to a narrower educational "specialism" manifested in the English tradition.[25] At times, Brodie seems to be very aware of this tradition of the "democratic intellect," as for instance, she readily becomes pupil herself in the attempt to learn Greek from her chosen pupils as they are initiated into this language on entering the senior school. Brodie's Latin explanation of the term *education* also recalls the historic emphasis in Scotland on a classical knowledge in which careful etymology (as a subset of the philosophy of Common Sense, which Davie sees epistemologically underpinning Scottish "generalism") is prized over systematic, potentially florid, fluency. Brodie speaks exactly to the Scottish common sense educational agenda as espoused by Davie:

The word "education" comes from the root *e* from ex, out, and *duco*, I lead. It means a leading out. To me, education is a leading out of what is already there in the pupil's soul. To Miss Mackay it is a putting in of something that is not there, and that is not what I call education, I call it intrusion, from the Latin root prefix in meaning in and the stem *trudo*, I thrust. Miss Mackay's method is to thrust a lot of information into the pupil's head; mine is a leading out of knowledge, and that is true education as proved by the root meaning. (37)

Here we find Jean Brodie determined to appear as a Scottish teacher in traditionally authoritative manner. As we learn more, however, we realize that Brodie's demeanor in this regard perhaps has to do with the fact that her own educational attainments (especially when compared to those of the hated, younger Miss Mackay) are modest and her position as a minimally qualified female teacher at Marcia Blaine school is an unusual consequence of the social and cultural flux of the interwar years. We might also note, however, that Brodie's "leading out" is a function not dissimilar from Dougal Douglas's exorcism of moral propensities. As ever with Spark, the identity we might think we are fairly certainly dealing with is never far from revealing itself to be something differently edged.

Brodie, in the passage above, is seen clinging to a realism or a literalism, but she also practices linguistic transformation (this is one of several ways in the novel where we again encounter shape changing). Objecting to her girls using the words *comic* and *social* as nouns when these should be adjectives, Brodie utilizes the word *prime* to describe her abstract state of maturity and so performs the same act of transmutation. If we are attuned to the social and historical particulars of the novel, however, we realize that Brodie is not gratuitously willful but fighting to mark out a space in which she can exist. *The Prime of Miss Jean Brodie* marks a trend in Spark's novels of beginning to view cultural particulars much more sympathetically than in her often severely *contemptus mundi* mode in novels previously such as *The Comforters* or *The Ballad of Peckham Rye*. The beginning of chapter three of *The Prime of Miss Jean Brodie* brilliantly contextualizes Brodie in the interwar years (marking yet again an inter-terrain of the kind in which Spark specializes). Given the decade in which the novel appears, we find a poignant reminder that the freedoms of thought, particularly female thought, that began to ensue during the 1960s were a revisiting of social trends that had been apparent in the 1930s and that were later dampened down by the unified "homefront" of World War Two. We are shown women like Brodie at "Edinburgh grocers' shops arguing with the Manager at three in the afternoon on every subject from the authenticity of the Scriptures to the question of what the word 'guaranteed' on a jam-jar really meant" (42). These are women of (yet again in an oxymoronic identity) "war-bereaved spinsterhood" (42), so that the catastrophic loss of "manpower" (literally, but also in terms of authority) allows them, it is implied, a fairly sudden partial liberation. Brodie herself, we should be aware, is unlikely to have become a schoolteacher, instead becoming a housewife, had her lover not died during World War One. Given her opportunity, Brodie is determined to grab it, simultaneously working hard to appear like a dominie and exercising fictions that neatly shore up her position. Thus, her dead lover, Hugh Carruthers, is narrated fictively by Brodie to her girls as a man of the country with a store of wise sayings so that he might be seen to be a stereotypical version of Robert Bums. If, indeed, Hugh ever existed he is an excuse for Brodie's single-state and her dedication to her girls. Later his story is invested with his dual talents for singing and art, as a codified way for the teacher to indicate her entanglements with her colleagues, Gordon Lowther and Teddy Lloyd. What we have, then, is Brodie occupying a fragile space where fiction is her safeguard against forces that would not easily concede to Brodie her chosen career or her love life.

Calvinism becomes part of the theme of the mystery of identity in *The Prime of Miss Jean Brodie.* We see this especially in the apprehensions of Sandy Stranger, who with her name and her mixed Scottish-English parentage is an outsider to some extent. Sandy contemplates Calvinism:

Fully to savour her position, Sandy would go and stand outside St Giles Cathedral or the Tolbooth, and contemplate these emblems of a dark and terrible salvation which made the fires of the damned seem very merry to the imagination by contrast, and much preferable. Nobody in her life, at home or school, had ever spoken of Calvinism except as a joke that had once been taken seriously. . . . All she was conscious of now was that some quality of life peculiar to Edinburgh and nowhere else had been going on unbeknown to her all the time, and however undesirable it might be, she felt deprived of it; however undesirable, she desired to know what it was, and to cease to be protected from it by enlightened people. (108)

For Sandy, Edinburgh is suffused with a unique quality, even though Calvinism has seemingly ceased to have much of an existence on the surface of life. In fact, it is Sandy's inexperience that leads her to believe that things are so very different in her home locale. She herself, at this point, is inhabiting the stereotype of the cold, dour Scottish metaphysical mind (worse, apparently, in its conceptions than the "fires of the damned"). Sandy wishes to encounter Calvinism, which very much like her imaginative forays into *Kidnapped* or *Jane Eyre* or her other fantasies of being a heroine of one kind or another, is all too vividly realized in her growing perception of Jean Brodie. Fundamentally craving excitement, she brings to life a dead text (something not without irony given Spark's own practice in this mode) and uses it as an explanation for Brodie's behavior.

Sandy "savours" the fact that she stands out with Calvinism, but she nonetheless activates the idea of this religion. We should be aware of the full passage, too often precipitously drawn upon by critics of Spark, which contains Sandy's crucial identification of Jean Brodie:

She thinks she is Providence, thought Sandy, she thinks she is the God of Calvin, she sees the beginning and the end. And Sandy thought, too, the woman is an unconscious Lesbian. And many theories from the books of psychology categorized Miss Brodie, but failed to obliterate her image from the canvases of one-armed Teddy Lloyd. (120)

In seeing Brodie as a "Lesbian," Sandy is collaborating in the oppression of Brodie by a society that would like to mold her into an entirely conventional female type or castigate her for her deviation from such

a role. Sandy's theorizing, we are told by the narrator, is somewhat in-
discriminate and "fails to obliterate her image" in the paintings of the
man to whom Sandy becomes lover. What is suggested is that Sandy
cannot explain by any means the mysterious nature of Brodie's at-
traction for Lloyd (or, indeed, for others). The mature Sandy, from
the locus of her convent, comes to see Brodie as one whose "defective
sense of self-criticism" (86) ought to mark out the terrain of a "justified sinner" as "quite an innocent" (127). Sandy "clutche[s] the bars
of her grille," which might seem to indicate punishment for relaying
information to Miss Mackay about Brodie's flirtation with fascism
that leads to Brodie having to resign her post. However, when Sandy is
visited by Eunice, she is quite rightly hard-headed, saying of Brodie's
complaints of betrayal, "it is only possible to betray where loyalty is
due" (127). Sandy's own motivations in the downfall of her teacher are,
undoubtedly, selfish, but the harm that the teacher does in encouraging Joyce-Emily Hammond to foolishly go off and fight in the Span-
ish Civil War, and, perhaps even more seriously, her lack of charity in
the case of Mary MacGregor (whom she mocks) are sins of which
Brodie is certainly not "innocent." Sandy, in fact, might be read by
the end of the novel's events as undergoing the religious process of
"unselfing," something that is not necessarily without personal anxiety. She is divesting herself of images and stories of which previously
she has produced a surfeit.

We see Sandy undergo a more profound set of transformations
in the novel than Brodie, who for all her contradictory posturing remains a rather static character trapped in her own pathetic space.
Sandy's youthful imagination reaches a pitch with her obsessive apprehensions of Brodie. Paradoxically, it is Sandy who manifests the
mark of demonic enslavement, which the apprehension of being one
of the unco' guid is supposed to lead to. In a received image that goes
back at least as far as Christ driving the demon into a herd of swine
in the Gospel of Luke (9:33), she is seen to have pig-like eyes, and, in
another porcine comparison, Sandy extracts from Lloyd his Catholic
"religion as a pith from a husk" (123). She inspires in Brodie the greatest confidence of any of her "set" and self-fulfills the Calvinistic situation where Brodie is encouraged to feel in command of the situation

around her "so that [her] surprise at the end might be the nastier" (109). Sandy, embarrassed early on that her English mother calls her "darling," has longed for a Scottish identity and unbeknown to herself has taken one on. Later, in converting to Rome and becoming a nun, Sandy clearly shifts in her perception of Jean Brodie. Inspired by her teacher, she writes her treatise, "The Transfiguration of the Commonplace," so that Brodie now is seen as quasi-Catholic in wielding mundane materials (the various stereotypes and hackneyed stories that she employs) to bring about something that adds up to a bigger or transubstantiated total. We are told that Sandy's treatise is on psychology, but one might well assume, given the title, that its conclusions are more religious than psychological, asserting presumably the indefinable essence of the human person that the perception of other alone is never enabled nor entitled to view. It is with regard to such a reading that Sandy's desperately enclosed state as a nun makes sense. She is struggling to divest herself of worldly involvements since these necessarily mean making images and stories that can never show anything like the complete truth. It is not the case that the world is completely fallen and corrupt (so that, as in the scenario of *Confessions of a Justified Sinner,* moral actions are neither here nor there and those supposedly predestined to salvation can sin with impunity), but that human discrimination in the moral weighting of actions can never be absolute. It is in this subtle but profound difference between extreme Calvinism and orthodox Catholic belief that the warp and woof of *The Prime of Miss Jean Brodie* lies. The crude predetermined drama of the former and the endless story of the latter—wherein the battle between good and evil is never done and is never entirely predictable (an often surprising conflict that is the mark of so much of Spark's fictional *oeuvre*)—makes the essential difference

It is perhaps no coincidence that Muriel Spark's two most "Scottish" novels should be published in close proximity. In these she works through a rich vein of received images and ideas of her country as well as any contemporary Scottish writer. That she does not take notions of Scottish identity as essentially different in their human dynamics and artistic potential should come as no surprise given Spark's theocentric view of the world. Imaginatively, Scotland is a strong site of the dissonant and interpolated human reality that she conveys throughout her fictional *oeuvre*, where truth and transcendent identity can never be exactly located but are indicated through the imaginative aspirations both of Spark herself and her characters. Scottish material continues to surface in her work from time to time, such as the *Peter Pan* scenario in *The Hothouse by the East River* (1973), where the work of J. M. Barrie, the father of the supposedly diseased "kailyard" school, is craftily utilized to deconstruct the outwardly hardheaded reality of contemporary New York. By and large, though, "Scottish" elements feature in smaller, parodied ways, such as the treatment of moral awareness in *Symposium* (1990), where far from reliable characters say of Scotland that there "all the families are odd" and there "people are more capable of perpetrating good or evil than anywhere else."[26] This mischievous reiteration of the stereotype of the metaphysical Scot is joined by the appearance of Lord Lucan in Scotland in *Aiding and Abetting* (2001), an inversion of the infliction of Dougal Douglas on England, so that the notorious real life English aristocratic murderer is returned to an appropriate locus of dark (perhaps ballad) legend. Scotland is a place conjugated by Spark with many other sites and cultures in her work, and Scotland should be grateful that she utilizes it in her art so universally.

NOTES

1. See Inga Agustdottir's interview with Robin Jenkins in *In Scotland*, no. 1 (Autumn 1999): 13.

2. Scottish literary modernity has been so traumatized by the notion of nineteenth-century "Kailyard" (cabbage-patch) literature's supposed creation of an a-historical fantasyland where problematic social and cultural division are written out that it has clung for grim life (literally) to the ideal of a fiction of leftist social realism.

3. It is interesting that even James Kelman, the Scottish writer of impeccably leftwing credentials and most fêted as an "urban realist," has recently complained of the constraining Scottish ideological preference for "social realism" in fiction (see his comments in Kathleen Jamie, "The Voice of the Oppressed," *Scotland on Sunday* [February 19, 1999]).

4. Jenkins's principal distaste for Spark seems to arise from the fact that, apart from *The Prime of Miss Jean Brodie*, "all her other novels [are] set in Venice, they're set in London particularly" (*In Scotland*, 13).

5. References to Spark's short stories are from *The Collected Short Stories* (London: Penguin, 1994).

6. *Curriculum Vitae* (London: Constable, 1992), 11.

7. Alan Bold, *Muriel Spark* (London: Methuen, 1986), 26.

8. "Edinburgh-born," in *Critical Essays on Muriel Spark*, ed. Joseph Hynes (New York: G. K. Hall, 1992), 21 [reprinted from *New Statesman* 64 (August 10, 1962)].

9. Ibid., 22.

10. Ibid.

11. Cairns Craig, *The Modern Scottish Novel: Narrative and the National Imagination* (Edinburgh: Edinburgh University Press, 1999), 38.

12. Ibid., 39.

13. *The Comforters* (London: Penguin, 1963), 186.

14. *The Prime of Miss Jean Brodie* (London: Penguin, 1965), 125.

15. See also *Curriculum Vitae*, 204–5.

16. This point is very well crystallized in Barton Thomas Swaim, "Using Psychology: The Theories of C. G. Jung and the Early Novels of Muriel Spark" (MA thesis, University of South Carolina, 2000), 7–11.

17. Allan Massie, "Calvinism and Catholicism in Muriel Spark," and Trevor Royle, "Spark and Scotland," in *Muriel Spark: An Odd Capacity for Vision*, ed. Alan Bold (London: Vision, 1984), 98, 156–57.

18. Peter Kemp, *Muriel Spark* (London: Paul Elek, 1974); Allan Massie, *Muriel Spark* (Edinburgh: Ramsay Head Press, 1979); and Ruth Whittaker, *The Faith and Fiction of Muriel Spark* (London: Macmillan, 1982).

19. Muriel Spark, ed., *The Brontë Letters* (London: Peter Nevill, 1954), 51.

20. We see this in, for instance, J. F. Hendry, ed., *The Penguin Book of Scottish Short Stories* (London: Penguin, 1970), which selects Spark's "The House of the Famous Poet" for its *outré* qualities; in Moira Burgess, *The Other Voice* (Edinburgh: Polygon, 1987), which selects "The Black Madonna"; and in Carl MacDougall, ed., *The Devil and the Giro* (Edinburgh: Canongate, 1989), which selects the same. In the coincidence between the latter two cases one can see the abundant supply of Spark short fiction being "squeezed" to suit this "national" literary agenda.

21. With regard to the lesser known attributes of Boswell as a mimic, see Frederick A. Pottle, *James Boswell: The Earlier Years 1740–1769* (Heinemann: London, 1966), 63, 93, 180.

22. For my reading of Spark's developing usage of supernatural, including "supranatural," devices in her fiction, see, "The Remarkable Fictions of

Muriel Spark" in A *History of Scottish Women's Writing*, ed. Douglas Gifford and Dorothy McMillan (Edinburgh: Edinburgh University Press, 1997), 514–25.

23. *The Ballad of Peckham Rye* (London: Penguin, 1963), 102.

24. A good example of this type is to be found in "The Black Madonna," where Elizabeth the sister of trendy, progressive Catholic Lou Parker exists amidst a brood of illegitimate children, while Lou herself has her own child adopted because of the awkward appearance of her legitimate, but "throwback," daughter. In this story the Virgin icon, to which the Parkers make a petition after years of failure to produce children, has proved to be a dispenser of oxymoronic identity.

25. George Davie, *The Democratic Intellect* (Edinburgh: Edinburgh University Press, 1961).

26. *Symposium* (London: Constable, 1990), 87, 159.

# CHAPTER SIX

# Unrivalled Deftness

## The Novels of Muriel Spark

### FRANK KERMODE

When Muriel Spark's first novel, *The Comforters,* came out in 1957 there was an unusual stir of interest. She had as yet published no novel but was not unknown in literary circles, having previously published books on Mary Shelley and John Masefield, as well as editions of the letters of the Brontës, Newman and others. There was also an admirable volume of poems and a short story, "The Seraph and the Zambesi," which, in 1951, won first prize in a well-publicized *Observer* competition. More stories followed, and these successes led to her first venture into full-length fiction. *The Comforters* was at once recognized as a novel of unusual originality and skill; it was warmly praised by Graham Greene and Evelyn Waugh, and not merely out of sympathy for a newly converted Roman Catholic writer but from an understanding that here was an artist, writing fiction that has the quality, scope and variety of ambitious poetry, and which could be at the same time comic and deeply serious.

*The Comforters* is a novel that looks into the question as to what kind of truth can be told in a novel; in fact nearly all of Spark's fictions have this reflexive quality, though never in an ostentatiously theoretical fashion. *The Comforters* is always conscious of the fact that to make up fictive narratives is, in a way, a presumptuous activity, because the characters of a novelist, unlike those created by God, are not endowed with free will; she enjoys power at the expense of her characters. Caroline, the heroine of the book, resists the will of her creator, who nevertheless goes on creating coincidences, arbitrarily, sometimes impatiently, dealing with her characters as she pleases. A fascinated interest in the relation between life and plot persists in the later fiction, notably in the novella *Not to Disturb* (1971).

Spark's writings were now assured of attention, and she proceeded to publish novels with quite remarkable frequency. In *Robinson* (1958), *Memento Mori* (1959), *The Ballad of Peckham Rye* (1960) and *The Bachelors* (1960) it is possible to trace some permanent or recurring interests, but they are nevertheless all quite astonishingly original and ingenious, imbued not only with the author's preoccupation with the supernatural and with the shadier aspect of religious belief and various other kinds of crookedness, but also with her intelligent and unfailing contempt for stupidity and weakness. Sometimes it appears that for Dame Muriel one of the prime duties of the artist is to clear away as much as possible of the monstrous accumulation of stupidity in our world. Hence a certain ruthlessness of tone, a steady refusal to countenance failures of common sense. The dull or in other ways unworthy may be represented as negligible, even as unreal. Forgiveness, even of one's own creations, is not, in this case, a necessity of art. Muriel Spark's novels are rarely short of wit and high spirits, but they are sternly deficient in sentimentality. As Rebecca West remarked, this writer "observes reality more exactly" than others, and "lacks the cowardice which makes us refuse to admit its lack of correspondence with our expectations and desires."

Few writers have so natural a command of the techniques available to the modern novelist. One has the impression that for Spark there somehow exists, in advance of composition, a novel, or more usually a novella, which can be scanned as it were in a satellite's view of it, from above—a map, rather than a temporal sequence. It can be surveyed in all its parts and details, and it ignores the conventional notion that to write it down requires one to treat its events in their temporal order. From the outset the end may be just as visible as the beginning, and on the same page may be found conversations and revelations that took place, in the "real" time of the narrative, years apart. In these manoeuvres there may sometimes be a certain playfulness, serving as an indication of the writer's absolute control (though one device may be to confront that control with evidence of its fallibility).

Nothing is absolutely new in the novel; what we think of as the mainstream English novel had barely got under way before Sterne wrote *Tristram Shandy*. And two generations before Muriel Spark began her experiments Conrad and Ford Madox Ford were doing extraordinary things to persuade us that the proper order of a fiction may not be, perhaps rarely is, a mimicry of the notion that the momentum of a story depends on its sticking to what passes for the commonsense process of "Then . . . and then . . . and then." Yet Muriel Spark never sounds like these august predecessors, self-consciously exploratory; and she has a surer sense of the right order of things than Ford, who worked so hard at such matters as "progression of effects" and the interrelation of disparate narrative sections. It is true that she loves complicated plots and expounds them with the confidence of an expert thriller writer, giving, as she once said, "disjointed happenings a shape"; but to do that is only one of the techniques, and probably not the most interesting of them, at her disposal.

Nowhere are these powers more evident than in *The Prime of Miss Jean Brodie* (1961) and *The Girls of Slender Means* (1963). They are short books and they are often funny, but they have very serious themes. Exquisitely formed, they give pleasure by their very existence, by the way they illuminate with their own plots the plot of the world, the writer matching her own presumption of providential powers with a truth beyond them. The puzzle is that fictions, if we are not to think of them as lies, must offer a kind of truth; yet they must be seen as shadowed by a truth more absolute than any they can aspire to. Or, as she once put it, "I don't claim that my novels are truth. I claim that they are fiction, out of which a kind of truth emerges."

It is of course important that the truth is that of the Roman Catholic religion, an absolute truth, but treated quite unsentimentally in these books. God, as Barbara Vaughan discovers in *The Mandelbaum Gate,* Spark's longest novel, does not play by the human rules. Barbara is half-Christian, half-Jewish, and experiences the mysterious union of these religions in Jerusalem. She reflects that Jacob tricked Isaac into blessing him instead of Esau, and, having stolen his brother's inheritance, became the father of Israel. God doesn't necessarily play fair; it is one of the facts of life we have to live with. It is a recurrent theme, and is perhaps most explicit in *The Only Problem* (1984).

In *The Prime of Miss Jean Brodie* the order of telling may appear almost random. Attention moves from 1931, when this very odd teacher first gathers together her girls with the intention of shaping their lives, establishing them as the *crème de la crème,* to the postwar period, alighting at many separate points between the beginning and the end of the tale. Here are the girls in their first year, and here they are at the end of their schooling, six years later; and so to their final meetings with Sandy, or Sister Helena of the Transfiguration. But these disparate moments are denied strictly consecutive treatment. The tone of the narrative is one of amused and mannered irony, as in the recurrent use of the same tags to characterize the girls, especially Sandy, who is rarely mentioned without some allusion to her piggy eyes. For these she was merely "notorious"—her early fame depended on her beautiful (English, not Scottish) vowels. The effect of the repetitive mentions of Sandy's piggy eyes is almost Homeric. It could be hard to find anything like it in other modern novelists. The reader is left to relate Sandy's tiny eyes ("which it was astonishing that anyone could trust") to her subsequent conduct as the betrayer of Miss Brodie—though we know her to be precociously capable of treachery, for example at the expense of the unhappy scapegoat Mary Macgregor, who is famous only "for being stupid and always to blame." The other girls are famous for this or that: for sex, acrobatics, and so on. Brodie seeks to transfigure them, and they play their parts in her attempt to achieve this secular "Transfiguration of the Commonplace," later the title of Sandy's famous book.

Despite its boldness of method the novel has some old-fashioned virtues of plot. We may wonder why a strange girl, wearing the wrong uniform, is introduced near the beginning and then apparently disappears from the story; but she returns and turns out to be important to the plot. Mary Macgregor, as a young girl, is panic-stricken by the flaming Bunsen burners in the science laboratory, and at twenty-four she is burnt to death in a hotel fire. These events, years apart, are virtually simultaneous in the telling; in a single page we are taken back from the fire to the moment when, at ten years old, she is, no doubt wrongly, accused of spilling ink on the floor (at the beginning of Chapter 2). Spark has no compunction about repeating herself, even word for word (the last words in the book are an instance) if her overview of the fictional proceedings seems to demand it. There is what might be called a recursive quality about her narrative manner; but none of these apparently wanton departures from the normal procedures of duller novelists can be attributed to clumsiness; they are part of the story, and also part of the joke.

The unrivalled deftness of the narrative would be a source of pleasure in itself, but to praise that quality is to risk missing the more important point that the entire book is a testimony to the sheer, if somehow rather guilty, delight of the novelist in the possession of such powers. *Brodie* is charmingly and always relevantly funny. In the course of the story the girls grow from childhood to early maturity, questioning one another about sex as they are on their way to experiencing it. The characters of the two masters, art and music, are masterly sketches of obsession and abjection. That one of them lost an arm in World War I is a neat moment of historical placement, and, like Brodie's romance about her lost lover, is linked to the plight of all the spinsters of the period, their possible husbands killed in France. The children's walk through the Old Town of Edinburgh gives them a fleeting view of the poverty of the Thirties, the decade during which these girls are growing up: "Walk past quietly," says Miss Brodie. As middle-class girls they have no more direct knowledge of the unemployed—"the idle," as they were called in Scotland—than they have of sex.

The two themes come together in a Sparkian joke, as the girls study Tennyson's poem "The Lady of Shalott," which is sometimes regarded as an allegory of the menarche—a word that makes Miss Brodie's girls giggle.

"Down she came and found a boat
Beneath a willow left afloat,
And round about the prow she wrote
*The Lady of Shalott.*"

"By what means did your Ladyship write these words?"
Sandy inquired in her mind with her lips shut tight.

"There was a pot of white paint and a brush which happened
to be standing upon the grassy verge," replied the Lady of Shalott
graciously. "It was left there no doubt by some heedless member
of the Unemployed."

Meanwhile Miss Brodie follows her disastrous course. It is her
ignorant affection for Italian Fascism and for Hitler that precipitates
her fall, but her extraordinary teaching methods adumbrated it. Yet
the expression of her dangerously freethinking opinions cannot conceal her Edinburgh-Calvinist background, evident in her correct Sunday observance as in her fussing about manners and propriety.

In plotting the careers of her elite girls she imitates the predesti-
narian God and goes wrong in the process: "I do not think ever to be
betrayed," she boasts, and is as confident of her victory over her su-
periors as she is of the accuracy of her forecast for Sandy: "I fear you
will never belong to life's elite." God, as we know by hindsight (a
power freely conferred on us by Spark) has other plans, and a different idea of election. It might be said that Brodie's interests are on the
whole aesthetic, whereas God's are spiritual. Thus Sandy's conversion is facilitated by her loss of interest in the artist Teddy Lloyd as a
lover and her accidental absorption of his Catholic religion—another
of God's plots, and not one that could have occurred to Miss Brodie.
We learn of the early end of her prime, and of her life, in various places,
first in Chapter 3, later in grim conversations with Sister Helena in
the nunnery. Her end is everywhere implicit in her prime, as the end
of the story is implicit in the conduct of the whole.

Something of the manner of this remarkable book persists in
Spark's next novel, *The Girls of Slender Means.* Here, too, the tale is
of a conversion miraculously wrought. The story occupies the period
between the end of the war with Germany and the end of the war

with Japan, roughly May to August, 1945. We notice the familiar attention to detail in the rendering of that period of relief and rationing, a time of which it could be said, however inaccurately, that everybody in Britain had slender means. The girls at the May of Teck Club are mostly, though not without exception, of slender bodies, and on suitable occasions can wear the Schiaparelli dress, informally held in common. When the wartime bomb explodes in the garden and the building catches fire it is to recover this dress that Selina returns from the safety of the roof, through the aperture from which only thin girls can make their way.

Her action is noted by Nicholas, her lover; they had slept together through the summer on this roof, she arriving by the strait opening, he from the roof of the building next door. But now, seeing her emerge with the dress, Nicholas crosses himself. He is on his way to the martyrdom of which we have already, by means of Sparkian time-shifts, been made aware. Selina's action grants him a vision of evil that eventually changes his life, as Sandy's was changed by what remained of her feeling for a discarded lover. Another divine trick, another meditation on God's way of choosing his elite.

That was a pedestrian account, reducing the story to the kind of thing an ordinary writer might produce. Of course Spark is more than equal to the demands of realistic narrative, witness, for example, the force and accuracy with which she describes the effects of the bomb, with much detail of firefighting, rescue and disaster. But to speak of the novel thus is to falsify it. Once again, one has the sense of its having been conceived as a whole, so that the details of life in such a community, and in the strange post-war atmosphere of 1945, are already related to the whole, already cohere. Spark achieves the ambition of her butler-novelist in *Not to Disturb*—she makes everything pertain.

She likes to find occasions to quote poetry in her fiction, and in this book the elocutionist Joanna provides a sort of obbligato of anthology pieces. Her recitations assume great seriousness at the time of disaster, when she chooses Hopkins's "The Wreck of the Deutschland" and the Anglican liturgy for the appropriate day. The victims in Hopkins's poem were nuns, and the Anglican verses for the twenty-seventh day suit the scene of a collapsing house: " 'Except the Lord build the house: their labour is but lost that build it. / Except the

Lord keep the city: the watchman waketh but in vain.' Any day's liturgy would have been equally mesmeric. But the words for the right
day was Joanna's habit." She perishes with the house, and Nicholas,
after the event but long before his martyrdom, has to deal with her
father. He shows him the house; but there is little to see, and the old
man makes nothing of it, and despite his priesthood cannot find any
but the feeblest explanation of how such a fate should have over-
taken his daughter.

The inhabitants of the club are all sharply sketched and know-
able: the girl who pretended to have dates with the musical star Jack
Buchanan, the older ladies, permanent residents and not under thirty,
as they ought to have been by the rules of the institution. Jane Wright
is important though not slender; her dealings with shady publishers
bring Nicholas to the club. When we hear from her at the very beginning of the story the war is long over, and she is on the telephone
telling another May of Teck survivor about Nicholas's martyrdom. We
are not to expect events in sequence, but we are to understand their
place in the whole. We start in the battered London of 1945: "Long
ago in 1945 all the nice people in England were poor, allowing for exceptions . . . at least, that was a general axiom, the best of the rich
being poor in spirit." And we end in the park, at the rowdy and dangerous celebrations of VJ day. Nicholas protects Jane from the mob,
and as she stands, bedraggled, fixing her hair, Nicholas marvels at her
stamina, and will recall her "years later in the country of his death,"
as "an image of all the May of Teck establishment in its meek, unself-
conscious attitudes of poverty, long ago in 1945." The life of Nicholas has not yet gone forward to its conclusion, but the novel has, in
the middle of a sentence.

*The Girls of Slender Means* was followed by a very different book,
*The Mandelbaum Gate* (1965), and then by *The Public Image* (1968),
a dark tale of a film actress who sheds her fraudulent public image.
Two years later came *The Driver's Seat,* the most chilling and desperate
of all the novels. Written almost entirely in the present tense, it cannot
avoid reminding the reader of the French *nouveau roman,* especially
the novels of Alain Robbe-Grillet, which had appeared some years
earlier and were attracting much attention at the time. It is said that
Spark owed something in the conception of her narrative to Christine

Brooke-Rose, the most successful English exponent of what has come to be called post-modern experimental narrative, though Spark had certainly made her own experiments and cannot really have needed this model.

Indeed the atmosphere of this book is, as one realizes on reflection, quite different from Robbe-Grillet's habitual mysteries and puzzles. Sudden time-shifts and unapologetic repetitions were, as we've seen, a feature of her earlier writing; and she was already a mistress of the macabre, especially in her short stories. Here she extends an idea that might once have made such a tale into a longer narrative enacting a pathological obsession, represented with accuracy in the intensity and strangeness of the prose.

It seems that Spark remembered a newspaper story about a German woman, garishly dressed, who went to Rome and on her first evening walked into a park, was assaulted, tied up, raped and stabbed to death. She is reported as describing the book as "conceived at white heat . . . it is supposed to give the reader nightmares." It does not contain many jokes of the kind that enlivened some of the earlier fiction; there is, however, a satirical feminist speech by the slightly dotty Mrs Fiedke about the impudence of men in claiming equal rights with women: "the male sex is getting out of hand." Mostly such laughter as there is arises from Lise's sinisterly absurd clothes.

That a woman should wind up her life and choose, with the greatest care, her own murderer, is the material of dreams. That she should not only seek out and compel her assailant to kill her but lay down conditions—no rape permitted, only murder—is to go beyond human powers of foresight and planning. Much happens during her day that is merely the uncontrollable fuss of life, in shops and cars and cafés, even though the nightmare quality is enhanced by the weirdness of almost everybody Lise encounters—Mrs Fiedke, for instance, and the dangerous macrobiotic crank. Perhaps all this detail is irrelevant to her prime purpose, as she evidently believes; but she will discover in her last moments that she cannot control even the central event of her life. It is part of her tragedy that she cannot impose the terms of her own death; and the closing words of the book insist that it is truly tragic, awakening (in all but policemen): "fear and pity, pity and fear."

*The Driver's Seat is* among the most perfectly composed of modern novellas. By reason of its terrible subject and its unremitting onslaught on the reader's sensibility it stands a little apart from most of the other works. *Not to Disturb* appeared in the following year, and is fascinating in a quite different manner—a novel contemplating, in a comic spirit, the oddity of there being such things as stories and storytellers who, within sometimes unacknowledged limits, can control action and outcome. Five more novels, which must here be passed over, intervened before the publication of *The Only Problem* in 1984.

Dame Muriel had long been a student of the Book of Job. She published an article on "The Mystery of Job's Suffering" in 1955, and drew the title of her first novel, *The Comforters,* from the Bible story. What is the mystery of Job's suffering? It is clearly untrue to say, with the comforters, that he deserved it. Why, given that God is good and also omnipotent, should there be suffering, anyway? This may be regarded as the biggest, or only, problem. One answer, offered with great subtlety by Leibniz and ridiculed by Voltaire, is that this is the best of all possible worlds. Harvey, the protagonist in this novel, cannot accept such explanations; nor can Dame Muriel. Harvey thinks that if God permits suffering he must, "by the logic of his omnipotence, be the author of it." And all problems are, in the end, part of that greater problem.

Harvey is rich. He ends his marriage without undue suffering, and buys a house and then a chateau in France in order to have enough peace to work on his Job book. His choice of location is dictated by his wish to go to Epinal as often as he likes to see a painting by Georges de La Tour called "Job Visited by His Wife." The Bible credits Job's wife with only one sentence: "Dost thou still retain thine integrity? Curse God, and die." Job tells her not to speak as foolish women do, and goes on scratching his sores with a potsherd. But the painting, unlike any other of the same subject, shows Job's wife to be beautiful and tender, so Harvey wonders at the discrepancy between the biblical text and the picture. In fact the subject of the painting, dated about 1640, was long thought to be "The Clothing of the Naked." The female figure, being Compassion personified, is not at all bad-tempered; and looks rather like the angel in another of De La

Tour's works, the "Angel Appearing to St Joseph." The subject of the picture was identified, and the present title attached to it, as late as 1935. Only then did art historians begin to see the woman's face, assumed for centuries to be angelic, as in fact angry and cruel.

My own view, which is not Spark's, is that De La Tour was working from the Vulgate Latin text of the Bible. Its author, St. Jerome, was well aware that in the Hebrew text "bless God" was a euphemism for "curse God," which no scribe would write. But the Roman Catholic Church did not take the course followed by the vernacular translators (including the English) and render bless as "curse." Consequently a painter or his patron might read the passage in the Bible and see Job's wife as a tender though foolish woman, who, unable to bear his misery, advises Job to make his peace with God and seek a good end. The antithetical and more usual interpretation makes the woman gloat as if possessed by Satan: "Are you still going to be righteous? If you're going to die, curse God and get it off your chest first. It will do you good."

However, Spark's Harvey is right to conclude that "it was impossible not to wonder what the artist actually means." His difficulty is compounded by the fact that the woman in the picture resembles his discarded wife Effie, who also resembles her sister Ruth. The mystery of Job"s suffering becomes deeper and deeper as Effie's illegal adventures cause Harvey more and more trouble. It seems to Harvey that God comes out of the argument very badly with his boasting and shouting and bribery: if Job will admit he is vile he shall have back his sheep and camels and asses and seven sons and three daughters, one of them named Keren-happuch, which means Eye-Paint. (This last is a detail one would not expect Spark to miss, or indeed fail to repeat.)

One of the reporters who plague Harvey because of his wife's misdeeds is an old Swede, who alone of all the company knows what the Book of Job is. He asks Harvey whether to feel perfectly innocent while you are guilty in the eyes of the world is to find oneself in the position of Job. Harvey, ignoring such parallels as that of the comforters who beset him—Ruth, Nathan, Stewart—denies that he is so situated; he is not covered with boils, and so on. He adds that Job's problem was ignorance; nobody tried to explain his suffering to him. Job says he wants "to reason with God," but God won't "come out like a man and state his case." Since the Book of Job is so hostile to God the real wonder is how it ever got into the Bible. It is "the pivotal book of the Bible," yet there is nothing "moral" about it.

Typically, this central argument is set in the midst of a Sparkian plot of shoplifting, holdups, love affairs, Californian communes and other forms of human mess and muddle. But the point remains that all these problems are aspects of "the only problem worth discussing."

In the twenty years since the publication of *The Only Problem* Spark has produced five more novels and an autobiography. Another novel is said to be in preparation. All have, or will have, that amused, sceptical, satirical attitude to what she once called "the ridiculous nature of reality;" and all offer an image of life in the world that is virtually unique though perfectly reasonable—a quality that greatly enhances what we may surely take to be its permanent value.

NOTE

Frank Kermode, "Unrivalled Deftness: The Novels of Muriel Spark," originally appeared as the introduction to Muriel Spark, *The Prime of Miss Jean Brodie; The Girls of Slender Means; The Driver's Seat; The Only Problem* (New York: Everyman's Library, Random House, 2004). Reprinted by permission of Everyman's Library, Random House, 2004.

SELECT BIBLIOGRAPHY

Cheyette, Bryan. *Muriel Spark*, Northcote House, 2000.
Kemp, Peter. *Muriel Spark*, Paul Elek, 1974.

# CHAPTER SEVEN

# The Lightness of Muriel Spark's Novels

DAN GUNN

In May 2005 I was privileged to conduct a public interview with Muriel Spark at the American University of Paris, prior to her being awarded an honorary doctorate. The ensuing session with the audience raised many of the predictable questions: about the author's Scottish origins, her Catholicism, her sense of her own fiction as "poetic." The rhythm of to and fro was sprightly, until a colleague rose and started on a long and complex question—or series of questions as it became. Did Ms. Spark find that she had to inhabit her protagonists' mentality? Did she find that she built her novels up from an initial poetic core? Or on the contrary did she write a lengthy first draft, then edit the prose down to the sparse and elliptical sentences which characterize her work? After some minutes the queries had proliferated into an alarming multipronged interrogation which I realized it would take Muriel Spark the remainder of the evening to begin to answer adequately.

Our author took a short breath, before responding: "No, no, I don't bother with that sort of thing. It just comes out the way you see it. Nothing more. Next question?"

The audience's laughter was sufficiently protracted to permit me time to entertain several not-quite-random thoughts, thoughts which give rise, some years later, to what I wish to explore here. I could feel a weightlessness in the room, see a sudden freeing from gravity expressed in the audience's eyes, hear it in their hilarity. My mind raced back to the two passages from Spark's work which I had read to the audience shortly before, one from *Robinson*, the other from *The Finishing School*. I had read them as examples precisely of Spark's ability to be light even when she appeared to be heavy: for these were passages which, in the context of their respective novels, were notably protracted and oddly weighted.

What I intend, with Muriel Spark no longer here to make us laugh in person, is to try to do justice to that moment: to try, through two novels in particular, *Not to Disturb* and *Territorial Rights*, to express something of Muriel Spark's lightness, and why this is—unlike that of Milan Kundera—so very bearable. To do this I should like first to address once more those two curiously extended passages, ostensible *longueurs* coming each from one end of the author's career, and to do this through the best analysis of lightness I know, that given by Italo Calvino in the lectures he wrote shortly before his death and which are collected under the title *Six Memos for the Next Millennium*.


In *Robinson* few words are wasted to explain, still fewer to justify, the initial preposterous premise: three individuals have survived an airplane crash upon a tiny Pacific island which turns out to be controlled by and named after "Robinson," and little is offered to verisimilitude beyond a Treasure Island–style map and a quick "as you know" (275). Wherever one might expect description, ratiocination, retrospection on the recent traumatic past, one finds future-oriented action and dialogue; until, in chapter 5, after so much rapidity and so many lacunae, the pace alters dramatically and several whole pages are devoted to how to teach a cat called Bluebell to play ping-pong. Described with a quite uncharacteristic step-by-step thoroughness, the pedagogical procedure turns the text into a feline training manual, of which I can give only the opening:

To teach a cat to play ping-pong you have first to win the confidence and approval of the cat. Bluebell was the second cat I had undertaken to teach; I found her more amenable than the first, which had been a male.

Ping-pong with a cat is a simplified and more individualistic form of the proper game. You play it close to the ground, and you imagine the net.

Gaining a cat's confidence is different from gaining the confidence of any other animal. Food is not the simple answer. You have to be prepared to play with it for as long as two hours on end. To gain the initial interest of a cat, I always place a piece of paper over my head and face and utter miaows and other cat noises. This is irresistible to most cats, who come nosing up to see what is going on behind the paper. The next phase involves soft whispering alternately with the whistling of high-pitched tunes.

I thought *Bluebells of Scotland* would be appropriate to Bluebell. She was enchanted. It made her purr and rise on her hind legs. (305)

Bang in the middle of *The Finishing School*, forming its virtual centerpiece and occupying seven pages (where such length would seem an unimaginable luxury to the characters whose lusts, ambitions, and fears are being dealt with in the most summary manner), comes an account of the school fashion show, of which I give only a taster, from its middle section:

But then came Lionel Haas himself, relieved from his double duty as lighting assistant, to Rowland. He wore a flowered shirt and shorts, satin, with a dark background, a pair of long, white-rimmed sun glasses, a soft panama hat and gold leather sandals. Picking up his seaside summery statement, Pallas Kapelas followed wearing a minimal grey bikini. She wore rimless sun glasses and she, too, wore gold sandals. Less confident than the girls who had preceded them, both Lionel and Pallas none the less put on an attractive performance, with much elegant elbow and footwork.

> Opal Gross, being tiny, had thought well to project her presence with an enormous, high, cone-shaped hat, covered with flowers, feathers, shells, heads of corn and small pine cones. She wore a simple Greek-style tunic that she had brought back from her Aegean holiday, with bare legs and feet. As Chris announced Opal he observed over the top of her hat the faces of Nina and Israel Brown smiling at each other with extreme affability at the same time as they joyfully applauded.
>
> Pansy Leghorn or Leg was also a small girl, but she had decided to be herself in her shell-pink taffeta evening dress, and shoes to match. She wore a pearl tiara and carried a very large box of chocolates under her left arm. As she kicked her skirts out on the cat-walk, there flashed glimpses of a black frilled petticoat. (76–77)

Abruptly, no detail is too minute, no accessory too accessory, almost as if Spark had discovered that *description* were vital after all; as if Stendhalian spareness (which I often detect within her prose) had been dropped in favor of the methodical anthropological plod of a Sir Walter Scott.

In what he calls a "lightness of thoughtfulness," Calvino locates three principal distinguishing characteristics. "First there is a lightening of language whereby meaning is conveyed through a verbal texture that seems weightless, until the meaning itself takes on the same rarefied consistency" (16). The brief example he uses to illustrate this is taken from Emily Dickinson's verse. A second characteristic consists of "the narration of a train of thought or psychological process in which subtle and imperceptible elements are at work, or any kind of description that involves a high degree of abstraction" (17). Calvino's illustrations come from Henry James, from Celtic mythology, from atomism, and from Shakespeare, by all of which he seeks to indicate "the subtle forces connecting macrocosm and microcosm" (19), a metamorphic intimation of infinite linkedness. A third characteristic is given by "a visual image of lightness that acquires emblematic value." The example he gives is "the scene in which Don Quixote drives his lance through the sail of a windmill and is hoisted up into the air" (17). Behind all three characteristics there is one prior and crucial example, that of the poet Guido Cavalcanti as depicted by Boccaccio. Cavalcanti has refused to join the revels of wealthy young Florentines, preferring the company of the dead in a graveyard. The revellers, offended, have cornered him, seeking a quarrel, whereupon Cavalcanti first reminds them that they too are in death's grip; then, "leggerissimo" as he is, he vaults over a tombstone and escapes, leaving Calvino to comment on "the sudden agile leap of the poet-philosopher who raises himself above the weight of the world, showing that with all his gravity he has the secret of lightness, and that what many consider to be the vitality of the times—noisy, aggressive, revving and roaring—belongs to the realm of death" (12).

To return to Calvino's first trait of lightness, in the context now of my two untypical passages by Spark, we might initially find little that is poetical in a feline training manual. Yet for Calvino the language of lightness is not vague, but "for me goes with precision and determination"—just such precision as is found here (16). And the style, both purposive and precise, is at the same time increasingly divorced from instrumentality, as words cease to signify in their conventional prosaic ways, and the cat instructor passes from instruction to whispering, to a "lion growl" (306); passes from sense into sound. The fashion show, equally, is not presented in an ostensibly poetic manner, but rather as a list: "First . . . followed by . . . No. 3 . . . then came . . ." (75–76). Yet it may be this very adherence to form, whereby the nine models parade almost like lines of verse, that in fact yields the poetic, at least as I understand the poetic to inhere in Spark's art. Upon this poetic basis to her fiction Spark always insisted, as here in the 2003 foreword to *All the Poems of Muriel Spark*:

> Although most of my life has been devoted to fiction, I have always thought of myself as a poet. I do not write "poetic" prose, but feel that my outlook on life and my perception of events are those of a poet. Whether in prose or verse, all creative writing is mysteriously connected with music and I always hope this factor is apparent throughout my work. (xii)

Just in case in the present instance we were not to notice what Calvino calls the "lightening" of "verbal texture," the expressive difficulties of one particular pupil are evoked while she is parading, difficulties which dictate that sound again takes over from sense: "Mary was totally unable to spell or write in any language, including her own. She could start a letter Dear Dad, but never got as far as Dad, being unsure whether to put Dere, Dear, Deer, or maybe Dior" (*Finishing School* 75).

As to Calvino's second trait, involving imperceptible connections and metamorphic possibilities, when *Robinson*'s protagonist trains Bluebell to play ping-pong she herself undergoes a transformation as a range of unusual correspondences opens: woman enchants cat, then becomes cat, growling; while cat becomes almost human, "an encouraging pupil, an enthusiast" (306). The metamorphic élan is stifled only by the return of human motivation, as the cat's owner Robinson, "a great bore," reminds the cat of its ostensible purpose, as a mouser. Spark's "bores" will always be those who, like Robinson here, limit the freedom of play by insisting on prosaic functionality. In the fashion show from *The Finishing School*, a group of often awkward, antagonistic, hesitant, or overassertive pupil models—no model pupils these—are brought together in a ritual as cunningly improvised as it is jubilantly enacted. They are changed by their new roles, as is the very setting: "The room had been transformed into the image of a veritable fashion-house" (72–73). Even robust Joan Archer is transformed upon the appropriately named *cat*walk: "very swingy" she becomes, her aspiration to become an actress no longer fanciful; while Chris, who is watching her, "thought she might be a good Mary Queen of Scots in the motion picture of his novel" (76). The sense of each of these pupils being in some way "transfigured" (to borrow a word which looms large in *The Prime of Miss Jean Brodie*), of their having been uplifted into a larger ceremony or meaning, a poetical *event*, is only highlighted when the whole show is repeated, *da capo*, "more quickly and boisterously" (79).

The third of Calvino's traits of lightness, the gestural, may be far from obvious in *Robinson*, where the protagonist has landed on earth from her airplane in obeisance to gravity at its most literal and authoritarian. Yet by the time she has befriended Bluebell, the airiness of ping-pong is already onomatopoeically lifting the text upwards again: "She often leapt beautifully . . . making flying leaps . . . With my middle finger and thumb I pinged the ball into Bluebell's box. It bounced against the walls. The cat sprang at it and batted it back" (305–6). In *The Finishing School* the fashion show takes place on a runway constructed of elements liberated from their earthly duties: "The cat-walk itself was composed of two long kitchen table tops which were conveniently separable from their legs, as were most of the college tables. They were mounted on wooden boxes and flanked by clusters of plants" (73). The parade is thus almost organically suspended above the earth, permitting the first model, Princess Tilly, who herself is "tall, with her dark hair piled up," to raise her "high-stepping legs in their stiletto heels" (74).

If behind Calvino's discussion of lightness stands—or rather leaps—Guido Cavalcanti exiting the graveyard, then before moving on to discuss *Not to Disturb* and *Territorial Rights* I should perhaps reveal that behind my own discussion stand—or fly—images from the beginning and end of *Loitering with Intent*. As this novel starts, Fleur Talbot has retired to eat her lunch: "One day in the middle of the twentieth century I sat in an old graveyard which had not yet been demolished, in the Kensington area of London, when a young policeman stepped off the path and came over to me" (7). After offering him a sandwich, Fleur explains that she is writing a poem, while her avowal of her poetic mission is for me somehow caught up by the oddly floating tone of "One day in the middle of the twentieth century," and by the subsequent almost-run-on sentences. Fleur does not leap over the gravestones, but she does not need to, for her "morale was high" (7). Nor does the morale sag, even if Fleur does have to steer her way through a literally murderous situation, with Sir Quentin Oliver and his Autobiographical Association, toward her memorable ending:

> The other day when I had looked in on Dottie, in her little flat, and had a row with her on the subject of my wriggling out of real life, unlike herself, I came out into the court-yard exasperated as usual. Some small boys were playing football, and the ball came flying straight towards me. I kicked it with a chance grace, which,

if I had studied the affair and tried hard, I never could have done. Away into the air it went, and landed in the small boy's waiting hands. The boy grinned. And so, having entered the fullness of my years, from there by the grace of God I go on my way rejoicing. (158)

The ball arrives through the air in a perfect realization of Calvino's gestural Cavalcanti. And it arrives in fulfillment of Fleur's own poetic procedure in fiction, just as "characters and situations, images and phrases" have come to her for the novel she is writing, "as if from nowhere into my range of perception" (13).

The amorality nearly everywhere displayed in *Not to Disturb* and *Territorial Rights* might seem in and of itself to account for the lightness these two novels exude, as the characters free themselves from their bonds and duties; were it not that this argument cuts two ways, with an evil emerging from this freedom which is anything but elevating, and that ties the works to what is *base*, threatening even to drag us into a downward infernal spiral. What I should like to do, by using Calvino's three traits again, is to indicate rather less obvious ways in which lightness is achieved, and in the process, I hope, show a larger and "poetic" conception informing these two works.

*Territorial Rights* is written in very much the usual brisk Spark style, with just the precision Calvino somewhat paradoxically requires for his "weightless language." However, this precision barely conceals the fact that language often corresponds only slightly, when at all, to whatever it is to which it appears to be alluding—and this from the outset. Robert Leaver checks in to the Pensione Sofia in Venice with the words of Curran, his wealthy older lover, in his ears: "Goodbye, goodbye, goodbye, good*bye*" (6). He glosses the tone to himself, budding novelist that he is: "It was as if the older man had said, 'You bore me. You can't even leave in good style. You haven't any slightest savvy about partings. You've always bored me. *Goodbye very much*. Good-*bye*'" (6). Fifteen pages later, Curran is in Venice, in pursuit of Robert. "What brings you to Venice?" Robert asks him over dinner at

Harry's Bar. "Force of will," Curran responds, "as if there had been no 'Goodbye, goodbye, good*bye*'" (21). *Goodbye* can signify hello; *will* can equal weakness. Curran loathes to be called Mr. Curran or Mark Curran, his self-consciousness reaching beyond mere vanity to a deception founded on self-deception. For if "he drove into Venice very much aware of being Curran" (15), his very determination to protect the nugget of his name will be what makes him Robert's ideal blackmail victim.

Identity is moot in *Territorial Rights*. Each of the two sisters who run the Pensione Sofia is fanatical about possession of her half of the garden, yet they are themselves "almost interchangeable" (14). Robert's mother employs Global-Equip Security Services (GESS) to trace the adulterous activities of her husband in Venice; said GESS turn out to be specialists in "persuasion," using the information gleaned from their clients in order to blackmail those whose secrets they now possess. Serge, sometime boyfriend of Bulgarian defector Lina Panchev, "unaware that the same story that can repel can also enchant" (74), tells Lina of the horrors of Western capitalism. Lina hears his invective as invitation. Another interloper in Venice, Leo, puts it most concisely: "I don't myself see that there's much to choose between the injured party and the other parties. It's all one and the same isn't it?" (81). Robert, evil incarnate, brings the only moment of joy to his miserable mother Anthea when he sends her a diamond and sapphire bracelet, which is booty from his latest heist. Effects and causes part ways; heroes turn into villains; doubles proliferate in a manner that points toward Calvino or J. L. Borges, and beyond them to a specifically Scottish tradition of which Spark is just the most illustrious recent example and in which the paramount figure is beloved of all three writers: R. L. Stevenson.

Spark's own narrative, or the novel's language, both permits and colludes in this process by which a strange abstraction is created out of precision. When Robert is asked when he will see Curran for the first time in Venice, he responds "Tomorrow, in the evening." The narrative continues, "Tomorrow, in the evening, Robert walked . . ." (20), as if to emphasize the thinness of the gap between character and narrator. Robert's father, Arnold Leaver, has come to Venice for an affair with Mary Tiller, but he cannot shed the tic of repeating "My wife Anthea"; as Curran puts it, "as if he had other wives by other names" (46). Arnold is, precisely, unable to *leave-her*. Like Curran with his pared-down name, he is at risk of being reduced to a tic, a trope, a verbal fetish which will stand in his stead. Umberto Eco has famously suggested that the "postmodern attitude" is that of "a man who loves a very cultivated woman and knows he cannot say to her, 'I love you madly,' because he knows that she knows (and that she knows that he knows) that these words have already been written by Barbara Cartland." Eco has supplied a possible palliative: "Still, there is a solution. He can say 'As Barbara Cartland would put it, I love you madly'" (530–31). Perhaps surprisingly, when asked by Martin McQuillan whether she considered herself a modernist writer, Spark answered, "Maybe Post-modernist"; though she immediately qualified this claim in exactly the postmodern manner: "They say postmodernist, mostly, whatever that means" (216).

What Curran and Arnold Leaver find and produce in language is a series of poor fits between desire and expression, which proliferate to encompass practically everyone. Robert himself, who arrives in Venice with "only half a mind to feel enchanted" (5), tries to escape into a language-world free from tourist guidebook quotation through claims to be conducting research in art history. But his thesis on Santa Maria Formosa, with its cod-scholarly formulations, is just as ritualized as the guidebooks he shuns. Lina's speech and cadence are foreign, of course, but as Grace Gregory observes, "even for here, where everyone's a foreigner she's a foreigner" (162). A letter arrives announcing the severance of her dissident's allowance: "Isn't it true, Lina, that you believe in nothing and know nothing of our struggle?" (181): her discourse of dissidence is merely a convenient way to curry Western favor, which, when it dries up, finds her returning to Bulgaria, "where she was put to happy use as a first rate example of a repentant dissident" (238). The telephone is much in use in this novel, detaching words from their utterer, to a satirical end reminiscent of Evelyn Waugh, but also producing an eerie effect more reminiscent of the telephone in Franz Kafka or in Marcel Proust (or indeed in Spark's own *Memento Mori*). And into the narrative itself penetrate foreign texts, interruptions such as the GESS brochure which flattens language so severely that subject and object, here protector and extorter, become tellingly conflated: "Uniformed • Armed Guards • Plainclothes • Negligence" (53). And of the interruptions, novels produce the most numerous examples of all. The novel which Anthea Leaver is reading to distract herself from her husband's adultery intrudes on four occasions, revealing how its narrator has failed to learn Fleur Talbot's lesson of "how little one needs, in the art of writing, to convey the lot, and how a lot of words, on the other hand, can convey so little" (*Loitering* 60). And if Anthea's novel is a ballast trying to hold Spark's novel down, then that which Robert intends to write is trying to out-fly it. For it embellishes the facts in a way that Robert intends to be provocative but which is in fact dictated by its author's sensationalism, even as it is constrained by his ineptitude. When Robert writes "1945 AD The Allies take Venice and the Germans go away" (148), that "go away" displays not just inexperience but the purpose or motivation which defeats the novelistic. His motive is blackmail, and his plot is clichéd in such a way that it can only lead to quotation, as if the author, Robert, were himself now being cited by tawdry convention (and this when, to cite Fleur again as our guide to the genuinely novelistic, "I didn't go in for motives, I never have" [61]). Of Robert's fondness for "AD" Violet de Winter notes: "It sounds creepy, like a history book or a memorial stone" (152). It is as if even the dates crucial to Robert's narrative were fictional or reported; as if history were "history." Robert's purposeful attempt to root his narrative in fact leaves his fiction tied to the ground, anchored to the memorial stone of his own career as a novelist.

*Not to Disturb* opens with Lister, the inverted Jeeves figure, out to destroy his master rather than assist him, citing fatalistically: "'Their life,' says Lister, 'a general mist of error. Their death, a hideous storm of terror.—I quote from *The Duchess of Malfi* by John Webster, an English dramatist of old'" (5). He goes on to cite, among others, Hamlet, Prospero, Freud, Marie-Antoinette, Edward Fitzgerald, the Bible, and Andrew Marvell. Lister summons the literary canon in order to indicate to his fellow servants the inevitability of the catastrophe about to engulf Baron and Baroness Klopstock and their shared lover Victor Passerat, and to intimate thereby that they will not die but have in fact already "died." Yet even though Lister may be Spark's master-citer, there is a sense—and this sense marks for me Spark's distance from the more playful postmodernism of Umberto Eco and perhaps of Calvino too—in which he is himself subject to the process he masters; he is playful perhaps, but also irresistibly played. This reversal begins, as is characteristic in Spark, with the name. Deviating for a second to another of Spark's novels, we find Miss Brodie has inherited her name from her forebear Deacon Brodie; she is at least aware of the dividedness implied by this, while Sandy Stranger, her nemesis, seems unaware of being a stranger to herself. By citing Miss Brodie in denunciation of her former teacher to the authorities, Sandy does not free herself, any more than she does by becoming Sister Helena of the Transfiguration, given the "Transfiguration of the Commonplace" for which she becomes famous itself appears to be an unconscious citation of Miss Brodie's pedagogy. Lister, here, the maker of lists who does not listen, may have no stranger to resist him by pointing to how he is himself being named or "cited." Yet he has a stranger within himself, starting with his proper name, which is anything but his property.

Who is speaking when Lister says, of John Webster, "an English dramatist of old"? Or when, telling of his master's death as "one remove from sex, as in Henry James," he describes James as "an English American who travelled"? The fact that Lister is more linguistically acute than Robert Leaver (with his "AD"s) does not relieve him. When he starts upon his autobiography, which Mr. McGuire is taping so as to sell it to the press when the night is over, he is interrupted by Mr. McGuire who directs him to "make it more colloquial": "Don't say 'a boy of fourteen,' say 'a boy, fourteen,' like that, Lister" (41). Lister rejoins that "style can be left to the journalists" (42). Yet he cannot liberate himself from the thraldom of tabloid cliché with its motives imputed by pop-psychology. "'When I was a boy, fourteen,' Lister goes on, 'I decided to leave England. There was a bit of trouble over me having to do with Eleanor under the grand piano, she being my aunt and only nine. Dating from that traumatic experience, Eleanor conceived an inverted avuncular fixation'" (42). Mr. McGuire interrupts again, perturbed morally rather than stylistically this time: "'It isn't right,' says Mr. McGuire, turning off the machine" (42). Lister, not heeding Mr. McGuire's tone, rejoins, "It isn't true, but that's not to say it isn't right" (42)—*right* here being what is dictated by the decorum of the mediatized narratives to which, prior to selling it to the highest bidder, he has already dedicated his intimate memoirs, has already *sold out*. Seconds later he will speak of the deaths of his master and mistress as "the last thing we expected," these deaths being yet to occur. Lister's awareness that truth is fiction which works, is a quotation which knows itself *per se*, does not free him from Eco's postmodern barb. For there is no Lister other than the one thus spoken, thus cited. Nor is Lister's dilemma circumvented by the characters in less formal or directorial roles than the butler, those more obviously driven by youth and its hormones, as is hilariously demonstrated in the scene where the sprightly Hadrian, Heloise, and Pablo dance together (54–58) while confabulating on how others fail to "relate" or "correspond" or "coordinate"—slaves to jargon quite as much as is Lister, their mentor and guide. Ingenuousness is no innocence, as we are reminded when Heloise plays Little Red Riding Hood and is "eaten up by Lister's understudy" (56) in the pornographic home-movie that Mr. Samuel has been shooting. This Heloise not only lacks her literary archetype's virtue, but, though she lives on the banks of Lake Leman like Rousseau's heroine, she lacks her passion too, and is unable to hazard more than an approximate guess as to who is the father of her unborn child.

So much of *Not to Disturb* is dialogue spoken by characters who are quoting (while themselves being quoted) that the language of Spark's narrator remains marginal; and, such as it is, it seems far from being free from the conditions besetting character and speech. The novel wears its gothic on its sleeve, as "the wind now whistles round the house and the remote shutters bang as another latent storm wakes up" (73). Yet it resists the fixed distances of irony, still more resolutely refusing those of parody or satire, and nowhere more forcefully than through its single dominant trope: its use of the present tense of narration (a trope it shares with *The Driver's Seat* and *The Hothouse by the East River* as well as with the early novels of Alain Robbe-Grillet by which Spark said she was influenced). We shall shortly see what effect this has on Lister's attack on "vulgar chronology" (40), when we turn to the second of Calvino's traits and examine its implications for the arch-plotter. For now, I wish only to point to the verbal texture produced by this insistent present, which inscribes an openness or anti-teleological unpredictability in the very heart of the overdeterminations of citation; a quasi-archival neutrality of tone when what is being reconstructed is being constructed at the very same time through a thoroughly unliterary, a downright *antipoetical* style; what Roland Barthes might have called a "writing degree zero," which in its precise imprecision offers what I'd like to suggest is central to Spark's "poetic" novelistic vision. And if the narrator is not free to deal out history—or is free to deal out *only* that, event by event, in mock-grim sequentiality; the figure appears reversible—then perhaps this is true of the author as well. The name of the novel is not what any frequenter of hotels might expect, "Do not Disturb." In his essay on the novel in *Theorizing Muriel Spark*, Willy Maley comments on the title's "odd grammar, like a phrase taken out of context" and suggests that "the repetition of the title, in various guises, throughout the novel, adds to its eerie and unorthodox accent and intonation, and extends the impression of a world that is unbalanced, unhinged and out of joint" (173). What Maley neglects to note is that the title in fact reads like an awkward translation, as it might be from French or Italian (*"Ne pas déranger"* or *"Non disturbare"*) where the infinitive can become imperative in its negative form. The title serves to usher us in to a world where the original is missing, where translation, itself a sort of citation or plagiarism doomed to failure, is virtually omnipresent; where even the author seems to lack authority and where that very lack adds to an echoing—or floating—sense of foreignness, of the *stranger* in our midst.

When seeking further to characterize his second, metamorphic, sense of lightness, Calvino refers to Celtic mythology with its "delicate natural forces, with their elves and fairies." He invokes Shakespeare—not just Ariel and Puck, but "that particular and existential inflection that makes it possible for Shakespeare's characters to distance themselves from their own drama, thus dissolving it into melancholy and irony" (19). It is in relation to this second trait that Spark's propensity to the supernatural could usefully be examined, and perhaps also her lightly worn but deeply structuring Catholicism. Even in the novels I am reading here, which are less pervaded by the supernatural and religion than many, a sense of magical connectedness is present. While Calvino's further sense, of a sadness leavened into melancholy, of an awareness of the limits to drama and plot, is all the more important in that the novels under consideration here contain some of Spark's most dogged and ambitious plotters.

Fleur Talbot, in *Loitering with Intent*, is an accomplished novelist by the time she writes of her experiences lived in 1949: "In a novel the author invents characters and arranges them in a convenient order. Now that I come to write biographically I have to tell of whatever actually happened and whoever naturally turns up" (43). Fleur flirts with the possibility of playing god, dictating her coevals' destinies in a way that aligns her perilously with Sir Quentin the "sado-puritan" (59). What saves her from an apotheosis of fantasized omnipotence, and indeed from the melancholy which besets most of Spark's plotters, is not least the clarity conferred by her métier, which demands that she be alert to "whoever naturally turns up": "I do dearly love a turn of events," she writes as she faces another surprise (145). She may claim that "in a novel the author invents characters and arranges them in convenient order" (43), but this only begs the question: Whose convenience? For as she also indicates, she writes not "so that the reader would think me a nice person, but in order that my sets of words should convey ideas of truth and wonder" (59). She may well say that "the true novelist, one who understands the work as a continuous poem, is a myth-maker" (100), but as we know, myths are not made by fiat or by individual hands. Spark herself has commented, in her celebrated interview with Frank Kermode, on how myth practically makes itself, stating that "If I think of a plot, I take it for granted that that's a myth" (Kermode 29). She then elaborates in terms that shed light backwards on the present tense of narration in *Not to Disturb* and forward on the passivity required of the novelist if she is to stop short of "sado-puritanism" and reveal the connectedness within the world:

> I think that the novelist is out just to say what happened. I express it in the past tense, but in the actual process, as far as I am

concerned, it happens in the present tense. Things just happen and one records what has happened a few seconds later. I don't mean, of course, that one is that recording instrument that Blake thought of himself, just a kind of medium between the angels and the creatures, but I do know events occur in my mind, and I record them. (32)

In the roll call of Spark's "sado-puritans" none is more charismatic than Lister in *Not to Disturb*, and this not least because, licentious amoral pornographer that he is, his puritanism has divested itself of any ethical appurtenance in order to focus on its essence in temporality. In writing the future, Lister links more explicitly even than Jean Brodie to the Calvinism represented by John Knox, while Spark points to her Scottish origins and to James Hogg whose *The Private Memoirs and Confessions of a Justified Sinner* (1824) is *the* exemplary text on the fascination and folly of such predestination as is permitted by fundamentalist Presbyterianism (or Antinomianism). " 'Let us not split hairs,' says Lister, 'between the past, present and future tenses'" (6). Vatically, Lister predicts and professes: "But what's done is about to be done and the future has come to pass" (9). The "crime of passion" that is soon to be committed is reduced to grotesque puppetry: "To all intents and purposes, they're already dead although as a matter of banal fact, the night's business has still to accomplish itself" (12). As Victor Passerat arrives, Lister comments, crushing life with his preterite: "He walked to his death most gingerly" (11). Not just for its Rousseauesque associations is the novel set on Lake Leman by Geneva, home as this city was to John Calvin. In this novel Lister's control of predestination is so complete that, as I have suggested, he practically usurps his own narrator. Speaking of the proleptic imagination which links Spark to Miss Brodie, Cairns Craig in *The Modern Scottish Novel* gives a brilliant analysis of how predestination is both the engine and the brake within Spark's infernal machine:

Brodie's Calvinist self-election parodies the author's awareness of how the novel, by its very form, replicates the world as envisaged by Calvin, since it presents reality not as an open future in which human beings have choices to make but as a fixed plot over which the author broods like "the God of Calvin," able to see "the beginning and the end." Calvinism presents the universe as though it were a novel already written by God. . . . The paradox which *The Prime of Miss Jean Brodie* exploits is that Spark's anti-Calvinist novel can only come into existence by acknowledging its own formal complicity with the ontological assumptions of the Calvinist universe. (204–5)

As Craig points out, Jean Brodie's proleptic imagining is curbed by Sandy Stranger, whose own over-fertile imagination is in turn curbed by her withdrawal from the world, by the bars of her nun's cell which she grips. To this I would wish now to add that Spark's own proleptic drive is chastened by the melancholy pervading the dull awfulness and waste of the protagonists' lives, the very failure of self-consciousness on both sides of the sectarian divide: Miss Brodie, "more fuming, now, with Christian morals, than John Knox," and Sandy who "had entered the Catholic Church, in whose ranks she had found quite a number of Fascists much less agreeable than Miss Brodie" (125).

It perfectly fits Craig's insight that Lister should be the most attractive character in *Not to Disturb*, and the most diabolic. He ties the world to his imagination even as he reveals his imagination's limits, reveals everyone's almost solipsistic isolation even as he reveals that all are united in his plot. And he does this while himself being anything but jubilant; he is, rather, melancholy in the manner Calvino suggests certain Shakespearean characters to be—"a gloomy shopkeeper" as he is described (84). "We are such stuff / As dreams are made on": Calvino cites Shakespeare's most powerful plotter at the moment Prospero is admitting the limits of his master plot (19). And Spark has Lister quote the same (86), though not now in order to abjure any rough magic but rather to sustain it. Yet as I have suggested, even Lister has his limits, signaled by the "vulgar chronology" he eschews, the "banal facts" of actuality. "There is a vast difference," he says, "between events that arise from and those that merely follow after each other. Those that arise are preferable" (68). Despite his preferences, despite his affection for the preterite, vulgarity and banality are imported by the insistent forensic present of narration, the sense of events "merely following after each other" (which present curbs his imagination as much as it does that of Lise in *The Driver's Seat*). Two friends of Victor Passerat turn up in a Mini and refuse to leave. Theo the gateman turns out to be anything but all-seeing, despite his name. Lister has to admit that "my forecasts are only approximate" (64), even as he claims that "It was quite unforeseen, but one foresees the unforeseen" (66). And even Lister is connected to others in ways he cannot control, to his niece, for example ("Their faces are long and similar" [27]), who refuses to marry him because, as she puts it, affirming precisely the ungovernable links that Calvino invokes, "I stand by the Table of Kindred and Affinity" (30). The Baron's idiot brother turns out to be the heir to the Klopstock dynasty and is married off to Heloise, who turns out to be a Klopstock too: patronym and patrimony flattened into coincidence, co-incidence indeed, which as we shall see when we turn now to *Territorial Rights*, is one of the principal binding agents within Spark's poetic-novelistic mythology.

Practically everyone is a plotter in *Territorial Rights*, and blackmail is their chief mechanism. The term itself originates from the home of one of Spark's most commonly cited literary influences, the Debatable Lands, origin of her beloved Border Ballads (the *OED* gives the following as its first meaning: "A tribute formerly extracted from farmers and small owners in the border counties of England and Scotland"). Through blackmail ontology and epistemology fight a duel, by which the blackmailer is paid to eliminate contradiction, enshrine hypocrisy, ensure the monotony of probity (blackmail of which Muriel Spark says, "I see it and I suffer from it. I always call people's bluff" [McQuillan 225]). Robert Leaver uses it as a lever on his future, challenging his own past, in the form of Curran, to reveal the secrets within *his own* past. When blackmail fails he retreats to the cruder extortion of robbery and terrorism, just as he moves from anxiety and apology to a discovery of his delight in crime, and of his true "talent" as a criminal (the word is used repeatedly). Robert moves beyond conscience, hence beyond blackmail, embodying the protean spirit—

switching names, appearance, the gender of his sexual objects. He is as joyous as instinct untrammelled by repression. Grace glosses the ironic *Bildungsroman* that Robert ensures the novel has become: "The really professional evil-doers love it. . . . The unhappy ones are only the guilty amateurs and the neurotics" (235). Yet the narrative has a way of signalling a limit to Robert's wishes, a ballast upon his lability, and this from the outset. For no sooner does he arrive in Venice seeking Lina Panchev than he bumps into her; his investigative drive is subverted by the first of almost countless coincidences the novel contains. Robert checks in to the very hotel where Lina's father happens to be buried. Robert's father happens to check in to the same hotel. Robert's mother happens to contact GESS, which happens to employ Violet de Winter, who happens to be friends with Curran, who happens to be Robert's lover and Lina's father's former acquaintance . . . *Happens to*: the very flouting of plausibility required by novelistic verisimilitude serves paradoxically to inscribe the *happening*—the sense of an event which takes place beyond plot, a "poetic" event as I wish to claim. Robert's behavior takes him beyond moral propriety. By declining to adhere to any single character, by moving sideways rather than forwards, by revealing the hidden connections that lie beyond Curran's "force of will," by vaunting the co-incidental—Spark's narrative flouts not just moral propriety, but every other sense of propriety as well. This includes property, what is proper to a particular character, and whatever confers upon a character essence or individuality.

Nowhere is this clearer than in one of the novel's chief narrative drives, which bears upon filiation. If, as Peter Brooks has suggested, "paternity is a dominant issue within the great tradition of the nineteenth-century novel (extending well into the twentieth century)" (63), then Robert and Lina represent two poles within this great tradition: Robert fleeing his father, Lina struggling to find her father's earthly remains. As we first meet him, Robert is escaping from the ubiquitous surrogate-father Curran, but he runs straight into his real father's purview. When told by Lina that if his father were dead he would be seeking his grave, Robert replies, "I would dance on it." Yet in the end he does not dance but has to watch his own father dancing on another father's grave. Behind the repudiation, family resemblances

form up, as the father's duplicity and self-righteousness are magnified
into the amorality and egotism of the son. There is more than a little
truth to the song which is overheard: "My Heart Belongs to Daddy"
(96). The weight of the past, of what Peter Brooks educes as the concerns behind his "great tradition"—"with authority, legitimacy, the
conflict of generations, and the transmission of wisdom" (63)—is not
so easily shirked. In the end, all Robert does is to substitute, not shed,
his father-figures: declining from his hypocrite father to the unscrupu-
lous Curran; to the "Butcher" by whom he is adopted and who calls
him "*figlio mio*" (218); to a criminal "talent-spotter" who employs him
for a heist; to a further "talent-spotter" who recruits him as a terrorist. While Spark, declining to tie her narrative to any individual, to
make her narrative father or son to anyone, takes her own resolutely
un-proprietorial principle almost *ad absurdum* in her conclusion. By
allotting a short sharp block of prose to each of her characters, as if in
a business résumé or a forensic report, she drops her characters un-
graciously, so allowing her silence to soar; in relinquishing her novelistic responsibility—novels are not supposed to end this way!—she
signals her willingness to abjure her own rough magic.

In turning to the third and final trait of Calvino's lightness—"a visual
image of lightness that acquires emblematic value"—I would like to
pass briefly by way of another Italian writer who may serve to con-
firm that behind the weight of solid buildings and the inevitability of
moral decline there may be lightness: one whom I have rarely seen
aligned with Spark, yet from whom I suspect she learned; one whose
masterwork, published in 1959, has been read as such a manifesto of
the futility of action that it has given rise to a new word in the Italian
language, *gattopardesco*, signifying something like the impossibility
of change. Giuseppe Tomasi di Lampedusa's *The Leopard* (*Il Gat-
topardo*) may be a less obvious precursor of Spark's novels than those
of, say, Evelyn Waugh, but the "decline and fall" described therein
ends just as ineluctably in a "handful of dust." "Our sensuality," says
the Prince of Salina, the eponymous Leopard, "is a hankering for
oblivion"; "sleep, that is what Sicilians want, and they will always

hate anyone who tries to wake them" (206). The very terms are prac-tically glossed by Lister, when he comments on his masters: "How urgently does an overwhelming obsession with life lead to suicide! Really, it's best to be half-awake and half-aware" (13). The Leopard's comments on the mendacity of his subordinates who are eating away at his property and territorial rights could be the Baron Klopstock's, were he capable of such lucidity: "We were the Leopards, the Lions; those who'll take our place will be little jackals, hyenas" (214).

It would require more space than I have before me to show how the politics, and *a fortiori* the aesthetics, of *The Leopard* are not as baldly conservative or nostalgic or pessimistic as has been commonly portrayed (a demonstration which might return me to the hostile at-titude of Lampedusa's contemporaries to his work, including on the part of the Sicilian writer to whom Spark is more often compared, Leonardo Sciascia). Here, it may suffice to remark that this novel ex-plores decadence—the word itself containing, in its *cadere*, a down-ward trajectory—and moral abjection quite as intensively as do Spark's mature works. Yet, despite its time spent in palaces, despite being rooted in a dying past, *The Leopard* is as suspicious of any idealiza-tion of paradise lost as is Spark's work; it contains a score of prolepses (leaping forward to Eisenstein, to psychoanalysis, to bus transport, to the bomb that will almost destroy the Salina palace in 1943) that lead me to view it as a veritable training ground for *The Prime of Miss Jean Brodie*. Calvino suggests that the moon, in poetry, "brings with it a sensation of lightness, suspension, a silent calm enchantment" (24). When the star-gazing Leopard dies, his very obliteration is an ascen-sion of a secular sort, as he is taken by his beloved Venus, who "looked lovelier than she ever had when glimpsed in stellar space" (292). The novel's final part projects, through the Prince's surviving spinster sis-ters, the very picture of loss of value, desire, truth, that has transformed the Salina palace into a gilded prison. The sisters' religious relics are revealed by the new ecclesiastical bureaucracy, in exactly the spirit of Spark, to be frauds, mere gristle and bone. And to cap it all the novel ends with the Prince's beloved and life-affirming dog, Bendicó, the most obvious image of lightness, stuffed and about to be thrown out of the window. Yet, in keeping with my wish to read this novel as instructive for reading Spark, even though it has been viewed as the emblem of freighted commitment to the past, I wish to follow Bendicó as he falls: "his form recomposed itself for an instant; in the air one could have seen dancing a quadruped with long whiskers, and its right foreleg seemed to be raised in imprecation." And when the dog hits the courtyard whence the rubbish-collector will remove him, he still, in the novel's final sentence, refuses fully to stay down: "Then all found peace in a heap of livid dust" (320).

"Not to Disturb" could be the Prince of Salina's motto, and certainly the novel of this title—to turn to it a final time—is quite as firmly grounded in stones and succession as is *The Leopard*. Yet the Klopstock castle proves rapidly to be faux-gothic rather than genuinely ancestral; it is only eleven years old and is filled with imported miniaturised valuables. Masonry and décor dissolve into stage set, which process itself partakes of a tradition shared by kings and popes, as Lister claims: "They take everything, like stage-companies who need their props. With royalty, of course, it is largely a matter of stage production" (28). And in the castle's upper storey resides a figure who, if indebted to a gothic tradition of madwomen in attics, is more irrepressibly present—and in the present—than anyone, a Bendicó of sorts, if more equine than canine: "The zestful cretin's eyes fall first on Irene. He neighs jubilantly through his large teeth and shakes his long white wavy hair." His very apparel seems to promise elevation and speed: "He wears a jump-suit of dark red velvet fastened from crotch to collar-bone with a zip-fastener" (74). True to this promise, the idiot Klopstock breaks free: "He rips the whole zip-fastener from the stuff of his suit and exultantly dances out of the garment . . . capering lustily with carols" (80). This is, of course, something like a parody of the life-instinct, of Cavalcanti's leap over the tombstone. The natural is barely permitted entrance to this novel (still less the supernatural), and when it enters it too falls squarely "within the realm of predestination," as Lister puts it (37). The Baroness, once a desirable woman, has now "let herself go to rack and ruin" (35); leaving Theo's wife Clara to comment, "She shouldn't have let go her shape. Why did she suddenly start to go natural? She must have started to be sincere with someone" (35). Yet a storm does blow up, and however predetermined it is by gothic convention, its ripped zip-fastener still links human to something like suprahuman, releasing death and life at once: "lightning, which strikes the clump of trees so that the two friends huddled there are killed instantly without pain, zig-zags across the lawns, illuminating the lily-pond and the sunken rose garden like a self-stricken photographer, and like a zip-fastener ripped from its garment by a sexual maniac, it is flung slapdash across Lake Leman and back to skim the rooftops of the house" (86). One of Lister's last requests is that "we don't want to be disturbed" (95), raising the ominous specter of forthcoming repetition. Yet the final words find the servants asleep in their beds, "while outside the house the sunlight is laughing on the walls" (96): a quiet lifting of the pall of Lister's particular melancholy and a reminder, at the last, of the common root linking illumination and levity, lightning and lightening, light and the light.

Both words of the title *Territorial Rights* threaten to hold what follows down to earth. Lina feels she has the rights of a dissident as well as "residential rights" in Venice (66). Grace feels that as a former matron of a boys' school, "it's my right to know" (136). Curran feels it is his right to conceal, to pretend, to rewrite history. Mr. B. of GESS, who is the one who uses the expression "territorial rights," reveals that though nameless—unless it is *because* he is nameless—he indeed has rights to the power of "G," which is to say globally (165). Even Lord Byron, according to Mr. B, when in Venice, "exercised, if I may say, his human rights" (169). Everyone believes in his or her own right; nobody believes in responsibility. Passports, those emblems of mobility and mutability explored with such prescience in another north Italian novel, Stendhal's *La Chartreuse de Parme* (1839), confer the right to cross territories external and possibly internal. But they may at the same time possess their ostensible owners. Arnold Leaver cites his doctor in order to demonstrate his right to escape England and his wife. However, his passport being shared with his wife, it ensures he carries her with him. Robert feels it is his right to snoop, to lie, to extort, to murder, to terrorize (heedless of how he may be emulating recruits to the notorious Baader-Meinhof group or the Red Brigade). Yet for Robert, his territorial rights turn into territorial *rites*, as he divests himself of allegiance to place and patronym, a shedding taken to its apogee when he teams up with the criminal Anna, who "never used a surname unless absolutely necessary, in which case she had a choice of surnames inscribed on a choice of documents and identification papers" (214). And no right ties its owner more firmly to the ground than that claimed by the two sisters at the Pensione Sofia— and *into* the ground, since the sisters' commitment is to what is buried in their garden, the corpse of Lina's father. Giorgio, Robert's adopted father, claims that this corpse is a still point in a turning world, a master-signifier when all else is ambiguous: "That's concrete," he says. "Everything else is anything you like" (218). Yet he ignores his own name and role in saying this: ignores that he is "the Butcher" who has helped slice the body in two, producing an originary doubling which proliferates from this ground into a multiplicity of plots and plotting, of suspicion and interpretation.

When Robert manipulates Lina to dance on Victor Panchev's grave, he fulfills his role as one of Spark's nastier "sado-puritans." But he also, almost as much as Calvino's Cavalcanti vaulting the tombstone, releases a gesture of lightness whose ironic trammels are themselves curtailed by the fact that Lina dances with Robert's father, offering him finally, after all his disappointments, "a Venetian adventure," one which ensures that Robert's mocking laughter emerges as "a convulsed sound" (197). When he flees Venice to pursue his newfound career as a criminal, Robert may be embracing mobility, but he also lands on "what the Venetians call *terra ferma*" (225). He leaves the territory which itself is the denial of *terr*-itory, a city more implausible than even the most implausible of Spark's coincidences. Venice may be several and variable, since as Mary Tiller says, "the beauty, the great beauty, of Venice simply changes when one has some worry on one's mind" (131). Yet it remains staunchly resistant to the weight of contemporary projections, inscrutable even to one such as Violet de Winter who claims to be "someone who knows the place, who knows the past," but who fails to monitor the goings-on in her own house (100). This city may contain something of the ruthlessness of Shakespeare's merchants, and of anti-Semitism (as we see when Lina throws herself in the canal to cleanse herself after sex with the Jewish Leo); but it contains something of Belmont too, its light "opalescent," its colors "pink and grey," a city floating on its almost magical sense of its own suspension (109). The novel ends far from what Calvino calls the "revving and roaring" of "the vitality of the times": "the canals lapped on the sides of the banks, the palaces of Venice rode in great state and the mosaics stood with the same patience that had gone into their formation, piece by small piece" (240). The city of Venice is in every sense *imponderable*. And like its famed mosaics, which take the multiple and seemingly random, and, in some evolutionary way which we appear to have lost, create from them a poetic whole, so the novel "rides," curiously weightless and undemanding, patient in its own quiet certainty, before it goes on its way rejoicing.

## WORKS CITED

Brooks, Peter. *Reading for the Plot: Design and Intention in Narrative*. New York: Alfred A. Knopf, 1984.

Calvino, Italo. *Six Memos for the Next Millennium*. Cambridge, MA: Harvard University Press, 1988.

Craig, Cairns. *The Modern Scottish Novel: Narrative and the National Imagination*. Edinburgh: Edinburgh University Press, 1999.

Eco, Umberto. *The Name of the Rose, Including Postscript to the Name of the Rose*. Trans. William Weaver. New York: Harcourt Brace, 1994.

Kermode, Frank. "Muriel Spark's House of Fiction." *Critical Essays on Muriel Spark*. Ed. Joseph Hynes. New York: G. K. Hall, 1992.

Maley, Willy. "Not to Deconstruct? Righting and Deference in *Not to Disturb*." *Theorizing Muriel Spark*. Ed. Martin McQuillan. Basingstoke: Palgrave, 2002.

McQuillan, Martin, ed. *Theorizing Muriel Spark*. Basingstoke: Palgrave, 2002.

Spark, Muriel. *All the Poems of Muriel Spark*. New York: New Directions, 2004.

———. *The Finishing School*. London: Penguin Viking, 2004.

———. *Loitering with Intent*. London: Penguin, 1995.

———. *Not to Disturb*. London: Penguin, 1974.

———. *The Prime of Miss Jean Brodie*. London: Penguin, 1965.

———. *Robinson. Muriel Spark Omnibus*. Vol. 4. London: Constable, 1997.

———. *Territorial Rights*. London: Penguin, 1991.

Tomasi di Lampedusa, Giuseppe. *The Leopard*. Trans. Archibald Colquhoun. New York: Pantheon Books, 1960.

# CHAPTER EIGHT

# Muriel Spark and the Peters Pan

## JOHN GLAVIN

Since this chapter is going to end with theology, it starts with a parable; it is a virtual parable suited to the writer who gave us "The House of the Famous Poet," a story that starts on a train and ends, notably, on a train with a virtual funeral. It's a somewhat Hitchcockian parable: it sports strangers on a train. And it's also semi-Ovidian: it features goddesses in disguise.

In the summer of 1981, in the bar of an English train, a man accosts a woman. Nothing unusual or strange there. He detains her, insisting he knows her—in fact, that he recognizes her as the novelist Margaret Drabble. "How can you tell," she replies "that I'm not Doris Lessing, Muriel Spark, or even Iris Murdoch?" He is not to be denied: "Margaret, I'd know you anywhere" (Conradi 527).

This stranger on a train gets it partly right. The woman is a writer. But she is not the writer Margaret Drabble. Nevertheless, she tries to help him, narrowing the correct choice to one of the three reigning female divinities of postwar British fiction. Still, our louche demi-Paris misreads his moment.

Ah, you will think, it really was, then, Muriel Spark. (This is, after all, a chapter called "Muriel Spark and the Peters Pan.") But there you, like the stranger/swain, would be wrong. It was Iris Murdoch.

At least, that is what Peter J. Conradi, Murdoch's biographer and good friend, contends. But how, with divinities like these, can he be sure? I assume no one would mistake Doris Lessing for either Iris Murdoch or Muriel Spark. But between Murdoch and Spark how do we always and certainly tell? Is there any sign, a mark, that can make us sure we could "anywhere" tell the author of *Existentialists and Mystics* from the writer of *Memento Mori*? If you can write "The Seraph and the Zambesi," may you also not author *Nuns and Soldiers*? If you can call a semi-autobiographical novel *Loitering with Intent*, are you not someone whose novels might be analyzed (by Barbara Huesel) in a study called *Patterned Aimlessness*? Or, in other, and more useful, words, can beginning with a virtual overlap between Murdoch and Spark help us to see something important, central, or essential to Muriel Spark and her achievement in fiction?

That is the question this essay tries to answer. Hence a revision in its title. It's now "Muriel Spark, Iris Murdoch, and the Peters Pan."

In 1973 Muriel Spark published her twelfth novel, *The Hothouse by the East River*. The climactic moment in its plot turns on an off-off-Broadway octogenarian production of Barrie's *Peter Pan*, a performance the planning for which runs throughout the earlier chapters. In 1975 Iris Murdoch published her seventeenth novel, *A Word Child*. The novel also significantly deploys Peter Pan, particularly in siting the trysting place of its serio-comic lovers, Hilary and Kitty, at the Peter Pan statue/shrine in Kensington Gardens. But the connection goes well beyond the icon. Murdoch's entire novel wittily functions as an extended adaptation of Barrie's weird, spectral Peter Pan novel, *Peter Pan in Kensington Gardens*, which is much less well known than the play.

I was struck by the uncanny chance of these two in many ways paired novelists using the same material within so short a period of time, and I wondered if Iris Murdoch might deliberately be replying to or answering Muriel Spark.

Here is the text of the letter I received from Iris Murdoch in reply to that question.

March 16 [1988]

> Dear Mr. Glavin,
>
> thank you for your letter. I am afraid I have not read the novel of Muriel Spark to which you refer. I can't recall in which respects my Peter Pan remarks, that is my characters' *very various*, remarks and desires, referred to the novel as well as to the play. The novel is certainly worth reading if one is interested in the wonderful dramatic myth.
>
> All best wishes to your studies,
> Yours sincerely
> Iris Murdoch
> I'm afraid this letter is not very helpful. Do write if you want to.
> I'm glad you've liked the novels.

There was of course no need to apologize. I find the letter "very helpful," much more helpful than if my surmise had been correct. Iris Murdoch in conscious dialogue with Muriel Spark is one, relatively simple and clear, thing. Murkier is the more interesting and complex question of why these two writers would have decided at the same time that Barrie's "wonderful dramatic myth" had something crucial to say to the novel and their readers. And most interesting and murkiest: that they would each mount, as they did, such profoundly divergent takes on that myth, one using the play, the other the novel. Making the rounds of that intersection—Murdoch on Barrie crossing Spark on Barrie—uncovers, I want to claim, how we might indeed recognize Muriel Spark anywhere.

## PETER AND IRIS IN KENSINGTON GARDENS

Readers of an essay on Muriel Spark can be assumed to know *The Hothouse by the East River*. And readers of all kinds are familiar with at least the outlines of *Peter Pan* the play. But I don't think I can assume a comparable familiarity with either *A Word Child* or *Peter Pan in Kensington Gardens*.

To summarize *A Word Child*: Hilary Burde, an orphaned, violent, scholarship boy, a whiz at languages and thus a word child, goes up to Oxford where he manages to win a fellowship, largely through the mentorship of the slightly older, wealthy, and well-born Gunnar Jopling. Alas, Hilary and Gunnar's wife, Anne, fall in love. They drive off together but reckless, rushing Hilary crashes the car and Anne dies. His life and university career ruined, Hilary leaves Oxford to take a low-level bureaucratic job in an obscure government ministry, consoled only by his adored sister, Crystal. Years pass. Unexpectedly, Gunnar is appointed to head Hilary's department. Gunnar's exotic second wife, Lady Kitty, persuades Hilary to approach Gunnar to attempt reconciliation. The peacemaking fails but Hilary and Kitty now fall in love. Clued by a letter from Hilary's jealous mistress, Thomasina, Gunnar discovers them together on a jetty near the Joplings' Chelsea house. In the ensuing struggle Kitty falls to her death in the freezing Thames. The novel ends with a brace of church scenes. Hilary mourns Kitty, and incidentally T. S. Eliot, in St. Stephen's Church, where Eliot's memorial tablet can be found. In another church he watches his sister, unexpectedly, marry her long-time faithful suitor, Arthur Fisch, on Christmas Eve. And then, as the bells of St. Mary Abbots ring in Christmas Day, Hilary, "standing at the corner of Kensington Church Street" (391), hears Thomasina declare that she intends to marry him.

*Peter Pan in Kensington Gardens* is the earlier of Barrie's two Peter Pan novels. Published in 1906, two years after the prodigious success of the play in 1904, its stories are both earlier than and different from the play's, the sequel to which is actually the second of Barrie's Peter Pan novels, *Peter and Wendy* (1911).

The Peter of Kensington Gardens bears little resemblance to the Peter of the Never Land. A week after he is born this Peter flies from his house into Kensington Gardens. Landing on an island in the pond in the middle of the Gardens, Peter finds himself scorned by the fairies, who revel there at night. The birds are kinder. They help him to cope with the fact that he can no longer fly. Eventually, they enable him to leave the island by fashioning a boat from a thrush's nest. Sailing on the nest, he finally reaches the Gardens proper where he gradually gains acceptance from the fairies because of his inborn skill at the panpipes. They grant him two wishes. The first wish returns him to his nursery only to find his crib occupied by another child, carefully tended by his mother. Peter chooses not to disturb his mother and returns to the garden. But he cannot resist the memory of his mother. He uses his second wish to go back again to the nursery. This time he calls out to his mother, but she cannot hear him. He flies back "sobbing, to the Gardens, and he never saw his dear again. . . . The iron bars are up for life" (76). The remaining chapters dwell mostly on an Oedipal romance with a Wendy-type called Maimie, who also stays late in the gardens. She loves Peter, but then she leaves him. The final words of the little novel, not unexpectedly, are: "It is all rather sad" (126).

Murdoch's novel, in effect, stretches on an axis defined by the tension between this Peter, the perennial outcast baby of the novel, and the better known Peter of the play, the blithe, insouciant boy. On the one hand, the more naïve characters keep trying to appropriate for themselves and their romances the boy Peter's story and powers, his "blameless simplicity" (338). Enthusiastically, they join in planning the play as the office Christmas panto. But as their personal lives collide and crash into ruin, they are forced to surrender the plan. On the other hand, the smarter, more jaded figures dismiss this Peter from the start as a lure, a deeply suspect figure of bad faith. "Peter personifies spirituality," Gunnar pompously insists, "irrevocably caught in childhood . . . which cannot surrender its pretensions. . . . the apotheosis of an immature spirituality" (227). He is intelligently approached only as a "being from somewhere else" (227). Thus, while his statue in the gardens can mark the spot where Hilary centers his fantasy-romance with Kitty—"we had reached my objective, the Peter Pan statue" (191)—Peter himself figures always as an asymptote, forever eluding, indeed taunting, Hilary's aspirations. "Behind [Lady Kitty] upon his wet pedestal of beasts and fairies, polished and sanctified by the hands of children, towered beyond their reach the sinister boy, listening" (197). In a literally crystallizing moment the novel admits that Peter can stand for those yet unscarred by time as "a monument to innocence, as unsmirched as the very children who came to dig with little wooly mittened hands for the rabbits and the mice whom they knew so well." But for adults "Peter Pan, heaped with snow," can never be more or other than "a scarcely decipherable crystal mound" (339) who is *sinister* because he models aspirations no adult life can ever possess.

Hilary's own life story, however, re-reads in an almost literal way that of the baby Peter, the protagonist of Barrie's novel. One literally a child, the other metaphorically a word-child, both exile themselves from bourgeois domesticity into lives of painful, unbroken isolation. Peter manages to please the great ones of his fairy world by his skill on the pipes; Hilary achieves roughly the same results through his parallel skill with languages. As a result each gets a first and then a second chance at happiness, always with another man's wife. Peter has his two returns to the nursery; Hilary his two attempts at his mentor Gunnar's wives. Neither succeeds either time. In his final attempt Peter flies to the window only to find it closed and barred. "Peter called, 'Mother! mother!' But she heard him not; in vain he beat his little limbs against the iron bars. He had to fly back, sobbing, to the Gardens" (76). In *A Word Child* this scene seems to mutate into Hilary's crucial screen dream, which he can narrate to himself only through a punning play on his own name: "I dreamt that Tommy, or was it some other woman, in the guise of a water-bird with beautiful eyes was battering battering battering on the glass trying to get in" (213). But for both there's no getting in, nor any getting out. "Ah, Peter!" Barrie's narrator laments after the passage on the barred windows, "we who have made the great mistake, how differently we should all act at the second chance. But Solomon [Caw, Peter's crow mentor] was right—there is no second chance, not for most of us. When we reach the window it is Lock-Out Time" (76).

"Lock-Out Time" might as easily have served for Murdoch's title. As Hilary says of himself: "There are no miracles, no redemptions, no moments of healing, no transfiguring changes in one's relation to the past. There is nothing but accepting the beastliness and defending one-self" (290–91). Hilary, like Peter, is the "Betwixt-and-Between" that Simon Caw terms the newly exiled child, not "exactly a human" (29), but nothing else either, a "Poor little half-and-half" (28). Half in and half out of both the actual Kensington Gardens (Peter islanded in the pond, Hilary just north of it in shabby Bayswater) and also all the kinds of integrated community the Gardens figure. Professionally Hilary is betwixt and between two worlds: highly educated but debarred by Anne Jopling's death from the university career in which he could usefully deploy his formidable intelligence. Similarly, he is trapped between social classes: prepared by Oxford to move within the Establishment, which his mediocre income and status now permit him merely to visit. Driving both these rifts, he is torn between incessant longing for erotic and romantic satisfaction, on the one hand, and, on the other, a narcissistic rage, rooted in his early orphaned state, that regularly compels him to destroy in pique the individuals he loves. Finally, behind all of these other fissures, Murdoch suggests an even wider theological tear. Hilary longs to believe in a beneficent, immanent God who might deliver redemption from ruin, but this is also a God in whom Hilary insists it is good that he cannot believe (290). And yet such a God furnishes the only pattern for every other sort of desire: "as I walked along I began to think about Kitty . . . as a mystic thinks God with a thought which goes beyond thinking and becomes being" (193). Like the baby Peter, who leaves the nursery with no means of return, Hilary lives out an unredeemable pattern in which "such things happen to men, lives . . . thus ruined, thus tainted and darkened and irrevocably spoilt, wrong turnings . . . taken and persisted in, and those who make one mistake wreck all the rest out of frenzy" (221).

*A Word Child* concludes with the doubled memorials, to the fallen Lady Kitty and to the late T. S. Eliot. Peter's story ends also with "two innocent graves," those of Walter Stephen Matthews and Phoebe Phelps, "two babes, who had fallen unnoticed from their perambulators" (125). "It is," indeed, "all rather sad" (Barrie 126).

But not so, Muriel Spark. Not so at all.

## PETER AND MURIEL IN NEW YORK

Turning now to Spark I find myself returning to Hitchcock. Not this time to *Strangers on a Train* but to *Vertigo*. The title of its French source, *D'Entre les Morts* (*From Among the Dead*), could, of course, also serve as a title for *Hothouse,* which shares *Vertigo*'s focus on the obsessed man who, refusing to allow a woman to remain dead, summons absence into presence and reduces presence to devastating absence. Seen in this way, we confront in Spark's novel apparently another version of Murdoch's Betwixt and Between, another novel of a male protagonist's deeply flawed, indeed disastrous, attempt at a Second Chance. But fascinating as that overlap is, it is finally less significant than the crucial differences between their Betwixts and Betweens that not only separate Murdoch's novel from Spark's but that also difference crucially Murdoch and Spark themselves. Differences that break out along lines we can distinguish as the carceral and the virtual.

For most of *Hothouse* Paul Hazlett might well be read as the troubled but successful version of Hilary Burden. He's what Hilary can never quite become: the Peter of the play—a paranoid, aggressive dictator, managing the lives of both the Lost (Boys) and the found (Other). Hilary manages his version of this domestic tyranny through a cruel rotation of days on which he sees each of the other characters in turn, ruthlessly spigotting their affections and his attention. But the superiority of the Joplings and his tenuous economic position combine fairly quickly to erode his authority and control. Not so Paul, who summons and sustains his English comrades for several decades of extended fantasy in the Never Land of New York. "What is now?" Paul in a panic asks, and answers: "Now is never, never" (59).

Paul's superiority derives from his virtual status. Hilary, his alter-ego, is trapped in an economy of mimesis (hence my use of carceral). He can learn languages without number but he has no ability to generate texts. He can desire, both bliss and status, but only as the second-hand and ultimately second-rate copy of another man's, Gunnar Jopling's, marriages and career. He is thus a figure from the Lacanian mirror, identifying as self only what he finds imaged elsewhere. Paul, however, centers all narrative, and all desire, through and toward himself, exactly like the play's Peter. Almost all the other characters in the novel—Elsa, Poppy, Klaus—*are* because Paul has pulled them into, and kept them within, his invention of their virtual expat experience. Paul, neither quite alive nor quite dead, is so tellingly powerful just because—again like the Peter of the play—he is, to take an apt phrase from Anne Friedberg's *The Virtual Window*, "liminally immaterial" (19).

A virtual window is of course almost the first thing we learn about in *Hothouse*: the "window-thing" (11) in the Hazletts' apartment through which light casts shadows "unnaturally" (7). That window offers readers a first clue to the task Spark's novel shares with Friedberg's theoretical project: exploring a virtual dynamic that counters and contests a hegemony of the actual. Friedberg does not treat fiction, limiting her exploration to the visual. Nevertheless, she helps us uncover deep connections between Spark's work and earlier twentieth-century analyses of virtuality, particularly that of Henri Bergson. We now tend to associate interest in the virtual with a postmodern aesthetic that some theorists have persuasively labeled neo-Baroque (Ndalianis; Giovannotti and Korotkin). But the neo-Baroque departs radically from the model of virtuality that shapes Spark's fictions. The postmodern, technologically generated neo-Baroque, like the more solid Baroque from which it takes its name, "strategically makes ambiguous the boundaries that distinguish reality from illusion" (Ndalianis 28). Spark's virtual, like the high modernisms of cubism and surrealism, insists on patrolling those boundaries with a crisp and vigilant precision. Clearly, someone who initiated her career with the Baudelarian poem "Fanfarlo," the short story "The Seraph and the Zambesi," and the novel *The Comforters* owes deep debts to high modernism, particularly to its insistence that the virtual image resist any mimetic claim that it should copy or echo something merely or crudely *real*. Indeed, so powerfully do linkages emerge between Muriel Spark's fiction and Friedberg's reading of Bergson's contemporaries and heirs that I find myself tempted to label her, despite her post–World War II debut, as the last to emerge of the great interwar British novelists.

Far from blurring the difference between them, Bergson aligns the virtual "with the possible . . . over and against the actual and the real" (Freidberg 141). The actual belongs to the realm of *being*. But being can be known only insofar as we can image it—that is, only as we encounter it within the realm of the perceived. To perceive, Bergson insists in *Matter and Memory* (1896), we must "obscure some . . . aspects" of an object, even to the point that we "diminish it by the greater part of itself, so that the remainder, instead of being encased in its surrounds as a *thing*, should detach itself from them as a *picture*" (cited by Friedberg 142). Bergson enunciates here a claim that is key to Spark: we cannot know the actual, we can know only the virtual, only that which we image in (this is Bergson's own metaphor) a kind of mental photograph. The Platonic and post-Platonic privilege of the actual over the virtual is thus reversed. As Bergson argues: "the real action passes through, the virtual action remains" (cited by Friedberg 143).

In that phrase Bergson could seem to predict Paul's role in *Hothouse*. The *real action* of the characters' lives, their spying and lovemaking in wartime Britain, ends with their shared death in the bombed train. But their *virtual action remains* to become the plot of the book, their shared serio-comic life in postwar New York. Of course, Paul appears to have no idea that he, or anyone else, is virtual. Indeed, he robustly contests that claim until the very last pages of the book, the *totentanz* through the nighttime metropolis. Though he acts like the play's Peter, Paul prefers to think like that conventional realist Hilary Burden, a Hilary who has somehow managed to convey his car crash into a successful, prosperous future with a loving and loyal spouse. But Paul is a Bergsonian-manqué at best. He has managed narcissistically to stumble into rather than rationally to access the virtual. In fact, the heroine of the virtual, and of the novel itself, is Elsa, the "Highest common Factor" (37). She is Bergson's, and I want to argue Spark's, paradigm. Paul is, merely and finally, Elsa's grotesque parody.

Paul parodies—and corrupts—the virtual by conflating it with power. Like all of the negative figures in Spark's work, Jean Brodie most indelibly, he is intent not simply on *knowing* but on using knowing as control. His jealous desire to know is insatiable, in both the "real" past plot and in the current virtual story. "'His intellect has a hundred eyes,' his mother wrote" (60). "It was you with your terrible and jealous dreams who set the whole edifice soaring," Elsa tells him as, finally, the truth of the virtual breaks through (113). In the past, as he proudly tells his son Peregrine, he tracked down and jailed his rival, Kiel (73). In the virtual present, he rigorously—and farcically—polices Elsa's behavior and the behavior of anyone with whom she has contact. In this, of course, he is entirely unlike the Peter of the play, who though willful is programmatically generous and ultimately unselfish when Wendy chooses to return home. Particularly in his magical ability to fly and to confer flight, Peter epitomizes the power of the virtual: its evanescence, its flicker, the speed with which it summons and then vanishes, leaving no trace. The kind of virtual Paul deploys works instead to control, define, limit, stabilize, essentialize. Peter is always cool; Paul's virtual perspires. In terms suggested by the "window thing," it re-imposes the very perspectival framing from which the virtual should grant freedom.

Elsa, on the contrary, yokes virtuality to unknowing, as it is described in the anonymous *Cloud of Unknowing*, the medieval mystical treatise central to Spark's imagination. *Cloud* is deeply suspicious of any claim to *know*, what mystical theology terms the *kataphatic*. Unknowing (the *apophatic*) affirms nothing. Rather, as a "privation of knowing" (21), it relies on a collection of strategies that share a trust in "darkness," suspending all teleologies of will and desire, severely limiting any claim to understand or grasp, to state or assert. Refusing to claim, unknowing deploys language indirectly and playfully, riddling, teasing, toying with allusion, trusting in tropes that prefer "a manner of speaking" (*Hothouse* 12) to declaration. Unknowing works, in a word, *virtually*.

These characteristics of unknowing are all at work in the following brief but typical exchange between Elsa and her shrink Garven Bey, one of the novel's prime "vivisectors of the mind" (12):

> "[W]e've got a good bit of ground to cover yet, Elsa, you know."
>
> She says, as if to irritate him, "Why do you say 'cover'? Isn't that a peculiar word for you to use? I thought psychiatry was meant to uncover something. But you say 'cover'. You said: 'we've got a good bit of ground to cover yet'—."
>
> "I know, I know." He places his hands out before him, palms downward, to hush her up. He then explains the meaning of "cover up" in its current social usage; he explains bitterly with extreme care.
>
> She says, "You aren't getting annoyed, are you?"
>
> "Me? No."

She says, "I came to Carthage where there bubbled around me in my ears a cauldron of unholy loves."

"Elsa," he says, "just take it easy. Relax, you have to relax."

Arriving home she says, "I managed to rattle Garven again today." (13)

Under Elsa's elusive and allusive interrogatories, the apophatic alternative to Garven's kataphatic declaratives, the knowing antithesis of cover and uncover suddenly yields to "cover up." Given the date of the novel and its American setting, this can only refer to the mother of all cover-ups, Watergate. Garven is thus induced unwittingly to reveal Paul as a Nixonian uber-manipulator, uncovered by his blundering, incompetent accomplice. Garven's "I know, I know" is merely *bitter*, hushing power's unavailing attempt to conceal its own undoing. Elsa thus continues throughout the novel's postwar plot to do her wartime job, unscrambling the "scrambler," piercing the "harrowing noise [that] all but prevents the speakers from hearing each other," "to hear the voice at the other end," the voice that gives the information needed to survive (63). This is just the reverse of Paul, trapped and tortured by the incessant dialogue waging war within his own brain.

But Paul she treats much more gently than she does Garven and his ilk because, of course, she loves Paul. The *Cloud* depends on a simple, stark dichotomy: "all rational creatures . . . have in them, each one individually, one chief working power, which is called a knowing power and another chief working power called a loving power" (17). For the *Cloud*'s author this loving power points the mystic's way to God. *Hothouse* ingeniously refocuses unknowing from the divine to the human, from the mystical to the erotic. With Rowan Williams, Spark insists that "the reality of existence is not to be defined as what intelligence can master by grasping structures" (Williams 168). Refusing to grasp, resisting critique, Elsa instead redeems Paul, from himself and from the limbo into which he has drawn her, by a love that willingly suspends its power to counter and condemn. She offers him (here we come back to Friedberg) a window that is also a screen. She subtly, slyly invents a virtual Kiel in just the way he has invented all the rest of their virtual life. And through that window he can discover, slowly, on his own, a finally and fully accurate projection of the mad thing he has himself desired. "'If Pierre doesn't exist and I'm dead,' she says, 'I don't see how I could have ruined his show. Use your logic'" (113).

Pierre's show returns us to *Peter Pan*. The novel stages the play as a multiplex of ramifying virtuality. It is a play, and therefore a virtual action, produced by Paul, who is virtual; it is directed by Peregrine, the virtual son of a virtual father, and performed by virtual actors like Miles Bunting, who are performing Paul's fantasy of virtuality: that the old can find a Never Land in which they are forever young. All of this Elsa literally squelches with her rotten tomatoes. This is the moment to bring the performance, on and off stage, to a close because, finally, Paul is prepared to concede the ways in which it is "sick" (109): "Those people are not real. My son, my wife, my daughter, do not exist" (111). He has been steadily brought by Elsa's unknowing kindness to admit the truth: "your mother and I were killed by a bomb in the spring of 1944" (163).

But the novel does not end with *Peter Pan*. Rather its long, final *totentanz* waits on Paul willingly to concede the departure from the Never Land. He cannot be forced out, nor is he punished or even humiliated for what he has tried to do. At the end Elsa and Paul are like the couple celebrating their wedding anniversary, united in a tender and tighter bond. Up through the novel's final moments, she waits on him to see his way clear. And he depends on her virtually Vergilian guidance. Here is the novel's closing, exquisite-in-miniature Liebestod.

> "Come, Elsa," Paul says, "we can go back with them. They've been very patient really."
> She turns to the car, he following her, watching as she moves how she trails her faithful and lithe cloud of unknowing across the pavement. (168)

Elsa waits on Paul and Paul ends loved because Spark is targeting in this novel not virtuality but its knowing corruption. With virtuality itself she is entirely sympathetic: hence the creation of her dazzling heroine, Elsa, the virtuoso of virtuality. In fact, Elsa here functions, I would argue, as a kind of stand-in for Spark herself, who not only also left the United Kingdom (where she too did secret wartime work) for a new life in New York but whose entire story, from the moment Muriel Sarah Camberg, secretary, moved to Rhodesia and became Muriel Spark, is a narrative of self-invention.

One way to read *Hothouse*, then, is to see it as a novel in which the characters flee, unwittingly but with cause, the world of *A Word Child*. Imagine Lady Kitty not only surviving but becoming her story's heroine and saving her men and you've arrived not only at *Hothouse by the East River* but at a core distinction that allows us finally to determine whom the stranger encountered on the train.

*A Word Child* can imagine but it cannot support virtuality like Paul's and Elsa's. Like the baby Peter in the garden, no one in Murdoch's novel may sustain the invention of a new self. The clamp of history, the grid of class restrain every attempt. Hilary tries by the sheer power of words to break free from his past only to find that past repeatedly reclaiming and damning him as Gunnar's poor copy. But what's true for the bottom is also true for the top. Ironically, Gunnar himself is as trapped by the patterns of that past as his poor imitator. And Lady Kitty, despite her beauty, her wealth, her glamour, ends by freezing to death in the Thames mudflats, held down by her own fur coat. In *A Word Child* Murdoch captures, nimbly, inimitably, the sad world of Britain between Churchill and Thatcher—a Britain as powerless to shake off the dead mode of the past as to invent a vital alternative. It's a world in which it is always dusk in a dreary, gray-brown, and damp November with power cuts: "a thick gathered gray congested awfulness" (294) that resists in Murdoch's astonishing, solecistic prose even the elementary shape conferred by commas and chapters. It's a world of offices in which no work is ever done, and in which no work is expected, because nothing can be made to happen that would compensate for the effort involved in trying. A world that inevitably ends, like Barrie's pattern book, in grave stones.

It's that world Paul and Elsa, and Spark, flee, inventing and reinventing themselves. Better, they say in their different ways, the sustained liminality of the expat than any place within the established order of the United Kingdom. It is Spark, then, who is the sturdy Word Child, who not only supports herself by the power to spin narrative but invents herself, repeatedly, in the process. In fact, self-invention emerges as the tonic theme that continues throughout Spark's career as a novelist: the ethics, and the dangers, of virtuality, and in this novel, her only love story, virtuality's erotics.

Aspects of Muriel Spark's Roman Catholicism will and should always remain, at least for me, a mystery. She was a practicing Catholic but invariably *good* Catholics furnish her best targets for ripe satire—like Elsa with the tomatoes. Nevertheless, while not claiming to penetrate the mystery, I do think, in closing, that this novel might shed some light on her core beliefs. Elsa's relation to Paul seems to affirm Rowan Williams's claim that "Christian belief . . . assumes in all sorts of ways that liberty and dependence are not mutually exclusive" (147). One of those sorts of ways, indeed an astonishing version of one of those ways, seems to me to be Muriel Spark's vision of the virtual. Emerging from the crucible of failed marriage and world war, Muriel Sarah Camberg insisted fiercely on the liberty to invent that virtual figure, the international literary celebrity Muriel Spark. But that liberty was never for her the same as independence. Like her alter-ego Mrs. Hawkins (in *A Far Cry from Kensington*), she preferred to live in other people's houses. In her life as in her art the virtual frees the self not only *from* every claim of overdetermination; it also frees the self *for* a dependence, as long as that is a dependence freely chosen, neither duty nor obligation. Admittedly, dependence freely chosen, freed from constraint, is a virtual dependence. But as Spark's fiction, and action, insist, all the richer as such. Certainly, virtuality freed Muriel Spark not only in terms of who to be and how to live but also to choose what to believe. Even more significantly, it freed her to choose how, not to save herself but to be saved.

And that is why—to return to our opening parable—it had to be Iris Murdoch and not Muriel Spark in the bar of that train. Because though Muriel Spark might have allowed herself to be accosted, she would never permit herself to be detained.

WORKS CITED

Anonymous. *The Cloud of Unknowing*. Ed. Emilie Griffin. San Francisco: HarperCollins, 1981.

Barrie, J. M. *Peter Pan in Kensington Gardens*. New York: Weathervane Books, 1975.

————. *Peter Pan Or The Boy Who Would Not Grow Up*. New York: Scribner's, 1928.

Conradi, Peter. *Iris Murdoch: A Life*. New York: Norton, 2001.

Friedberg, Anne. *The Virtual Window: From Alberti to Microsoft*. Cambridge, MA: MIT Press, 2006.

Giovannotti, Micaela, and Joyce B. Korotkin. *Neo-Baroque!* Milano: Edizioni Charta, 2005.

Huesel, Barbara. *Patterned Aimlessness*. Athens: Georgia University Press, 1995.

Murdoch, Iris. *A Word Child*. London: Chatto and Windus, 1975.

Ndalianis, Angela. *Neo-Baroque Aesthetics and Contemporary Entertainment*. Cambridge, MA: MIT Press, 2004.

Spark, Muriel. *The Hothouse by the East River*. London: Macmillan, 1973.

Williams, Rowan. *On Christian Theology*. Oxford: Blackwell, 2000.

# CHAPTER NINE

# Elliptical and Inconsequential Ladies

Muriel Spark, Jane Bowles, Penelope Fitzgerald,

and the *texte contestant*

DAVID MALCOLM

## THE METAFICTIONAL SPARK

Critics have frequently pointed to metafictional concerns in Muriel Spark's fiction, and Spark herself has acknowledged her self-conscious concern with the traditions, conventions, problems, and possibilities of novel writing (McQuillan 12). This essay considers two substantial ways in which Spark's texts breach the conventions of the traditional novel, thereby laying bare those conventions and deautomatizing traditional story material and genre. These are ellipsis and inconsequence, and they will be discussed in relation to three of her novels from the 1970s and 1980s: *Territorial Rights* (1979), *The Only Problem* (1984), and *A Far Cry from Kensington* (1988). This essay also compares Spark's narrative technique (ellipsis) and patterning of motif (inconsequence) with strategies employed by two other women writers—

Jane Bowles and Penelope Fitzgerald. The essay suggests a continuity of tradition among these writers and also a shared contestation of tradition.

Spark is consistently seen as one of the more consciously metafictional of British novelists in the second half of the twentieth century. Although many critics, such as Bryan Cheyette, focus on other aspects of her novels, there is a critical consensus on this topic. For example, Alan Bold writes that Spark "regularly . . . exposes as fraudulent the realistic foundations of fiction" (119). Martin McQuillan suggests that her fiction questions "the very categories of character and anecdote as they are associated with the bourgeois novel" (17) and that she comments "on the inadequacies of closure as a totalizing trope in literary and social narrative" (18). (One does not have to accept McQuillan's terminology to see what he is getting at here.) Allan Massie and Norman Page both place Spark's work within the tradition of innovative and antitraditional fiction that includes that of Ronald Firbank and Henry Green (Massie 9–11; Page 119). Ruth Whittaker associates Spark's novels with the innovations of the French *nouveau roman* and with U.S. experimental fiction (6) and argues that parts of her work "are to do with the exposure of fictions" (12). Gerardine Meaney sums the matter up by declaring that Spark's "relationship to the novel is one of radical interrogation" (190).[1]

The theoretical basis for the discussion of Spark's work in this essay is formalist. It assumes that within fiction we can observe texts that draw attention to their own organization and fictiveness in certain ways and can, thus, be called self-referential. Self-referentiality is also often accompanied by an autothematic focus, that is, a thematized concern with the claims and disabilities of narrative texts.[2] One of the many functions of such metafictional concerns (apart from scrutinizing the prerogatives and pretensions of narrative) within novels is to refresh (to deautomatize) a well-established, *fade* story material (for example, a plot of detection, of youthful psychological development, or of marital discord). The passages of the novel, or novels, that Anthea Leaver reads to put herself to sleep at night (Spark, *Territorial Rights* 64, 174, 234) are meant to present a type of traditional, tediously familiar fiction, a species of text that Spark wishes to distance herself from and the story material of which she wishes to refresh by a variety of techniques.[3]

## ELLIPSIS AND INCONSEQUENCE

The two techniques focused on here are ellipsis and inconsequence. Ellipsis has been extensively discussed, especially within narratological approaches to fiction. Gerald Prince defines it as follows: "When there is no part of the narrative (no words or sentences, for example) corresponding to (representing) narratively pertinent situations and events that took time, ellipsis obtains" (*A Dictionary* 25). The importance of narrative gaps and omissions (and their disruptive force) has been discussed elsewhere by Prince and by Gérard Genette, Mieke Bal, and Shlomith Rimmon-Kenan.[4] Its importance as a narrative device can be seen in discussions of texts as widely (and wildly) different from each other as, for example, in Gabriel Josipovici's analyses of the "peculiarly fragmentary and elliptical mode of narration" of the Bible (23), or in expositions of technique in George Eliot's or Ronald Firbank's work (Hardy 23–24; Malcolm, "Laying It Bare and Being Naughty" 133–57).

"Inconsequence" is less familiar as a term in analysis of narratives, although it is not unknown. For example, when Bal writes of character predictability in fiction, she is addressing the issue of consequence and inconsequence (82–85). The same is true of Prince's discussion of textual "legibility," in which the ease with which a text can be read is related not just to the presence or absence of information but to the facility with which logical connections can be seen among events (*Narratology* 133–35). Philip Sturgess also addresses the issue of logical connections among events and its importance for the reading of narratives (39n, 40n). In this essay inconsequence has to do with a lack of logical or conventionally accepted sequence, and the presence of the seemingly irrelevant, disconnected, anomalous, and paradoxical—on the level of events, on that of individual phrases, and, occasionally, on that of narration. I would contend that a large number of ellipses and a prominent lack of consequence in a narrative has a disruptive force. The traditional norm in fiction is to minimize the former and to avoid the latter, and, thus, a text that flaunts both can be seen as *contestant* vis-à-vis tradition and established convention. It can also be seen as highly self-referential, possibly autothematic, and deautomatizing.[5]


## ELLIPSIS AND INCONSEQUENTIALITY IN SPARK'S FICTION

Gerard Carruthers notes that "economy" is "a favorite term of Spark's" (517), and critics frequently point to ellipses and omissions as constitutive features of her fiction.[6] Douglas Gifford, Sarah Dunnington, and Alan MacGillivray associate her work with the notably elliptical genre of the traditional Scottish ballad and refer to her tendency toward "laconic understatement" (969–70). Certainly the three novels under discussion here are full of holes, although they cluster most prominently in *The Only Problem*.

   Nevertheless, the narrative of *Territorial Rights* is marked by ellipses. Thus, Euphemia's and Katerina's activities in the garden of the Pensione Sofia are introduced in an enigmatic and elliptical way: "It seemed that the trouble between the two was about the autumn leaves" (12). On first encountering this sentence, the reader knows neither what the trouble is, nor whom it concerns—only subsequent passages elucidate. On the next page, the reader is informed that "This was two days after Robert's arrival" and is thus made aware of an omission of action (13). Similarly, Mary Tiller's and Arnold Leaver's departure from the pensione is only revealed after it has occurred in the course of a conversation with Curran (38). A few pages later, Mary makes an appointment to see Curran "About seven tomorrow evening in the bar" (43). There follows a blank space, and then the narrator resumes "About seven next evening . . . ," the repetition emphasizing the several hours that have been skipped over. Such ellipses are typical. Robert's words to Lina about (the reader must assume, for the narrator does not say) Mary Tiller are not even summarized, but rather their delivery is recounted (68); only one side of Curran's telephone conversation with Violet is given (123–24); an entire past and future relationship is elliptically presented when Anthea Leaver is phoned by a friend whose friendship she loses by her snappy response (204); the reader suddenly learns, with no preliminaries or preparation, that Robert and Anna, the terrorist, make love "whenever they wanted to" (221); the nature of the "adventures" that Mary and Grace pursue after Venice is quite opaque (239). The reader is meant to be conscious of many things omitted throughout the novel.

This is most particularly true of *The Only Problem*. Critical commentary often points to a seeming insubstantiality in this novel.[7] This perception is in large measure due to the narrator's fondness for ellipsis. Thus, at the beginning of chapter 3, the reader is informed that Ruth has moved in with Harvey, along with Effie's baby (39). One is not told how or why Ruth does so, nor has any substantial information about the baby been given previously. Harvey's having written to Edward is a secret both from Ruth and the reader (47), and Ruth's relationship with Harvey is elliptically and enigmatically presented in passing in a letter she writes to her husband (51). The purchase of the château is given as a *fait accompli*, with all intervening stages omitted (55). The fact that Ruth has received a letter from Effie is mentioned only in passing and out of chronological sequence (57). Harvey's feelings about Ruth and the baby are presented laconically and only some time after the consequences of those feelings have affected the action (62).

Harvey's feelings toward his wife are hidden in veils of ellipsis and obliqueness, only to break out at times. For example, he reflects on La Tour's painting of Job's wife, assumes that the painter intends him to think that "Job and his wife are deeply in love," and then (in a disruptive piece of free indirect speech) bursts out "Oh, Effie, Effie, Effie" (78–79). The omissions are clear here, and multiple: the reader has no preparation for this eruption of feeling; nor, indeed, does the reader really know the tone of Harvey's ejaculation (despair, sorrow, ecstasy?). Indeed, Harvey's emotions seem frequently to come from nowhere, without very much narrational preparation or subsequent narrational gloss. After Ruth leaves, he notices his hand is shaking but does not know why (117). A whole aspect of his attitude toward

Effie becomes apparent only when his lawyer asks him if he still loves her, and when he shows that he is sexually jealous of the terrorists with whom Effie associates (124). Harvey's own reflection that if Effie is, indeed, a terrorist, "I would feel I had failed her in action" (152), comes suddenly and without any explanation from the narrator. The reader is left to puzzle over what he/she has not been told, and, appropriately, one of Harvey's own repeated phrases is that "Nobody told me" (87, 88, 101, 102, 106). Ellipses put the reader in the same position. Why does the housemaid/police lady Anne-Marie react in the way she does, with anger and despair (118, 134, 186, 187)? What has been omitted by the narrator? This bamboozling of the reader reaches a sharp point in Harvey's exchange with Stewart in chapter 8.

> "But this is something different from a divorce case. Don't you realize what's happened?"
> "I'm afraid I do," said Stewart. (127)

The ellipsis-loving narrator does not offer much help here.

A similar strategy of omission is also apparent in *A Far Cry from Kensington*, although it is much less prominent than in the two earlier novels. The narrator, Mrs. Hawkins, frequently fails to provide information about feelings and events in a chronological sequence. For example, she does not inform the reader of her depression when out of work until some time after she has recounted her long bus journeys during that time (120). The reader only learns of her hunger and the distress that her diet causes her in an aside (102), and she never directly addresses the matter of her religious feelings (127). When she and William go to bed with each other, the reader is meant to be surprised by the vast ellipsis that has preceded this event (129). He/she has been told nothing of William's feelings, or of any earlier advances he had made, nor indeed of Mrs. Hawkins's interest in the young medical student. Similarly her emotions concerning this turn in her life are given at best obliquely. The reader only learns that she has changed her hairstyle because the information is elicited in a conversation (133). Although there may be many fewer local examples of ellipsis in *A Far Cry from Kensington*, one is tempted to see the whole novel as a vast piece of ellipsis. What is Mrs. Hawkins not telling the reader? Why is her hostility toward Hector Bartlett so intense and unremitting? How culpable is she in Wanda's suicide; after all, she knows about Bartlett's fake press cuttings (168)?

Clearly ellipsis depends on the reader's active engagement with the text. In the term Roman Ingarden employs, the presence of "spots of indeterminacy" (*Unbestimmtheitsstellen* in the German original, and *miejsca niedookre lenia* in Ingarden's native Polish)—which are present in all literary texts—is particularly foregrounded by ellipsis. The reader is asked continually to consider what has been omitted, what has not been said. His/her active engagement with the text is requested, indeed provoked, and a competent reading of the text requires such activity. Ellipsis, it could be argued, makes a paradigmatic point about the relationship of reader to story material and its realization.[8]

But it is inconsequence, on every level of the text, that most distinctively marks these three novels. In *Territorial Rights*, when Robert Leaver observes Katerina and Euphemia arguing in the pensione garden, the narrator notes that "the witness at the window could have perceived here and there only a few familiar landmarks of rational discourse" (12). This points to the way in which the text is pervaded by anomaly, paradox, and lack of consequence. For example, in chapter 1, the reader learns that the novel is set in "off-season" Venice and starts on "a sunny day in October" (5). It is not the tourist season; it is autumn but sunny; everything is not quite foursquare. At the Pensione Sophia one of the sisters addresses Robert in English; he replies in Italian (7). Nearby stand the Italian Communist Party headquarters, anomalously "ornate and ancient . . . with its painted façade" (9). In the next paragraph, Robert asks for directions to an address; his interlocutor paradoxically (although, the narrator explains, not foolishly) "asked where this address was" (9). From the first few pages, the novel becomes a jamboree of inconsequentialities. Lina finds that Robert laughs in English (11); Curran signs his letters inappropriately (15); Lina's flat defies gravity, and when Robert first visits her, she greets him with the seemingly unmotivated "Did you bring your torch?"— a welcome that "was no sort of welcome at all" (17). Curran describes Robert's treatment of his father as "in the civilized sense, unnatural"

(34); the reader learns of cookery classes in Leaver senior's boy's school (42); and a street in a Birmingham suburb is described as "glorious" (51). Such inconsequentialities and paradoxes (a glorious suburban street in Birmingham—even Larkin would baulk) mark the entire novel: the ships in the Venetian lagoon are at an oxymoronic "static gallop" (85); Lina seeks cleansing from pollution in a Venetian canal (156); Grace lies down under the table after lunch (much to the surprise of other guests at the pensione) (162); Anthea accuses her of making right wrong (164); and when Robert is confined by his supposed kidnappers, he feels free, in "a trap" but "out of the trap" simultaneously (219).

Inconsequentiality is apparent constantly in *The Only Problem*. At one point, Harvey reflects about scholarly approaches to the Book of Job: "But moving passages about for no other reason than that they are more logical is no good for the *Book of Job*. It doesn't make it come clear. The *Book of Job* will never come clear" (132). A great deal in *The Only Problem* is not "logical" and will not "come clear." This is the case from the first pages. As Edward approaches Harvey's home, he thinks that it "wasn't what he had expected," although "Nothing ever is" and he cannot remember "exactly what he had expected" (9). The grass grows inconsequentially by Harvey's house (9, 55), and Harvey uses the back door as his front door (11). Conversational moves are frequently illogical. When Edward arrives, Harvey declares that his telegram was too long; "I can see you're busy," replies Edward (12). Edward praises Effie, and Harvey replies, "If you want a loan why don't you ask for it?" (26). When Edward leaves, he envies Harvey the nonexistent girl that Harvey pretends lives with him (33).

As in *Territorial Rights*, examples of inconsequentiality in *The Only Problem* can be multiplied. They are local, such as the ones mentioned above, and also over-arching. Harvey's leaving of Effie because of a piece of chocolate is an anomaly that pervades the text (17), as is the view of responsibility and justice that recurs throughout: for example, when Ruth makes Harvey responsible for Clara's birth (41) and when Harvey urges that "We do not get what we merit" (144). This sequence of motifs is capped at the novel's close by Harvey's insistence that Job's "tragedy was that of the happy ending" (186)—an ending that he also suffers (188–89). It is apparent also, both in local verbal terms and in relation to the whole action of the novel, in Harvey's words over Effie's body. "Yes," he declares, he does recognize his wife, "but this isn't my wife" (187).

There is, however, a further degree of anomaly in *The Only Problem*, this time on the level of narration. On occasion, the novel cracks narrational logic. It does this by moving from a third-person, substantially omniscient, narrator to free direct speech. One example is in Harvey's outburst while reflecting on the La Tour painting (discussed above). Other examples are scattered throughout the text and usually concern Harvey's point of view. For example, when Nathan arrives at the château, "Harvey noticed the edges of Christmas-wrapped parcels sticking up from the bottom of the pack. My God, he has come for Christmas. Harvey looked at Ruth: did she invite him? Ruth fluttered about with her thanks and her chatter" (59–60). The seamless moving from omniscient third person to free direct speech should give the reader a jolt. Why is there no "he thought" or "he said to himself," why no quotation marks? A few pages earlier there is a similar example in which Ruth moves into free direct speech (57–58), and later there is Harvey's ejaculation ("The rich!" [81]). Even when Harvey's thoughts are preceded by a narratorial "he thought," those reflections are not enclosed in quotation marks and are not transformed into indirect speech (62, 100, 103).

Such narrational anomalies only occur sparingly in *A Far Cry from Kensington*, but there are present—for example, in Mrs. Hawkin's ejaculations concerning Wanda, "Oh God! She might milk this event for the rest of her life" (36), and her outburst about Mabel's death, "Oh Mabel, come back; come back, Mabel, and persecute me again" (87). Here in the midst of events that are being narrated at considerable temporal distance, the response of the narrator, as it was at that past moment, is given as if it were immediate and now (at the time of narration). (This contrasts with the consequentially placed emotional response to being at "a far cry" from the Kensington past in the first chapter [6].)

However, like the two other novels discussed above, *A Far Cry from Kensington* is a rich repository of the paradoxical. Mrs. Hawkins lies awake "listening to the silence" (5) and "looking at the darkness" (5), both activities that at least contain germs of inconsequentiality. Mrs. Hawkins's names are presented as anomalous; she is really too young to be called Mrs. Hawkins; is she Agnes or Nancy? (129, 156, 162). The first publisher she works for is called Ullswater and York, although there is no connection with those places (15), and the man with the raincoat, employed by the creditors of the bankrupt firm to stand outside the publisher's, seems to have no logical purpose (21). The couple who live next door to Milly's house find matter for a quarrel only because "it gave rationality to the couple's mutual need to dispute" (18), and, instead of intervening, Milly, Mrs. Hawkins, and the policeman sit and eat chocolates, "watching the show" (18). Wanda is a guilty victim (38); Abigail's boyfriend works at Lloyd's and manages "a small pioneer rock-and-roll group" (156, 162); the American political exiles are not what Mrs. Hawkins expects at all (155, 156), and there is no explanation ever given of their row that devastates their office (185). Many inconsequentialities are centered on the narrator. Her names themselves are anomalous; her loathing of Hector Bartlett seems unmotivated; she does not leave the table with the ladies after a formal dinner at her employer's (96); her not going to Father Stanislaus (an omission of some importance, for he might have saved Wanda) is irrational (133–34); radionics itself is strikingly irrational (152); and the narrator's explanation of what happened between Bartlett and Wanda is, to some extent, inspired and inconsequential guesswork, something the narrator herself stresses (152).

Thus, ellipsis and inconsequentiality are central elements in Spark's novels of the late 1970s and the 1980s. *Territorial Rights*, *The Only Problem*, and *A Far Cry from Kensington* place substantial demands on their implied readers. They must be aware of gaps in the realization of the story material in these texts and work to fill in the fabular lacunae of which they are made teasingly aware. Similarly, the attentive reader must be aware of the flood of inconsequentiality that bursts through at many levels of the texts—in dialogue, in action, in narration, in character names, in characters' thought processes. Danielle Escudié's remark about *The Hothouse by the East River* that it is "un récit qui progresse par ellipses" (a narrative that progresses by ellipses) seems apropos, as, indeed, is her comment on Spark's work in general: "elle truffe ses contes d'invraisemblances" (she stuffs her tales with improbabilities) (201, 197; translation by the author).


## TRADITION AND CONTESTATION

As Ingarden points out, "*Unbestimmtheitsstellen*" ("spots of indeterminacy") are a key feature of any story (246–54). "[N]arratives by their nature are riddled with gaps," notes H. Porter Abbott (90), and he argues that an important part of the reader's activity is to fill in and interpret these gaps where possible. Although one must bear in mind that some gaps are "cruxes" that are extremely difficult to complete, and that much interpretation of the relevant narrative depends on how the reader chooses to do so (90–95). With regard to consequentiality (and inconsequentiality), in a now somewhat neglected text, *On Realism* (1973), J. P. Stern sees one of the defining features of realism (one of what Martin Swales calls "drei Merkmale realistischer Kunst" [three features of realist art] [Swales 14]) as the represented world's "consequential logic and circumstantiality" (Stern 28).[9] Abbott goes further when he argues that coherent causation—"the qualities of 'continuity' and 'narrative coherence,'" meaning that the narrative "hangs together" (45)—is something that many different types of narrative offer, providing a sense of order and stability to readers (41–46).

Thus gaps that can be filled in and coherence and consequentiality can be seen as integral parts of any well-made narrative of various kinds. This is particularly true of the nineteenth-century realist tradition. As the third-person narrator asks in *Bleak House* (and he answers the question):

> What connexion can there be, between the place in Lincolnshire, the house in town, the Mercury in powder, and the whereabout of Jo the outlaw with the broom, who had that distant ray of light upon him when he swept the churchyard-step? What connexion can there have been between many people in the innumerable histories of this world, who, from opposite sides of great gulfs, have, nevertheless, been very curiously brought together! (272)

The narrator in *Middlemarch* is interested in "this particular web" of character relations (170). Earlier she has insisted:

> any one watching keenly the stealthy convergence of human lots, sees a slow preparation of effects from one life on another, which tells like a calculated irony on the indifference or the frozen stare with which we look at our unintroduced neighbor. Destiny stands by sarcastic with our dramatis personae folded in her hand. (122)

For both Dickens and Eliot, the gaps must be filled in as much as possible, the coherent links established, and they are. Other examples from this tradition could be multiplied.

It is notable that writers concerned to contest and deautomatize the conventions of the realist text have frequently resorted, *inter alia*, to reversals of narrative gap filling and consequentiality. I have written on this subject with regard to Ronald Firbank and Henry Green. For example, in Firbank's *Sorrow in Sunlight* (1924), how Miss McAdam from Aberdeen might become the outrageous ballet-mistress of the lubricious Cunan Opera is scarcely suggested. Her ensembles are "daring," even by Cunan standards (Firbank 166). This is not to say that such a life course (Aberdeen to Cuna-Cuna) is inherently improbable, but rather that the narrator does not bother to make it probable at all (Malcolm, "Laying Bare Conventions" 275). In Green's *Living* (1929), for example, Mr, Dupret's death (a major item in the story material) is recounted laconically thus (in a separate paragraph, and, indeed, in one set off from the rest of the text by spacing): "Just then Mr Dupret in sleep, died, in sleep" (Green 288). Mr. Gates's striking of his daughter is passed over in five words (331), and his being arrested for disorderly conduct in a single sentence (344). Green is reminiscent of Firbank in his exiguous presentation of crucial events (Malcolm, "Laying It Bare and Being Naughty" 151).

Spark's fictions can, thus, in respect of their deployment of ellipsis and inconsequentiality, be seen to belong to a strong twentieth-century tradition of foregrounding, deautomatization, and contestation of crucial aspects of the protocols of realist fiction and even traditional narratives *tout court*. Pam Morris argues that realist texts aim at a transparency, an obfuscation of their created nature, and that one of the ways of shaking the hold of realism is to aim at self-referentiality and antitransparency, of the kind that Spark aims at through ellipsis and inconsequence (15, 30). This is an argument strongly echoed in the theoretical work of Lilian Furst (23–24) and Hayden White (5, 17). In the work of the latter, indeed, the only ethical position for the writer is to be aware of and to foreground narrative strategy.

## OTHER ELLIPTICAL AND INCONSEQUENTIAL LADIES

Ellipsis and inconsequentiality mark the novels of two other women writers, Jane Bowles and Penelope Fitzgerald, to the extent that one wants to suggest a shared tone of voice among them. These are writers who differ in nationality, productivity, status, and length of career, but in this respect they appear to share something.

Although Bowles is a marginal figure within U.S. literature, her writing has always had prominent admirers.[10] Bowles's major work, *Two Serious Ladies* (1943), recounts the sexual adventures of Miss Goering and Mrs. Copperfield, both of whom reject the sexual norms of the fictional world of the text and of the extratextual world of mid-twentieth-century U.S. society. Miss Goering engages in casual sex with chance-met men; Mrs. Copperfield enters a lesbian relationship with a Panamanian prostitute. "You're a horror," exclaims Mr. Copperfield when he learns that his wife wishes to stay in Panama with Pacifica (108). "You're crazy. . . . You're crazy and monstrous—*really*. Monstrous," whines one of Miss Goering's lovers when he learns that she intends to leave him for another man (188). *Two Serious Ladies* itself, however, also exhibits prodigies as a text, breaching traditional novel conventions in a variety of ways. Two of the ways it does so are through ellipsis and inconsequence.

Action is presented elliptically, and the narrative is marked by radical jumps in time.[11] For example, the text moves from Miss Goering's childhood to adulthood without even alluding to the intervening years (8). Miss Gamelon's moving in with Miss Goering and their first three months together are passed over in a few sentences (13), while Miss Goering's staying with Andy is passed over even more succinctly ("Miss Goering had been living with Andy for eight days" [171]). Such ellipses can occur with regard to shorter periods of time too. For example, in the Toby–Mrs. Quill episode, Toby leaves his intended victim, she reflects briefly on the meeting, and then suddenly the reader learns that some time has passed and the hotel terrace is now empty (88–89). This elliptical technique, too, is part of the novel's monstrosity, as Michelle Green suggests when she notes: "With its elliptical plot and elusive characters . . . *Two Serious Ladies* had proven too abstruse for most readers" (31).

Inconsequentiality and anomaly are apparent on the level of character and characters' utterances. Characters frequently engage in unexpected, often seemingly unmotivated and illogical, acts. For example, one wonders why Miss Goering accepts Miss Gamelon as a visitor (10). The reader is clearly meant to be in the dark, too, about why Arnold invites Miss Goering to his home (16) and falls in love with her (20). The anecdote Miss Goering tells of the man in the house that is being destroyed is utterly inconclusive and obscure as to the man's motives. In addition, the telling of the story itself is similarly unmotivated (17–18). Arnold's throwing a perfume bottle at Miss Gamelon is barely explained (115). The same is true of the fight in the bar observed by Miss Goering. It starts for little reason, becomes intense, and then peters out inconclusively (139–41).

Characters' language, too, seems to breach fictional conventions relating to consequence.[12] The slight elevation and formality of vocabulary in some pieces of direct speech (see, for example, 17, 19, 134–35) is itself odd and unexplained. But the way in which characters' utterances can take illogical, quite unexpected, and unmotivated turns is very striking. In *Two Serious Ladies* speech often lacks cohesion and coherence.[13] For example, early in the novel, Miss Goering's question to Miss Gamelon—"Have you a guardian angel?"—comes from nowhere (11). Later, Miss Goering's cohesive device seems quite deviant when she suggests: "Most people have a guardian angel; *that's why* they move slowly" (12; emphasis added). Mrs. Copperfield's speaking French in Spanish-speaking Panama shows a similar failure to grasp rules of discourse (64). Other characters show a similar disregard for coherence. For example, a Panamanian prostitute tells

Mrs. Copperfield: "I can never sleep late in the mornings . . . . I don't even like to sleep at night if I have anything better to do. My mother told me that I was nervous as a cat, but very healthy. I went to dancing school but I was too lazy to learn the steps" (100). The cohesive links between the first and second sentence are clear ("sleep"), and the third sentence might be said to follow logically from the first two. But the fourth sentence is neither linked cohesively nor in terms of coherence with the previous ones. Here, too, the text demonstrates a transgression, in this case linguistically, just as it embodies and illustrates transgression on the level of action.

Although Penelope Fitzgerald is a contemporary of Spark, her career as a novelist started much later in her life. However, by the time of her death in 2000, she had achieved a remarkable status as a major British novelist.[14] Like Bowles's work, her novels are not discussed in relation to Spark's; yet they show a striking similarity—particularly in terms of their fondness for ellipsis and inconsequence. This essay focuses on Fitzgerald's novel from 1990, entitled *The Gate of Angels*. Set in 1912, this novel presents the trials of Fred Fairly, a fellow at a Cambridge college, and the young working-class woman, Daisy Saunders, with whom he falls in love. The complex events of the novel separates and then brings them—enigmatically—together at its end, although there is no indication whether they will form a lasting relationship.

This is the major ellipsis in the novel, although there are others. For example, while Fred and two companions are on a walking tour of the Salzburg Alps, three young women visit them in their hotel room. Why they do so, and what happens in the room, can doubtless be imagined by the reader but is not presented directly and is, in fact, elided (26–27). The same is true of the motives for Fred's decision to stay at Cambridge, instead of going to Manchester. They are simply passed over (27). Another example of ellipsis appears in Fred's conversation with Mr. Ellsworthy, the stationmaster. The reasons for the latter's anger at Fred's questions are not given (35–36). However, the major ellipses are connected with the novel's end. How does Mrs. Turner know who Daisy is? How can the gate at St. Angelicus College, which is never opened, be open? And what will Fred and Daisy do when they meet (166–67)?

For inconsequence and anomaly, *The Gate of Angels* holds its own with Spark's and Bowles's novels. The novel starts with a storm that turns things upside down. Cyclists in inland Cambridge look like "sailors in peril" (9). Cows' horns are covered in branches, and some of the cows have fallen on their backs, still "munching," "exhibiting vast pale bellies intended by nature to be always hidden" (9). "A scene of disorder," the narrator notes, "in a university city devoted to logic and reason" (9). Examples abound throughout the text. Skippey cycles up to Fred in the storm and produces the unexpected remark, "Thought is blood" (10). The master of Angelicus asks a question to which he knows the answer (12, 13). Fred attends a meeting of the Disobligers' Society in the course of which—as is the custom of this society—he and another speaker have to defend a position that they utterly reject (14, 43, 47–48). Pope Benedict XIII, the founder of St. Angelicus, "had been declared not to be the Pope at all" (17). Fred's titles at the college of assistant organist and deputy steward "didn't mean that there was necessarily anyone above him to do the work" (20). Professor Wilson wipes off what he writes on the board as he writes it (22), and Fred's father's parishioners never come to consult him at the time scheduled (32). Conversations follow inconsequential paths (36, 120, 150); Fred gives a lecture unrelated to the topic announced (154); and Dr. Sage's madhouse does not contain the mad (156). Centrally, the claims of contemporary physicists are described by Professor Flowerdew (an inappropriate name for a professor of physics) as logically dubious: "Rutherford . . . claims to be able to show that it [the nuclear atom] exists, that this unobservable, consisting of unobservables, depending on exchanges of energy of which he can only say that he has no idea when or why they may take place, exists, and that we must take it to be the indivisible unit of matter" (161). Throughout the novel, the question is raised as to whether there is any order and any coherence in the universe—in physicists' description of material laws (24), in the providence and will of God (95), or in any purposeful intention underlying human events (104). The novel leaves the question open, and how the contingency and inconsequence of the novel's universe is seen to a large degree depends on the text's resolution, which is, of course, elliptical and unresolved.

## CONCLUSIONS AND FURTHER SUGGESTIONS

Thus, widespread use of ellipsis and the extensive occurrence of in-consequence can be noted in Spark's novels, and also in those of two other mid-twentieth-century women writers. The functions of such narrative technique and patterning of motif are multiple but are extensively shared among these novelists' work, certainly in the texts under discussions. These are, first, humor. The inconsequentialities of Spark's, Bowles's, and Fitzgerald's novels are clearly meant to be humorous, reversing as they do both characters' and readers' cultural and linguistic expectations. Second, a metafictional function of these elements is apparent in all the texts under consideration. They lay bare the nonelliptical conventions of much fiction and also the drive for consistency and consequence that underlies so much traditional, pre-twentieth-century fiction and much traditional twentieth-century fiction to boot. They reveal them as conventions by presenting radically different narratives marked by gaps and anomalies. Third, these elements deautomatize very familiar and traditional story materials. The love and revenge story materials of Spark's novels are familiar from thousands of narratives, as are the female emancipation plot of Bowles's novel and the *mésalliance* subject matter of Fitzgerald's. But the authors' technique refreshes material that would perhaps be all too familiar without it. Fourth, all five novels suggest a view of the world as inconsequential, one in which absurdities and paradoxes abound, and one in which individuals have to make the best interpretations they can based on partial and scarcely cohesive or coherent information. Fifth, it is notable that all the three writers discussed are women. It is worth asking whether the transgression of literary conventions to do with fullness of explanation and coherence particularly marks the writing of women novelists wishing to contest the norms of fiction and of society.[15] That male writers (Conrad, Joyce, Firbank, and Henry Green, for example) also call into question some of the conventions queried in Spark's, Bowles's, and Fitzgerald's novels must make one hesitate to suggest this. However, one can—elliptically but not, one hopes, inconsequentially—suggest that more work on this subject might well prove fruitful.[16]

Spark is often seen as *sui generis* within the history of postwar British fiction, and, while certainly a *rara avis*, she is not quite the hippogriff many critics make her out to be. Her exposure and contestation of many of the conventions of the novel tradition place her squarely in an honorable tradition of European letters that is as old as Cervantes, Fielding, Sterne, Austen, and Balzac (in his day as innovatory as Robbe-Grillet). She may also be seen, as I have tried to do in a preliminary fashion in this essay, within a particular quirky and challenging line of women's writing that is difficult, contestatory, and provocative; this is a lineage that includes other writers but within which Spark herself has achieved most, and that most disturbingly and acutely.

NOTES

1. Spark's comments in her 1963 interview with Frank Kermode are illuminating in this matter. See also Carruthers 515–16, 522; Escudié 198; Richmond; and Apostolu.

2. For a discussion of these terms, see Booth 205–9; Fowler 364–75; Jakobson 356; Prince, *A Dictionary* 48. Polish treatments of the topic are very illuminating but only for readers of Polish. See, for example, Sandauer, "O ewolucji" 453–65; Sandauer, "Samobójstwo Mitrydatesa" 468–512.

3. For discussions of these terms, see Zgorzelski 27; O'Toole and Shukman 29–30, 35.

4. See Prince, *Narratology* 135; Genette 106–9; Bal 71–73; Rimmon-Kenan 56, 127, 128–29.

5. For an interesting discussion of inconsequentiality in fiction, see Lem 88–109.

6. See, for example, Hynes 177; Kane 13; Whittaker 134.

7. See Wilson 4; Brookner 26; Updike 107.

8. See, for example, Ingarden 246–54.

9. This is an unjustly neglected and very suggestive study of literary realism. I must confess to an interest here. J. P. Stern supervised my PhD dissertation at University College London in the 1970s. I owe him a debt of gratitude.

10. See: Capote vi–vii; Sage x, xii.

11. Barabara Schinzel discusses this aspect of Bowles's writing on the level of syntax (17).

12. Schinzel examines "Änderungen in der Normgrammatik als Stilmittel zur Betonung" (changes in normative grammar as a stylistic means of emphasis) (85–88; translation by the author).

13. "Cohesion" refers to the way that texts are held together by internal linguistic connectors; "coherence" refers to the unity of subject matter. See Crystal 119; and Wales 65–67.

14. See, for example, Lively 56 and Bayley 13–14. For some hints that Fitzgerald may be a tradition-breaking novelist, see Bayley 14.

15. Meaney puts forward this argument with regard to Spark; see especially 176–90. In this respect, see also Julia Kristeva's insistence on the importance for women writers of "ce refus de la tradition" (this refusal of tradition) (1:11) and the adoption of "un autre alphabet, monstrueux cette fois" (another alphabet, this time a monstrous one) (2:15; translation by the author).

16. An obvious candidate for further discussion along these lines is Sybille Bedford, although probably only with reference to *A Legacy* (1956).

## WORKS CITED

Abbott, H. Porter. *The Cambridge Introduction to Narrative*. 2nd ed. Cambridge: Cambridge University Press, 2008.

Apostolu, Fotini E. *Seduction and Death in Muriel Spark's Fiction*. Westport, CT: Greenwood Press, 2001.

Bal, Mieke. *Narratology: Introduction to the Theory of Narrative*. Trans. Christine van Boheemen. Toronto: University of Toronto Press, 1985.

Bayley, John. "Innocents at Home." *New York Review of Books* 9 April 1992: 13–14.

Bold, Alan. *Muriel Spark*. Contemporary Writers. Ed. Malcolm Bradbury and Christopher Bigsby. London: Methuen, 1986.

Booth, Wayne C. *The Rhetoric of Fiction*. Chicago: University of Chicago Press, 1961.

Bowles, Jane. *Two Serious Ladies*. My Sister's Hand in Mine: An Expanded Edition of the Collected Works of Jane Bowles. Introd. Truman Capote. New York: Eco Press, 1978. 1–201.

Brookner, Anita. "How Effie Made Him Suffer." *New York Times Book Review* 15 July 1984: 1, 26.

Capote, Truman. Introduction. *My Sister's Hand in Mine: An Expanded Edition of the Collected Works of Jane Bowles*. New York: Eco Press, 1978. v–ix.

Carruthers, Gerard. "The Remarkable Fictions of Muriel Spark." *A History of Scottish Women's Writing*. Ed. Douglas Gifford and Dorothy McMillan. Edinburgh: Edinburgh University Press, 1997.

Cheyette, Bryan. *Muriel Spark*. Writers and Their Work. Tavistock: North-cote House/The British Council, 2000.

Crystal, David. *The Cambridge Encyclopedia of Language*. Cambridge: Cambridge University Press, 1987.

Dickens, Charles. *Bleak House*. 1853. Ed. Norman Page. Harmondsworth: Penguin, 1971.

Eliot, George. *Middlemarch*. 1872–1873. Ed. W. J. Harvey. Harmondsworth: Penguin, 1972.

Escudié, Danielle. *Messages chiffrés: Les contes de Muriel Spark*. Editions Ophrys, n.d.

Firbank, Ronald. *Three Novels: The Flower Beneath the Foot, Sorrow in Sunlight, and Concerning the Eccentricities of Cardinal Pirelli*. 1923. Introd. Alan Hollinghurst. London: Penguin, 2000.

Fitzgerald, Penelope. *The Gate of Angels*. 1990. London: Flamingo, 1991.

Fowler, Alastair. *Kinds of Literature: An Introduction to the Theory of Genres and Modes*. Oxford: Clarendon, 1982.

Furst, Lilian R. *All Is True: The Claims and Strategies of Realist Fiction*. Durham, NC: Duke University Press, 1995.

Genette, Gérard. *Narrative Discourse*. Trans. Jane E. Lewin. Oxford: Basil Blackwell, 1980.

Green, Henry. *Loving, Living, and Party Going*. 1929. Introd. John Updike. London: Picador, 1979.

Green, Michelle. *Paul Bowles and the Literary Renegades in Tangier*. London: Bloomsbury, 1992.

Gifford, Douglas, Sarah Dunnington, and Alan MacGillivray. *Scottish Literature: In English and Scots*. Edinburgh: Edinburgh University Press, 2002.

Hardy, Barbara. Introduction. *Daniel Deronda*. By George Eliot. Harmondsworth: Penguin, 1967.

Hynes, Joseph. "Muriel Spark and the Oxymoronic Vision." *Contemporary British Women Writers*. Ed. Robert E. Hosmer Jr. Basingstoke: Macmillan, 1993. 161–87.

Ingarden, Roman. *The Literary Work of Art*. 1931. Trans. George G. Grabowicz. Evanston, IL: Northwestern University Press, 1973.

Jakobson, Roman. "Closing Statement: Linguistics and Poetics." *Style in Language*. Ed. Thomas A. Sebeok. 1960. Cambridge, MA: MIT Press, 1966. 350–77.

Josipovici, Gabriel. *The Book of God: A Response to the Bible*. New Haven, CT: Yale University Press, 1988.

Kane, Richard C. *Iris Murdoch, Muriel Spark and John Fowles: Didactic Demons in Modern Fiction*. Teaneck, NJ: Fairleigh Dickinson University Press, 1988.

Kristeva, Julia. *Le génie féminin: La vie, la folie, les mots.* 3 vols. Paris: Fayard, 1999.

Lem, Stanisław. "O niekonsekwencji w literaturze." *Mój pogląd na literaturę. Rozprawy, szkice.* Kraków: Wydawnictwo Literackie, 2003. 88–109.

Lively, Penelope. "Five of the Best." *Encounter* 55.1 (Jan. 1981): 53–59.

Malcolm, David. "Laying Bare Conventions in Ronald Firbank's *Sorrow in Sunlight.*" *Conventions and Texts.* Ed. Andrzej Zgorzelski. Gdańsk: University of Gdańsk Press, 2003. 262–80.

———. "Laying It Bare and Being Naughty with the Novel: Ronald Firbank and Henry Green." *Critical Essays on Ronald Firbank, English Novelist, 1886–1926.* Ed. Gill Davies, David Malcolm, and John Simons. Lampeter: Edwin Mellen Press, 2004. 133–57.

Massie, Allan. *Muriel Spark.* Edinburgh: Ramsay Head Press, 1979.

McQuillan, Martin. "Introduction—'I Don't Know Anything about Freud': Muriel Spark Meets Contemporary Criticism." *Theorizing Muriel Spark: Gender, Race, Deconstruction.* Ed. Martin McQuillan. New York: Palgrave, 2002. 1–31.

Meaney, Gerardine. *(Un)like Subjects: Women, Theory, Fiction.* New York: Routledge, 1993.

Morris, Pam. *Realism.* The New Critical Idiom. New York: Routledge, 2003.

O'Toole, L. M., and Ann Shukman, eds. *Formalist Theory.* Vol. 4 of *Russian Poetics in Translation.* Oxford: Holdan Books, 1977.

Page, Norman. *Muriel Spark.* London: Macmillan, 1990.

Prince, Gerald. *A Dictionary of Narratology.* Aldershot: Scolar Press, 1988.

———. *Narratology: The Form and Functioning of Narrative.* Amsterdam: Mouton, 1982.

Richmond, Velma Bourgeois. *Muriel Spark.* New York: Frederick Ungar, 1984.

Rimmon-Kenan, Shlomith. *Narrative Fiction: Contemporary Poetics.* New York: Methuen, 1983.

Sage, Lorna. Introduction. *Two Serious Ladies.* By Jane Bowles. Harmondsworth: Penguin, 2000. v–xiii.

Sandauer, Artur. "O ewolucji sztuki narracyjnej w XX wieku." *Pisma zebrane.* Vol. 2. Warsaw: PIW, 1981. 453–65.

———. "Samobójstwo Mitrydatesa." *Pisma zebrane.* Vol. 2. Warsaw: PIW, 1981. 468–512.

Schinzel, Barbara. *Jane Bowles: Analyse der Kurzprosa.* Europäische Hochschulschriften Series 14, vol. 307. Vienna: Peter Lang, 1996.

Spark, Muriel. *A Far Cry from Kensington.* 1988. Harmonsworth: Penguin, 1989.

———. "The House of Fiction, VII. Interview with Frank Kermode." *Partisan Review* 30 (1963): 79–82.

———. *The Only Problem*. 1984. Harmondsworth: Penguin, 1995.

———. *Territorial Rights*. 1979. Harmondsworth: Penguin, 1991.

Stern, J. P. *On Realism*. Boston: Routledge and Kegan Paul, 1973.

Sturgess, Philip J. M. *Narrativity: Theory and Practice*. Oxford: Clarendon, 1992.

Swales, Martin. *Epochenbuch Realismus: Romane und Erzählungen*. Berlin: Erich Schmidt Verlag, 1997.

Updike, John. "A Romp with Job." *New Yorker* 23 July 1984: 104–7.

Wales, Katie. *A Dictionary of Stylistics*. 2nd ed. Harlow: Pearson, 2001.

White, Hayden. "Literary Theory and Historical Writing." *Figural Realism: Studies in the Mimetic Effect*. Baltimore, MD: Johns Hopkins University Press, 1999. 1–26.

Whittaker, Ruth. *The Faith and Fiction of Muriel Spark*. Basingstoke: Macmillan, 1982.

Wilson, A. N. "Suffering, Salvation and Sex." *Washington Post Book World* 1 July 1984: 4.

Zgorzelski, Andrzej. *Fantastyka. Utopia. Science fiction: Ze studiów nad rozwojem gatunków*. Warsaw: PWN, 1980.

# CHAPTER TEN

# Stonewalling Toffs

JOHN UPDIKE

Dr. Hildegard Wolf, a contemporary, unlicensed Paris psychiatrist, who was formerly a fraudulent stigmatic and miracle healer in Bavaria called Beate Pappenheim, and whose unusual psychiatric method commences with her talking about herself while the patient patiently listens, counts among her loyal clientele two gentlemen who both claim to be Lord Lucan, the fugitive English earl who disappeared from London on the night of November 7, 1974, having evidently battered to death a nanny whom he mistook for his wife. Upon this implausible—indeed, preposterous—premise, Muriel Spark builds a strangely gripping and gnomically illuminating short novel, *Aiding and Abetting*. Lord Lucan, a Note to Readers emphasizes, is or was an actual personage, who "has been 'sighted' in numerous parts of the world, predominantly central Africa." He was officially declared dead in 1999, though his body has never been found. In a sentence of typical aplomb, Spark assures the reader,

> What we know about "Lucky" Lucan, his words, his habits, his attitudes to people and to life, from his friends, photographs and police records, I have absorbed creatively, and metamorphosed into what I have written.

She additionally confides, "The parallel 'story' of a fake stigmatic woman is also based on fact."

Dame Muriel, it would seem, has been mulling the old scandal of Lord Lucan for some time. The need to consider a real event, with its much reported facts and lingering mysteries, gives this novel a less peremptory texture than she has accustomed us to; the figure of Lord Lucan deepens and complicates, as does the nature of the evil credited to him. Spark focuses upon those who, in the immediate wake of the murder and for, possibly, decades thereafter, helped the murderer escape and supplied him with funds. After putting his inadvertant victim's bloody body in a mailsack, Lucan assaulted his intended victim, his wife, with the same "length of lead piping, specially prepared to deaden the thuds"; she escaped, with severe head wounds, to the shelter of a nearby pub. Why wasn't a criminal so blatant and clumsy in his crimes quickly apprehended? A slight acquaintance of Lucan's, Dr. Joseph Murray, expresses this view twenty-five years later:

> The police were slow. The friends who aided and abetted Lucan ran rings around the police. Those police were used to lowlife criminals from the streets and from the rooming houses of Mayfair and Soho. Clever sharpsters, they were unnerved by the stonewalling toffs; they were not exactly abject, not at all. But they were hesitant, out of their depth.

The aiders and abetters acted, Murray thinks, out of a class loyalty that has become obsolete: "We are not the same people as we were a quarter of a century ago. . . . We cannot afford to be snobs. Since Lucan's day, snobs have been greatly emarginated." Old-fashioned snobbery empowered Lucan in his ill-planned crime: "It was not only that he was a member of the aristocracy, a prominent upper-class fellow, it was that he had pitched his life and all his living arrangements to that proposition. His proposition was: I am a seventh Earl, I am an aristocrat, therefore I can do what I like, I am untouchable." Later in the novel, the author adds to this analysis the fatalist psychology of a compulsive, self-ruinous gambler:

> Lucky Lucan believed in destiny. By virtue of destiny he was an earl. His wife had been destined to die, according to his mad

calculation. It was the madness of a gambler. . . . His sense of destiny obliterated the constant, well-known fact that the gambler loses and the bookie, the croupier or whoever, always wins in the end.

The novel's other characters, which proliferate as the plot develops ever newer kinks, are all in the grip of, if not murderous madness, obsessions and tics that snap them back and forth between Paris and London and Scotland and Mexico and darkest central Africa, where a fate as comically lurid as anything in Waugh (Evelyn) or Burroughs (William and Edgar Rice) puts the disturbances to rest, leaving the environment, in the book's chilly last words, "cleaner than usual." Ever since her first published, prize-winning short story, "The Seraph and the Zambesi," the dark magic of Africa has held for Spark an affinity with the dark magic of Catholicism, to which she is an unabashed, if antinomian, convert. "Beliefs are essential," one character admits, having asserted that "witch men can cure." So can fake stigmatics, who smear their hands and feet with their own menstrual blood. "What else," it is asked, "should a woman of imagination do with her menstrual blood?" Blood is Spark's dominant metaphor in *Aiding and Abetting*: one pagan African explains, "Christians worship the Lamb, unlike the Hindus who worship the Cow. They wash in the blood of a lamb," and the other responds, "I don't know about that. I should think it was a sticky way to be washed."

Sex, too, can be sticky, and reeks of bewitchment. In this novel Dr. Murray and a young lady named Lacey repeatedly just miss the object of their concerted search, as if by design: "Even a simple manhunt had been so peripheral to their love affair that they had let him slip time and again, and enjoyed it." If the novel has a hero, it is Hildegard's burly lover Jean-Pierre Roget, a resourceful "metal- and wood-worker" equal to all repairs. He is impervious to the machinations of the two Lord Lucans and unperturbed by Hildegard's rebuffs—she is one of Spark's bedevilled heroines, too harried to be considerate. Many puzzle pieces breezily fly together to make the quick-moving plot, but they interlock snugly. In her ninth decade, Spark has produced one of the best of her sui-generis novels, to rank with *The Comforters, The Bachelors, Memento Mori, The Prime of Miss Jean Brodie, The Driver's Seat, The Abbess of Crewe,* and *Loitering with Intent.*

Her language deserves an admiring word. Never ornate, it grows simpler. Has any writer since Hemingway placed more faith in the simple declarative sentence, the plain Anglo-Saxon noun? Hemingway's style sometimes gives the impression of striking a pose, whereas Spark's appears to be merely getting on with it, brushing aside everything she might say but doesn't care to. Decades of living in Italy may have rusted, or antiqued, her English idiom. We read that Lord Lucan "was a snob from his deepest gust"; that he "flourished a fly swat"; that "he stood up and out into the aisle to see them more clear"; that "DNA profiles and other new scientific perforations of bland surfaces were the enemy now." Of a minor character, as she picks up the telephone, we read, " 'Yes, speaking,' said the lady in the English tongue." The prose tends to be strict and briskly instructive. With Euclidean concision it delivers Hildegard's curious life story:

> She grew up on the pig farm. The sisters and brothers eventually married and went to live each in a house not far away. They continued in the pig business. Hildegard (then Beate) grew up, with all them around, among the pigs. She went to school, was clever. She fought herself free from her home. She found Heinrich. She made blood-money.

Perhaps, as Spark ages, her gnarly Scots roots thrust up through the ground of her long Continental residence. Certainly her prose is lifted by a trip that her lovers, Joe and Lacey, take to Caithness, in northern Scotland:

> The great lovely steep hills were all around them. The feeling of northern nature, a whole geography minding very much its own business, cautious, alien, cold and haughty, began here. The sky rolled darkly amid patches of white light. On they drove, north, north.

Unlike Ivy Compton-Burnett's clipped prose, which seemed fit
only for cranky, quibbling people pent up indoors in Victorian parlors,
Spark's can encompass, if curtly, whatever arises before it—the light-
struck landscape without, the bloody turns within.

NOTE

# CHAPTER ELEVEN

# In Sparkworld

JOHN LANCHESTER

A reader picking up Muriel Spark's first novel, *The Comforters,* at the time of its publication in 1957, might have noticed that the author was thirty-nine years old, and have thought that he was encountering the work of a late developer. It is not an impression that would have survived the reading of the book's first paragraphs:

> On the first day of his holiday Laurence Manders woke to hear his grandmother's voice below.
> "I'll have a large wholemeal. I've got my grandson stopping for a week, who's on the B.B.C. That's my daughter's boy, Lady Manders. He won't eat white bread, one of his fads."
> Laurence shouted from the window, "Grandmother, I adore white bread and I have no fads."

The reader immediately has a headful of questions—and part of what remains so fresh about *The Comforters* is that these questions all turn out to be centrally relevant to the book. Who is this batty old lady? Is she batty? Why is she so quick to let everyone know about her daughter's title? Does she just want to boast, or does she have some other reason for wanting to appear respectable? Why is Laurence so jumpy, and so eager to seem normal? How are we to judge who is crazy and who isn't? And then the most pressing question of all: To whom belongs this extraordinarily confident, assured, omniscient narrative voice?

It is part of the book's genius that this issue is the one on which the whole structure of *The Comforters* turns. Spark was early identified as a Catholic convert, and energetically praised right from the start by Graham Greene and Evelyn Waugh (who generously wrote that he preferred *The Comforters* to his own *The Ordeal of Gilbert Pinfold*). As a result of that, however, she has been misidentified as a figure from the time when, to quote Adrian Mitchell's "Oxford Hysteria of English Poetry," writers were leaving "the Communist Church to join the Catholic Party." But Spark could more accurately be seen as a sort of proto-postmodernist, a writer with a sharp and lasting interest in the arbitrariness of fictional conventions; a writer whose eager adoption of the conventions of the novel have always been accompanied by a wish to toy with, subvert, parody, and undermine them.

Spark's attitude to plot exemplifies this approach. Her stories always pose a set of questions. In the course of the novel most of them are resolved—a classic example being the central plot question of her great *Memento Mori,* from 1959: we finally learn the identity of the voice who rings old people and says to them, "Remember you must die." But once we have the answer—in this case, Death—the larger sense of mystery and strangeness in the book always remains, and we are left with a lingering feeling that the question we've had answered somehow misses a larger point. Spark satisfies our hunger for plot, and at the same time shows us the shortcoming of such things as plots— the extent of the human stuff that they ignore, and the troubling persistence of the questions they leave unasked.

The great flaw in postmodernism, however, has always been that the writer's enthusiasm to expose the fictionality of a fiction tends to be paralleled by the reader's consequent freedom not to care what happens in the book. Spark's way around this has always been to stress the realness of the real. This is not to say that she is a realist; but realism is one of the things she can do. This is the opening of *The Girls of Slender Means,* from 1963:

Long ago in 1945 all the nice people in England were poor, allowing for exceptions. The streets of the cities were lined with buildings in bad repair or in no repair at all, bomb-sites piled with
stony rubble, houses like giant teeth in which decay had been
drilled out, leaving only the cavity. Some bomb-ripped buildings
looked like the ruins of ancient castles until, at closer view, the
wallpapers of various quite normal rooms would be visible, room
above room, exposed, as on a stage, with one wall missing; sometimes a lavatory chain would dangle over nothing from a fourth-
or fifth-floor ceiling; most of all the staircases survived, like a
new art-form, leading up and up to an unspecified destination
that made unusual demands on the mind's eye. All the nice people
were poor; at least, that was a general axiom, the best of the rich
being poor in spirit.

Has any novelist ever been as consistently good at openings as
Muriel Spark? There is no denying that this is the real London of
1945—the sense of the depressed, half-ruined city is almost physically
palpable. Her London is as much the real London as her Edinburgh in
*The Prime of Miss Jean Brodie* is the real Edinburgh (complete with
the "amazingly terrible" smell in the 1930s High Street). But there are
also hints that this all-too-real scene is a mental stage as much as it is
a physical one. All metaphors have, to some extent, an anti-realistic
effect: here the comparison with a giant mouth, while striking, begins to suggest that, behind the real ruined London, there is a prompt-
ing imagination at work; then there are those castles, which make us
think of fairy tales, and then the stage sets, which make us think of the-
ater, and then we are finally led toward an encounter with the fount of
all imagination, "the mind's eye." It is as if Spark wants to parallel the
emphasis on reality with a reminder that this is all a fiction, a writer's
story being recreated in the mind of a reader in the act of reading.

Why does she bother to do this? After all, we know the fiction is a
fiction; we aren't stupid. (Or rather, we may well be stupid, but we do
at least know that.) The need to gesture at the fictionality of her fictions is, I would suggest, rooted in Spark's Catholicism, and particularly in her wish not to compete with God. This is where her identification with the older generation of Catholic writers comes together

with what some of her admirers take to be postmodernism. In Spark's fiction, we are never allowed to forget that the author, and indeed the reader, is subordinate to the final Author; our fictions must not ever seem to compete with His. Spark does not arrogate to herself the same rights as the atheist Flaubert, who thought the novelist should be like God, "everywhere present, nowhere visible," or the atheist Joyce, who thought that the novelist should again be like God, "indifferent, paring his fingernails." Spark is thoroughly present everywhere in her books. She intrudes into the story, prompts and nudges and judges and jokes, as a way of signaling the provisionality, the human limitedness, of any particular fiction.

This is not just a theoretical issue for Spark, but something that is woven into the texts of all her books. The twenty-two novels she has written over forty-seven years have a wide range of geography and subject, from 1930s Edinburgh (*Jean Brodie*) to 1990s Paris (*Aiding and Abetting*), from demonological fantasists in South London (*The Ballad of Peckham Rye*) to a parody of Watergate and President Nixon's impeachment (*The Abbess of Crewe*). Within this range, there is a considerable continuity of tone, a remarkable consistency of quality, and a few favorite plot devices. Her books usually take place in a closed world, a school or convent or (as in *The Girls of Slender Means*) a hostel. There always is a central figure who is in the grip of a delusion, and is in some way trying to play God, whether it be Brodie with her schoolgirls or the Abbess with her nuns. The central character is usually not the only person to be deluded: many, or even most of the ancillary characters tend to be, to some degree, in the grip of fantasy or misapprehension. Any one of her books could take as its epigraph T. S. Eliot's line "humankind cannot bear too much reality"—though we should add the qualification that in Spark's world, it's by no means clear that humankind can bear any reality, ever.

So Spark's books take place in a world that is recognizably the real one we all share, and at the same time they have a sense that reality is stretched thin. "One has the impression," Frank Kermode has written, "that for Spark there somehow exists, in advance of composition, a novel, or more usually a novella, which can be scanned as it were in a satellite's view of it, from above." It is sometimes as if when Spark sits down to write she has beside her elbow a long, boring, detailed novel telling the story she is about to tell, and that she is writing a kind of freestyle version of the same story. She is free to hop backward and forward in time (one Spark trademark being the sudden disruptive glimpse long into the character's future), to break the reality frame of the book whenever she feels like it, to make jokes and jumpcuts and above all to leave out anything she does not feel interests her; no writer has ever taken more to heart Elmore Leonard's advice to "leave out the boring bits." This sense of a work behind the work gives her books their paradoxical feeling of substantial insubstantiality, of artistic willfulness coexisting with a deeper internal logic.

*The Finishing School* brings us Spark's latest beginning, and her newest reminder that fiction is fiction. This time, Spark opens her book by reflecting on the subject of beginnings, with her patented blend of realness and not-quite-realness:

> "You begin," he said, "by setting your scene. You have to *see* your scene, either in reality or in imagination. For instance, from here you can see across the lake. But on a day like this you can't see across the lake, it's too misty. You can't see the other side." Rowland took off his reading glasses to stare at his creative writing class whose parents' money was being thus spent: two boys and three girls around sixteen to seventeen years of age, some more, some a little less. "So," he said, "you must just write, when you set your scene, 'the other side of the lake was hidden in mist.' Or if you want to exercise imagination, on a day like today, you can write, 'The other side of the lake was just visible.' But as you are *setting* the scene, don't make any emphasis as yet. It's too soon, for instance, for you to write, 'The other side of the lake was hidden in the fucking mist.' That will come later. You are setting your scene. You don't want to make a point as yet."

The man setting the scene, as Spark sets her scene, is Rowland Mahler, the twenty-nine-year-old co-proprietor of a nine-pupil school whose unique selling point is that it moves around from year to year—not least, Spark implies, because of the opportunities this gives to skip out on unpaid bills. At present College Sunrise is based in Ouchy, part of Lausanne. For Rowland, the school is mainly an opportunity for him to get on with his novel; the only class that really interests him is the creative writing class with which the novel begins. Rowland's partner in owning and running the school is his wife, the efficient and sane Nina:

> To conserve his literary strength, as he put it, he left nearly all the office work to Nina, who spoke good French and was dealing with the bureaucratic side of the school and with the parents, employing a kind of impressive carelessness. She tended to crush any demands for full explanations on the part of the parents. This attitude, strangely enough, generally made them feel they were getting good money's worth.

Spark's novels often have a character who, while not being anything as banal as a hero or heroine, is nonetheless the author's favorite. Here, you feel, that character is Nina, who is attracted to academics, and whose fondest wish for Rowland is that he might eventually become head of an Oxford or Cambridge college. "She had wanted him to call himself Dr. Mahler, but he had sensed that the title would interfere with his main ambition: to write a wonderful novel." Nina particularly loves to teach her charges etiquette or, as she calls it, *comme il faut:* how to eat a plover's egg; why you must realize your husband is a crook if he takes you to Ascot; and what to do if you seek a career in international diplomacy:

> "In case you are thinking of getting a job at the United Nations," Nina told them, "I have picked up a bit of information which may be useful, even vital to you. A senior member of the U. N. Secretariat passed it on to me especially for you young people. First, if you, as a U. N. employee, are chased by an elephant stand still and wave a white handkerchief. This confuses the elephant's legs. Second, if chased by a large python, run away in a zigzag movement, as a python can't coordinate its head with its tail. If you have no time to run away, sit down with your back to a tree

and spread your legs. The python will hesitate, not knowing which leg to begin with. Get out your knife and cut its head off."

"Suppose there isn't a tree to lean against?" Lionel said.

"I've thought of that," said Nina, "but I haven't come up with an answer."

Spark, it is clear, is having fun in *The Finishing School*. The novel has something of the quality that Edward Said was interested in when he wrote about lateness in art. "Late" works are the pieces an artist produces toward the end of an oeuvre: they combine an absolute control and mastery with a kind of sketchiness, a speedy glossing-over of the aspects with which the artist can no longer be bothered. The human comedy is in this short book more purely comic than it often has been for Spark. She doesn't spare her characters any more than she ever does, but here the exposures and stupidities are at the lighter end of her palette.

It is somehow characteristic of Spark that she began her career by writing about central characters who were older than her—notably the one-foot-in-the-grave senior citizens of *Memento Mori*—and has now, at the age of eighty-six, written a book in which most of the characters are still in their teens. She has always loved the superswift, devastating character sketch—think of Mary Macgregor in *The Prime of Miss Jean Brodie,* "famous for being stupid and always to blame"— and she has great fun with the none-too-bright privileged children of College Sunrise. We meet filthy-rich Pallas Kapelas, "tall and swarthy and striking," whose father is "widely believed" to be a spy; Opal, whose father has suddenly run out of money and who wants to be a priest; Mary, "a blue-frocked, blue-eyed, fair Englishwoman in the making," whose ambition is "to open a village shop and sell ceramics and transparent scarves"; and gossipy Tilly, "known and registered at the school as Princess Tilly, but no one knew where she was Princess of." Near-illiterate Tilly wants to be a journalist. She is "writing a thesis on the massacre of the Nepalese royal family in recent years. She had met one of their remote cousins at the Plaza Hotel in New York. This gave her confidence to describe the already well-documented scene, as if she herself had been there."

One of the school's pupils stands out from the others. This is Chris Wiley, a red-haired, self-possessed seventeen-year-old who is writing a novel about that very Sparkian subject, Mary Queen of Scots. Chris has a theory about the exhaustively revisited topic of whether or not Mary was involved in the murder of her husband Lord Darnley: he intends to propose that Darnley was murdered as an act of revenge for his murder of Mary's secretary and friend, the musician David Rizzio. "Chris didn't trouble to believe this theory one way or another, but he felt it would make a good story. It was to be an excitingly written novel, in addition to its originality. It was to be popular." In the crushing flatness of that last sentence, we can tell just how bad Spark thinks Chris's book is likely to be.

A Spark novel isn't a Spark novel without a central character in the grip of delusions. Rowland, who is failing to make progress with his own writing, comes to be obsessed with Chris's book. Rowland is essentially a comic character, but his envy of Chris is not comic, and it is on this subject that *The Finishing School* strikes its darkest notes:

> What is jealousy? Jealousy is to say, what you have got is mine, it is mine, it is mine? Not quite. It is to say, I hate you because you have got what I have not got and desire. I want to be me, myself, but in your position, with your opportunities, your fascination, your looks, your abilities, your spiritual good.
>
> Chris, like any of us, would have been astonished if he had known that Rowland, through jealousy, had thought with some tormented satisfaction of Chris dying in his sleep.

This is the point where *The Finishing School* touches on Spark's great theme of man's presumptuousness. Rowland is entitled to want to write his own book, but not to want Chris not to write his; for Spark, it is God who allocates talent and success and good fortune. "Envy of Another's Spiritual Good," she tells us, "was the sin from which Rowland suffered. 'Suffered' is the right word, as it often is in cases where the perpetrators are in the clutches of their own distortions."

Under the influence of these feelings, Rowland begins to go insane. He can't stop thinking about Chris, and is possessed by the feeling that the younger man's book is being written at the expense of his own. When Rowland's father dies, he flies home for the funeral, and manages to forget his envy for a few days—but then he returns to the school, and to his obsession. "The nearer he got to Geneva, the closer came Chris. No longer a boy student, he was now a meaning, an explanation in himself." The background matter of Mary Queen of Scots, and the murders committed around her—"the causes of these homicides were jealousy, uncontrollable jealousy," Spark has a historian tell us—makes us feel that *The Finishing School* is moving toward a dark, violent ending.

That sense, however, is balanced by the comedy of the book, which has great fun with the fact that "every publisher wants a novel by a red-haired youth of seventeen with a smattering of history and a good opinion of himself." Spark has clearly noticed the increasing preoccupation in publishing with youth, looks, first books, and hype, and has great fun with it. "The book itself," a publisher tells Chris, "is actually a lot of shit." We believe him, and we note that this makes no difference to "the eventual flamboyant literary success of Chris himself, if not entirely of his book"—a distinction in which Spark gives a perfect summary of what often happens these days when the hugely touted first novel appears.

The comedy and fun of this is, in Sparkworld, no guarantee that the novel will not lurch toward darkness. Is Rowland going to kill Chris? He certainly broods about it enough. ("'I could kill him,' thought Rowland. 'But would that be enough?'") Dame Muriel, however, hardly ever takes us where we think we are going to go, and likes to leave us with our questions answered, and yet not feeling that her fictional stage has been left over-tidy. The denouement, or punchline, of *The Finishing School* is so good that I can't resist passing it on, though with a warning that anyone who reads books for their plots should stop right here. Nina begins to have an affair; it is obvious that her marriage to Rowland is over. He abandons his novel and announces, unpromisingly, that he is going to write a book about the school instead. The last twist comes in one of those sweeping final passages that Spark so loves, in which she distributes to her characters their final fates:

Rowland was to continue to run College Sunrise with some success.

After another year at Ouchy he moved to Ravenna where the school specialized in the study of mosaics. From there he moved to Istanbul where he met with many problems too complicated to narrate here. His book, *The School Observed,* was published satisfactorily, as was Chris's first novel, highly praised for its fine, youthful disregard of dry historical facts.

Chris proceeded to establish himself as a readable novelist and meanwhile joined Rowland at College Sunrise as soon as he was of age. After a year they engaged themselves in a Same-Sex Affirmation Ceremony, attended by friends and Chris's family.

Not happily ever after, necessarily; but as close as it gets in Sparkworld.

NOTE

John Lanchester, "In Sparkworld," originally appeared in the *New York Review of Books*, November 18, 2004. Reprinted by permission of *The New York Review of Books.*

# THE LIFE

# CHAPTER TWELVE

# Muriel Spark

## Scottish by Formation

ALAN TAYLOR

I had an appointment with Muriel Spark in Arezzo, the Tuscan town where Vasari, fabled for his lives of the Renaissance artists, was born and bred. "My friend Penelope Jardine and I will come to Arezzo," said Mrs. Spark's fax. "I suggest we have dinner there at the Continentale Hotel (not far from the station) and we can talk then. Daytimes are very hot." The month was July; the year 1990. It was the height of summer and the sun was a fireball. Not wanting to leave anything to chance, I arrived with two days to spare. There was plenty to see. In the old part of Arezzo, spared by Allied bombs in the Second World War, was the church of San Francesco, home to a suite of frescoes by Piero della Francesca. During the mid-afternoon I hid in the Continentale and watched an Italian soap opera. At six o'clock I took a stroll and by no grand design ended up at Vasari's house in a back street so packed with cars it was barely passable even on foot. The house was cool, palatial, and empty save for the custodian who shuffled round the rooms in my wake.

A fairly pious Catholic and a patriot whose allegiance was to the Medicis in Florence, Vasari divorced himself from the religious and political issues of his day; art was his obsession. In that place at that time, the nexus between Mrs. Spark and Vasari seemed obvious. Of course, no one with even a passing acquaintance with her work would say that Mrs. Spark ignored great world events. On the contrary, they inform her fiction to an extraordinary if subterranean degree. From the rise of fascism in *The Prime of Miss Jean Brodie* to her satire of the Watergate scandal in *The Abbess of Crewe*, she was always aware of what was going on. But she was never flatly topical: no one with her intellectual attitude to faith and its implications for the hereafter could be. Like Fleur Talbot, Mrs. Spark's alter ego in *Loitering with Intent*, her sense of herself as an artist was absolute: "That I was a woman and living in the 20th century were plain facts. That I was an artist was a conviction so strong that I never thought of doubting it then or since" (25). Even when Fleur makes love her mind is elsewhere, despite efforts to think of General de Gaulle. How like Vasari's hero, Uccello, I thought, droning on about the beauties of perspective while his wife tried to coax him into bed.

In the Piazza Guido Monaco, Arentines had come out to play. Old men, gnarled as walnuts, played cards or chess while their sons drank beer and their grandsons kicked a ball. The road round the square was a racing circuit. "There is carnage every night on the roads of Italy," said Mrs. Spark. She had arrived punctually at the Continentale and in impeccable Italian ordered a gin while Penelope Jardine—Penny—parked their car. They had been together for twenty years. For a long time Mrs. Spark had been based in Rome, to which she moved in 1968. Now she was sharing Penny's rambling house in the Val di Chiana, fifteen kilometers from Arezzo. Centuries ago the house had been inhabited by a priest—it was attached to a small chapel—who kept a harem, adding rooms as necessary to accommodate additional women. Now it offered books a home, some seven thousand of them. "I buy books," said Mrs. Spark penitentially, "I often advertise for books; I spend a fortune. I do need rare books from time to time. We have endless encyclopedias."

The two women seemed content in each other's company, the one often ending the other's sentences, the one deferring to the other when she couldn't put a finger on a fact or recollect a date. The notion that Mrs. Spark was some kind of recluse or eccentric seemed absurd. Inevitably, the idea of two women living together had raised prurient eyebrows. But why should it? Though Penny is a sculptor who has exhibited at the Royal Academy in London, she supplied the domestic and business circumstances that allowed Mrs. Spark to flourish. "Penny provides Muriel with emotional security," someone who knew them both told me.

Enough at least to be flirting at seventy-two. I mentioned that I had tried with only phrasebook Italian at my command to buy a suit in Florence. If I had told her that I'd been diagnosed with a terminal illness she couldn't have shown more concern. "Let's ask that dishy waiter who is the best *sarto* in Arezzo." While the man was summoned, she asked if my hair was as nature intended. It was, I confessed. "You don't do anything to it? Touch it up?" I said I paid a man called Alfie in Edinburgh to keep it out of my eyes and off my collar. "I never touch up mine either," she said majestically.

While the waiter was interrogated on the best tailor in town (an establishment, it transpired, that charges as much for a jacket as a maître d' would earn in six months) I studied Mrs. Spark. She wore her years like chiffon. Her hair, touched up or not, was red, as it was when she was a girl growing up in Edinburgh and before it was bleached under Rhodesian skies when she was in her early twenties. She was petite, with a gay and curious demeanor. She seemed to me someone to whom you could talk unguardedly, without fear of it ever being passed on, like a doctor or a priest. She dressed elegantly and expensively. Her dress was like a forest floor covered in yellow, black, and white leaves. Round her neck she had a string of white pearls and a yellow scarf. She had a reputation for being waspish, once making mincemeat of a BBC interviewer who asked a fatuous question. When I told her—sincerely—how much I admired her latest book, *Symposium*, her dark eyes lit up and her face creased with pleasure.

The life of a "constitutional exile" appeared to suit Mrs. Spark. No one, though, should be deceived into thinking that the road to Arezzo had been straight and smooth. Her autobiography, *Curriculum Vitae*, had yet to appear. When it did, in 1992, it ended just as Mrs. Spark's career as a writer was beginning with the publication in

1957 of her first novel, *The Comforters*. By then, she was thirty-nine and a relatively late starter, but, as she makes plain in the autobiography, her life up until that point was preparatory to becoming a writer. "Since I wrote my first novel," she wrote toward the end of *Curriculum Vitae*, "I have passed the years occupied with ever more work, many travels and adventures. Friends, famous and obscure, abound in my life-story. That will be the subject of another volume" (213).

That promised volume, however, never materialized. In Arezzo, Mrs. Spark was happy to revisit her distant past, which was full of obscure people, some of whom had gained prominence because of their association with her. We talked about her father, Bertie Camberg, a Jew who was born in Scotland and who ran away to sea when he was fourteen. "He got as far as Kirkwall [in the Orkney islands]," she said. Her mother was English and an Anglican. There was no hint of gypsy blood in her, she said, a falsehood first spread by Derek Stanford, her one-time lover and former collaborator. A memoir of her by him infuriated her and continued to cause anxiety because it was often quoted. He was one of the reasons why she had embarked on *Curriculum Vitae*. "He is the limit," she said. "He was very fond of me. Absolutely. But as soon as I got any form of success he went so sour. He sold all my letters to Texas University. Then he started writing books full of the wildest things about my life, and the whole thing I ignored. I never did a thing. I am much too busy and life is too short. However, I thought I would put the record straight. One critic picks it up and another and on it goes. He's a mythomaniac."

Bertie Camberg was an engineer with the North British Rubber Works. He was a betting man, fond of horse-racing, a hobby Mrs. Spark inherited; at one time she had a share in two horses, neither of which was conspicuously successful. Her mother, Sarah, she reckoned, could have been a Bruntsfield Madame Bovary. "Quite easily," she said. "She was craving for what she called the 'bright lights.'" In *Curriculum Vitae* she recreated in meticulous and loving detail the first five years of her life, a whiff of Nivea cream being her petite madeleine. "Sometimes," she wrote,

> I compare my early infancy with that of my friends whose very early lives were in the hands of nannies, who were surrounded by

servants and privilege. Those pre-school lives seem nothing like so abundant as mine was, nothing like so crammed with people and with amazing information. I was not set aside from adult social life, nor cosied up in a nursery, and taken for nice regular walks far from the madding crowd. I was witness to the whole passing scene. Perhaps no other life could ever be as rich as that first life, when, five years old, prepared and briefed to my full capacity, I was ready for school. (46–47)

In the 1920s and 1930s, Edinburgh, Scotland's precipitous capital, was a provincial, culturally inward, begrimed city. To a dyspeptic observer, such as the poet Edwin Muir, it was a place of "extraordinary and sordid contrasts" (9). It is true, and something of a cliché, that it was a divided city, in which *Jekyll and Hyde* was conceived, where wealth and poverty, licentiousness and rectitude, were bedmates. The air in Mrs. Spark's teenage years was sweet with the smell from the numerous breweries. *Haars*—bone-chilling mists—rolled in from the Firth of Forth to the north of the city, and the wind, which so discomfited an earlier denizen, Robert Louis Stevenson, seemed never to cease blowing. It was a city of lawyers and accountants, clergymen and teachers, of pen-pushers who made a living without getting dirt under their nails.

As a child, Mrs. Spark was aware of what she called "social nervousness." Though Edinburgh was not the worst-hit of Britain's major cities during the depression in the 1930s—largely because it was not primarily dependent on heavy industry—it was impossible to avoid the gulf between rich and poor. Men and women queued for their dole (welfare payments), and ex-servicemen, veterans of the First World War, busked in the streets. In *The Prime of Miss Jean Brodie*, the favored girls, the crème de la crème, are taken on a walk through Edinburgh's Old Town, with its cobbled streets, dark, narrow alleyways (known locally as closes), and vertiginous tenements, built long before Manhattan's canyons were conceived. It is an alien territory for the girls, "because none of their parents was so historically minded as to be moved to conduct their young into the reeking network of slums which the Old Town constituted in those years" (32). This was a part of Edinburgh that just over a century before had been abandoned

by the upwardly mobile and the gentry. Where once lived the aristocracy now there were "the idle." For Sandy Stranger, as it doubtless was
for Mrs. Spark, it is her "first experience of a foreign country, which
intimates itself by new smells and shapes and its new poor" (32). A
man sat on a cold pavement. Children without shoes on their feet
played in the street. Some boys shouted obscenities at Miss Brodie's
girls. The smell was awful. A man hit a woman. It was a scene that
would return in later life to haunt Sandy Stranger, as it did her creator.
Mrs. Spark came to realize, as Sandy did, that Edinburgh meant different things to different people. Similarly, Sandy also came to appreciate that there were other people's 1930s. Visiting her in the convent
where she now lives, a man who was at boarding school in Edinburgh
recalls how beautiful it was, "more beautiful then than it is now"
(34). His favorite part was the Old Town, the Grassmarket, where
Sandy first experienced a foreign country. "'Architecturally speaking
there is no finer sight in Europe,' he said" (34).

For Mrs. Spark, who lived on its south side in a middle-class
enclave immunized from deprivation, in close proximity to hills and
with an abundance of street life on her doorstep, Edinburgh was where
she was first "understood." The school she attended—James Gillespie's Girls' School—was formative and was to be immortalized as
Marcia Blaine in *The Prime*, becoming as famous as St. Trinian's and
Dotheboys Hall. Looking back, Mrs. Spark appreciated that it was
"more progressive" than she realized. If not quite the best days of
her life, her schooldays were "very pleasant, very enjoyable." Recalling Jean Brodie echoing the boast of the Jesuits—"Give me a girl at an
impressionable age, and she is mine for life"—I wondered if a bad
teacher could have killed her interest in writing and literature. She was
adamant. "No. I'd have written at home." Her first poem appeared in
a school magazine when she was nine, and one appeared annually
until the school broke its own rule and published five the same year
by the precocious student who would later describe herself as "the
school's poet and dreamer." With this status came "appropriate per-
quisites and concessions." In 1970, she wrote: "I took this for granted,
and have never since quite accustomed myself to the world's indifference to art and the process of art, and to the special needs of artists"
("Images" 152).

She lived in Edinburgh until she was nineteen. In an oft-quoted passage, written in a hotel where she waited as her father lay dying, she wrote: "It was Edinburgh that bred within me the conditions of exile; and what have I been doing since but moving from exile to exile. It has ceased to be a fate, it has become a calling" ("Images" 151). For Mrs. Spark, exile was not a negative condition but something she embraced, which allowed her the freedom and space and distance to write. Away from Edinburgh and Scotland, away from anywhere in which she felt constricted and obligated and beset, she could work uninterrupted by irritants. In that sense, her ethic was Presbyterian; life was what you made of it. What one achieved was by one's efforts. Take nothing for granted. Expect no favors; nor, for that matter, much in the way of thanks or praise.

In Scotland a commonly used phrase is "I kent his faither," meaning I know where he comes from, what his roots are, whose genes he possesses. It is used to keep people's feet on the ground, to stop them getting above themselves, and it is applied as much to international superstars as it is to ordinary Scots who have left their homeland to make a fortune or simply a better living. I kent his faither: literally, I knew his father. In other words, who is he to lord it over me? It is a sign that Scots see themselves as equals, irrespective of what they have achieved with their lives and whether they have stayed at home or gone to the moon or to London, which is more the norm. However, it is also evidence of an innate parochialism, a suspicion of success, and mean-minded envy. Inevitably, those who suffer most from the sentiment are those such as Mrs. Spark who have embraced exile—who, for whatever reason, have left. Of them, one often hears fellow Scots talk as if they have been jilted or abandoned, referring to those who have gone as if they are lesser Scots.

Mrs. Spark left because she was in love. In her teens, she said, she was constantly falling in love. "My best love affairs were when I was young—eighteen, nineteen—and I was surrounded by students. I had a really nice time then. But I had to be in—home—early." Surrounded by students she may have been but she did not go to university. It was certainly not for lack of academic collateral. Money, however, or rather the lack of it, may have been a factor. Having said that, Mrs. Spark, looking back on those years, regarded university as something of a luxury and a waste of precious time. Other, older girls who went to university, she noticed, appeared dull and earnest and gauche, lacking charm, one of her favorite words. "Charm," she wrote in *Curriculum Vitae*, "was shunned like the work of the devil" (102). So what if these girls could write an essay on John Donne—so could she. She did, though, take a course at Heriot-Watt College, which has since become a university, in précis-writing, schooling her early in finding the briefest way to express meaning. Few writers have been as parsimonious with words as she. Fewer still have written such short books layered geologically with significance. Often, she'd jokingly remark, she felt she was short-changing her readers, so anorexic were her novels. If she'd written *War and Peace* it would have been a tenth of the length. In *Loitering with Intent*, Fleur Talbot spoke for her when she said: "I've come to learn for myself how little one needs in the art of writing, to convey the lot, and how a lot of words, on the other hand convey so little" (82).

What Mrs. Spark was doing in those apprentice days was very practically and conscientiously banking the skills and the experience she would need when she could call herself a writer. In order to write about life, as she very firmly intended to do, she had first to live. Other skills she acquired were shorthand and typing, both of which she later found to be enormously useful. Thus she learned how to style letters and to present essays and stories. Also, as a professional eavesdropper, she was well aware how useful it is for future reference to be able quickly to take shorthand notes of "meetings, encounters, chance remarks overheard on a train, in a restaurant." She was, *pace* Isherwood, a camera with its shutter forever open. Nothing passed her by; still less escaped her gaze.

With each new month her horizons expanded. She longed to work in Princes Street, then, as today, Edinburgh's main, mile-long shopping thoroughfare, on one side of which were large department stores, each independently owned. On the other side, the south side, loomed Edinburgh castle perched atop a volcanic plug, simultaneously a symbol of impregnability and paranoia. Getting a job, however, proved difficult, not, she was eager to emphasize, because her Camberg surname marked her out as a Jew and therefore a target of anti-Semitism but because of her lack of experience and secretarial qualifications. Eventually she was taken on by William Small and Sons, one of the more pukka Edinburgh fashion emporia. It was a situation that suited her perfectly. Her employer was sweet and old-fashioned and she was allowed to help him choose fabrics, always urging on him the bolder designs, a taste that never left her. He was also a source of folk wisdom, of which she was an avid collector, such as "The majority of old people die in November." Open any of her novels and you will soon find a plethora of such apparently innocuous and banal sayings. In the world according to Muriel Spark, there is profundity in the commonplace.

Little by little, she was liberating herself; she was hungry to discover what lay beyond Edinburgh and its environs. Just how desperate she was to leave may be gauged by the manner in which she achieved it. Aged nineteen, in 1937, when war was so close you could almost touch it, she agreed to marry Sydney Oswald Spark, a teacher who was thirteen years her senior. Was she in love? "Not madly, no, but I thought it was nice to get away." In her autobiography she recalled that several of her friends were getting engaged and married. Perhaps that was why she was so keen to do the same. What her friends were not doing, though, was leaving Edinburgh for a new life in Rhodesia, which we now know as Zimbabwe. Her parents disapproved but to no avail. How could she turn her back on a man who brought her flowers when she was in bed with flu? The marriage was an unmitigated disaster. With the benefit of hindsight she made her personal motto, "Beware of men bearing flowers." "I was only married a short time," she said, as the sun sank over Arezzo and the sky turned black and blue like a bruise. "Love is madness. There is nothing you can do about it. You must wait till it passes; it's like any other obsession."

The same is probably true of pain. Sixty years on, the scars of Mrs. Spark's marriage to Sydney Oswald Spark had not healed completely. On that first meeting we did not talk much about it, nor did we on subsequent ones. It seemed such an intrusive subject. In *Curriculum Vitae* she related how in Rhodesia, her husband began to show the first signs of a nervous disorder that would haunt him for the rest of his life. After their son, Robin, was born she realized the marriage was doomed, and she sought a divorce on the grounds of desertion. Since her husband wouldn't divorce her, she divorced him. But she retained his surname. Camberg, she reasoned, was "comparatively flat." In contrast, Spark had a bit of oomph about it, a bit of life. It was an affirming, memorable surname. Moreover, it seemed to sum up her personality. No one was more sparky than Muriel Spark.

That much was clear on that evening in Arezzo. Invariably, when her name cropped up in the British press, the word *reclusive* was not far away. The popular image of her was of someone who rather resented the world and was something of a misanthrope. Nothing was further from the truth, as her novels testify. What she would concede was that whenever she felt her ability to write was in any way compromised she had to retreat, to remove herself from temptation and supplication, away from the hangers-on, pub bores, and spongers who would cling to her like barnacles, whether in London, where she repaired after the war, New York, or Rome. She drew an analogy with the forest fires that sweep Tuscany in the summer months. To prevent them spreading the firefighters make a *contra fuoco*, a counter-fire round the perimeter of the fire. "They say, 'so far and no farther. That fire is raging and devouring. It won't get past this stretch because it's burnt down.' And I think that's what I've had to do with my life; make a counter-fire, to stop the encroachment of really devouring demands." Thus she had managed to avoid the many "enemies of promise." The dread pram in the hall did not thwart her, as it has many women writers, neither did sex, success, sloth, or self-doubt. Regarding her vocation, she was unswerving.

Her nineteenth novel was called *Symposium*, taking its title from Plato's dialogue, in which guests at a banquet take it in turn to talk about love—mythically, sophistically, poetically, and, finally, comically. Socrates said that the priestess Diotima had taught him that it was possible for love to take an intellectual form, creating the desire to make things of beauty, including poetry. Set partly in London and Scotland, *Symposium* has as one of its themes madness. "Here in Scotland," says Magnus Murchie, "people are more capable of perpetrating good or evil than anywhere else. I don't know why, but so it is"

(159). The Murchies live in "a turreted edifice" near the golfing mecca of St Andrews, a game played both by Mrs. Spark and Mary, Queen of Scots. Magnus is mad, but during occasional bouts of lucidity he is allowed out of the mental institution to advise his family on how they should run their affairs. When one of them questions the wisdom of this, Magnus retorts:

> Who do you have but me? Out of my misfortune, out of my affliction I prognosticate and foreshadow. My divine affliction is your only guide. Remember the ballad:

> As I went down the water side
> None but my foe to be my guide
> None but my foe to be my guide. (81)

Mrs. Spark remembered the Border ballads from her youth and could recite many of them by heart. Like her novels and stories, they are remarkable for their sense of fatality and lack of sentimentality. The most awful things are reported matter-of-factly, needing no embroidery. Death and misfortune are not occasions for the lachrymose. They speak for themselves. Dating to an era before print, a ballad is a song that tells a story by allowing the events and the characters to speak for themselves. Authorial intervention is largely absent, leaving listeners or readers to draw their own conclusions. As Roderick Watson, a Scottish academic and poet, has written, "The ballads tell of fated lovers, or battles and blood feuds or visitations from the other world—the very stuff of popular taste; and yet their presentation of this romantic, violent or uncanny material is realistic, objective and concise. In fact it is just this trenchant impersonality which produces effects of great emotional hinterland" (133).

Watson could just as well be describing Mrs. Spark's work. *Symposium*, despite its classical underpinning, is a prose ballad, a scrupulously organized dance of death, a jaunty reel choreographed by the devil. Magnus, like his creator, likes to quote from the ballads, greeting his sister with a burst of, "O where hae ye been, my long, long love, These seven long years and more?" (140).

"What do you think of Magnus?" Mrs. Spark asked. I muttered something inadequate, perhaps suggesting that it was stretching credulity somewhat to have a madman as a familial mentor. "It's amazing how many people do go to bins [lunatic asylums], or to their mad relations," she whispered, "especially in Scotland." Over the intervening years I have often pondered that remark and have grown to accept its veracity. Certainly, the Scotland that Mrs. Spark grew up in was remarkable for its acceptance of lunatics, of whom even the smallest town had a smattering, some "barking," others merely oddly behaved. Who knows why there was such a preponderance? Hellfire-and-damnation religion? Generations of inbreeding? The constant harping on about ghosts and ghouls, witches and warlocks? What is undeniable is that in Mrs. Spark's work real and other worlds exist in tandem, as naturally as human beings and animals.

Though it was many years since she had left Scotland, Mrs. Spark still spoke with a pronounced Scottish accent. It hurt her, she said, to think that anyone might think her other than Scottish. "What are you if you're not Scottish?" asked Penny. In Scotland there is a tendency to measure one's Scottishness, as if it were weighed in carats. Scots who live outside the country of their birth live constantly in danger of deracination. We left the Continentale and went out into the Tuscan dusk, and Mrs. Spark and Ms. Jardine set off on their journey home. I bought a glass of chianti in the piazza and turned to my copy of Vasari and read about Brunelleschi, who, among other wonders, built Florence's dome. Swap genders and he could have been talking about Muriel Spark. "There are many men whom nature has made small and insignificant, but who are so fiercely consumed by emotion and ambition that they know no peace unless they are grappling with difficult or indeed almost impossible tasks and achieving astonishing results" (Vasari 133).

A few weeks after my article on the interview in Arezzo had appeared in the newspaper for which I then worked I received a complimentary letter from Penny, gently correcting a few errors and asking if I would be interested in looking after their house the following summer. It was put in such a way that I was made to feel I was doing them a favor. How could one refuse? Now Mrs. Spark magically metamorphosed into Muriel. It was the overture to a friendship that continued until her death and included the exchange of many letters, frequent sojourns in Tuscany, trips to New York, London, Prague and, finally, in 2004, to Scotland and Edinburgh. Muriel was an inveterate traveler, never happier than when climbing into the passenger seat of the Alfa Romeo and motoring thousands of miles. In 1995 I helped make a BBC documentary about her. What, I asked in a preparatory letter, was her achievement, her legacy? "I have realized myself," she wrote. "I have expressed something I brought into the world with me. I believe I have liberated the novel in many ways, showing how anything whatsoever can be narrated, any experience set down, including sheer damn cheek. I think I have opened doors and windows in the mind, and challenged fears—especially the most inhibiting fears about what a novel should be." As for her roots, her origins, her nationality, she said simply this: "I am Scottish by formation."

WORKS CITED

Muir, Edwin. *Scottish Journey*. London: William Heinemann, 1935.

Spark, Muriel. *Curriculum Vitae*. London: Constable, 1992.

———. *Loitering with Intent*. London: Bodley Head, 1981.

———. *The Prime of Miss Jean Brodie*. London: Penguin Books, 1965.

———. *Symposium*. London: Constable, 1990.

———. "What Images Return." *Memories of a Modern Scotland*. Ed. Karl Miller. London: Faber and Faber, 1970.

Vasari, Giorgio. *Lives of the Artists, Volume 1*. Trans. George Bull. London: Penguin, 1987.

Watson, Roderick. *The Literature of Scotland*. London: Macmillan, 1984.

# CHAPTER THIRTEEN

# Now You See Her, Now You Don't

DORIS LESSING

In 1950 the *Observer* Short Story Competition was won by Muriel Spark's "The Seraph and the Zambesi."

The social atmosphere has changed so much that it is hard, from our perspective of heedless hedonism, to recall those surly and combative days, at the height of the Cold War, which bred hatreds, suspicions, mendacity. World war was believed to be imminent, and it would be started by the Soviet Union or the United States, depending on which camp you were in. The Korean War, whose nastiness had been forgotten, despite the television series MASH which compared to the realities seemed like anodyne tomfooleries, poisoned our days and our nights. Britain was still pervaded by a greyish postwar air. Food rationing was only just ending. It was a threadbare cold time.

The advocates of Socialist Realism, whose progenitor was the Soviet Union, sneered at their opponent's views, described as Art for Art's Sake. Unreal debates flourished, such as "Graham Greene or Edith Sitwell?" and "C. P. Snow, yes! William Gerhardi—no!" wasting time and the spirit.

These protagonists were shortly to be seen off by the arrival of what was inaccurately but economically called the Kitchen Sink. Disgruntled Osborne, snarling Lucky Jim, not to mention a galaxy of clever young men and a woman or two, mostly from the northern lower classes, were on the way, and here were arriving swallows from Africa, heralding an explosion of writing.

Two periodicals had about them the aura of rightness, of finger-on-the-pulse, the *New Statesman* under Kingsley Martin and the *Observer* under David Astor. Everyone read them. It must not be assumed that winning the stylish *Observer* short story competition meant then what it would now. It was a prodigious debut. The elegant little tale could not have been further from the temper of the time, and I remember reading it with the exhilaration that comes from the unexpected, from agreeable surprise.

Surprising, too, was the experience it came out of. Everyone who visits that part of Africa sees the Victoria Falls. It is not possible to remain unmarked by it. Muriel herself says she found it a spiritual impact there. And she was no visitor, she knew the place well: Africa itself was in that tale.

She went out to Southern Rhodesia to marry, before the war. While I was growing up a certain brave figure would arrive in our land, the girl from Home who was going to marry a local lad. She was watched by a hundred cold and suspicious eyes: would she measure up or not? This meant, had she brought with her silly liberal ideas from Home that would spoil the kaffirs. Would she conform and become one of us? In her case, there must have been double wariness, since she was not marrying a Rhodesian but a teacher, from Home, trying out the new land.

Most immigrants conformed. They had to, having already cast their bread upon the stormy waters of the Slump which was driving so many young people out of Britain, and besides, the Second World War was already on the boil. Retreat was not easy. Muriel thoroughly disliked the place. It was an unpleasant society, for dissident whites, as well as for blacks. If you were not dedicated to sport, and to conversations that nearly always centered on the Native Problem—seen as being the faults of your black servants or labourers, if you were not prepared to see the white occupation of the country as "civilization" you were much on your own.

Now, I had been brought up with all that, I knew how to dissemble, and the cost if you didn't. I used to feel pity for the poor girls from Home, and even now I feel a kind of retrospective protectiveness for Muriel Spark, who couldn't have had any idea of what she was getting herself into. The marriage did badly, but not too much should be made of this. War marriages tend to fail.

And then there was Muriel, on her own and stuck because of the war. She did a variety of secretarial jobs. On Saturday nights she danced with the Royal Air Force (RAF) stationed in large numbers in various parts of Africa, not to mention Canada and Australia. They must have felt they were sharing exile with this fellow countrywoman. She tried to get a teaching job at the Dominican Convent in Salisbury but found the nun who interviewed her anti-Semitic and a bit of a Nazi. This was the same convent I was in, a decade before. Hard to imagine sane and humorous Muriel Spark anywhere near this unwholesome place. But she was in some pretty surprising places, Gwelo, for instance. There used to be a joke that Salisbury was a mix of a genteel English country town and the Wild West, but Gwelo lacked any kind of gentility, was a raw pioneer mining town. Most novelists do tend to get about a good bit before settling into the narrowed life of a working writer. Or perhaps we could agree that a novelist's talent may be allied to curiosity about other lives, or at least an aptitude for the varied and the strange. I cannot think of a better place to be than southern Africa in wartime to encounter wide varieties of people and situations. Muriel Spark was a good Scots girl from Edinburgh, and if she had never left we might have had different novels. Miss Brodie commenting from a distance on wartime Africa—now that's a thought. But here I am uncomfortably close to sharing Auden's thoughts on the subject: novelists are doomed to "suffer all the wrongs of man." And I don't really. This is the belief that if you haven't committed murder or gone off with a handsome fisherman to the Mediterranean then you can't write about murder or handsome fishermen.

Muriel, in Bulawayo, did as many different things as I did in Salisbury. We did not meet then, but we have since compared notes. With so many men "up north"—that is, fighting Rommel, and then going up into Europe with the Allied armies—women were easily getting jobs. Worth our weight in gold we were, I remember joking with female mates: intangible gold, of course. I can't imagine Muriel had much money to splash about any more than I had. If we had met then we would have had literature in common but perhaps not much else. I was much at home on soapboxes; some of them I now regret, others not, but that kind of thing was not her temperament. We found and treasured *New Writing*, John Lehman's wartime magazine, for it was in the bookshops. I was ordering books from London. They had to dodge the U-boats, in the precarious convoys. It would have been very nice indeed to have someone like her to discuss them with. She was already well on her road: winning a prize at the Eistedfodd for poetry.

Then the war was ending and what we were both doing was waiting. Waiting was what millions (and millions) of people were doing during those interminable postwar years. Refugees waited to get back to their homes, if they ever did. Children waited for their fathers, wives for their men, airmen waited for boats to take them home at last, sometimes for years. People stranded like Muriel, waited: there was no air travel for ordinary people then, it was boats that took people between continents. People like me, who had longed for years to leave Rhodesia for London, and whose leaving the war had postponed, waited. Waiting is what our generation is good at: we have learned the hard way. And though this memoir is not any kind of an attempt at literary criticism, I must mention the story *Robinson*, about a group of survivors on an island, waiting to be taken off, and the paranoias and fidgets and survival mechanisms that develop. There was Muriel in Bulawayo, waiting, and I in Salisbury, thinking it would never end, never; just as the war had seemed it must go on forever so now this awful postwar time could, and in *Robinson* they think like this too. It is always intriguing to watch writers sifting gold from muddy experience.

When she returned to London and was working in the tight little world of magazines and poetry magazines, all underfunded, just emerged from the war where so many little magazines had gone under. Her life then is in *A Far Cry from Kensington* and *Girls of Slender*

*Means.* What is interesting is how far that high-minded threadbare living is from the world of magazines now, so sleek and well fed.

I met her about then and it still seems improbable. Why I was in her flat in South London I don't know, but there she was, surrounded by heavy serious furniture and wearing clothes of the kind my mother would have described as "good." She did not mean by this fashionable, chic, but rather well-dressed, expensive, certainly ladylike. The description defines me as much as it does her. At that time I was meeting mostly the Comrades, for everyone was pink or red or had been and was now violently opposed. No one had any money, and we were in the Bohemian life which I cannot recommend too highly for hard times. They might return, and so it is well to remember that the rent for living in Bohemia is much less than for good furniture and clothes and a dependable roof. We lived from hand to mouth. Colourful we were, if a bit grimcrack; and here was Muriel, the essence of good taste, and that made it even harder to imagine her in raffish wartime Rhodesia.

The next glimpse I had was from newspapers and the posh magazines. Muriel Spark was living in Rome, living it up, her companions the rich and glittering. I liked that, particularly because at that time my life did not run to elegance, nor either, to much society. A small child kept me circumscribed. But was it true? We have all learned to disbelieve newspaper gossip about the famous. Muriel later told me a story about that time. The media were anxious to fasten some eccentricity on her, I forget what. Television turned up, positioned their cameras, and the interviewer put a question designed to elicit from her remarks on that subject, which in fact did not interest her. While she protested her indifference, the camera rested on the title of a book which could be seen as contradicting her, held it, and then panned fast down a shelf of books, too fast to let the viewer see the titles, so as to imply that all the books, like the first, were on that very subject. I have had the same trick played on me: The media, that likes to see itself as fearless and perspicacious exposers of hypocrisy and wrongdoing, roots about until they find evidence of some wrongthinking or doing. The interviewer asked me a question about—I think—the imminence of interplanetary tourist travel. I said I didn't believe in it, but the camera had rested on a title and then rushed down a shelf of books, and so there I was, like Muriel, made out to be a liar. Do not imagine that the golden boys and girls of television are ashamed of their little deceits.

A simple question to Muriel would have sufficed. Did you in fact live in the fast set, dressed in designer frocks? But that would spoil the fun. It adds to the jests of life to read that such and such a person, whom you know to be a recluse, regularly attends international festivals where Japanese fighting fish engage in combat, or that a rigidly socialist friend who is uninterested in food will eat lunch only in the Ivy. Thus the journalists' bitter fantasy lives spread nets of the wildest fiction.

However long Muriel spent in the smart set, she soon was living, and did for the rest of her life, in a secluded village in Italy, far from the froth of London's literary life. Her elegant, witty and shapely novels emerge from the dull plains of hard slog which alas are the proper terrain for novelists. Whenever meeting Muriel I was reminded of the sensible Scotswomen on the farms around us when I was a girl—an area now terrorised by Mugabe's thugs. It is agreeable to accept a cup of tea from the hand of the author of, let's say, *Territorial Rights*, jealous wives, spies, criminals, terrorists in training, the terrible tensions between communism in the West made into a witty tale—but what dark depths do lurk.

> Amid the chaos of war, when Russian liberators in Bulgaria followed upon German liberators, and in Italy the Allies finally liberated left, right and centre, the noble owner of the Villa Sofia in Venice died a natural death, while his friend Victor was killed. (68–69)

That young woman, sitting out the war in Southern Rhodesia, in a country seething with refugees, the bored RAF officers and Other Ranks, military staff coming and going, such movement, such restlessness, with the anguish of the battlefronts in our ears night and day from the radio—such a witness is well-qualified to write such tales.

Writing about Muriel one has at least to mention that she is a Catholic, while if it were Graham Greene, the fact would have to be central. Hard not to think he became a Catholic because it gave him such productive room for his talent for the lugubrious satisfactions of guilt. Nothing of the kind, for Muriel.

"The churches were so much more cheerful than others, so full of colour, glitter, incense and images" (*Aiding and Abetting* 20). This is the sparkle of aesthetic enjoyment, to be shared by unbelievers, but surely what attracted her were the opportunities for ironic comment on our hypocrisies, or perhaps like was simply calling to like, for the wise intelligence in her work does put her in the company of writers who share the long perspectives of Rome.

She was no stranger to the dark nights, the depths and the deeps. It is now too much of a commonplace to say that literature cannot match the bizarre extremes of everyday life. Usually in our time the attempt is made in science fiction, or magic realism—a phrase which, like "the kitchen sink," seems designed to avoid the toil of real definition—but Muriel Spark's contribution is to convey the bizarre within the form we have decided to call realism. In her penultimate book, *Aiding and Abetting*, let us take the scene where a woman decides to become a holy stigmatic, much to her profit, because she suffers profuse menstrual bleeding, and seizes her opportunities. "Blood, once let loose, gets all over the place. It sticks. It flows. It garishly advertises itself or accumulates in thick dark puddles. Once it gets going, there is no stopping blood" (109). And there is her characteristic dry smile, that puts a stop to excess.

Muriel was not always hard at work in Italy. Sometimes she came to England. One of the most pleasant days of my life was spent in the company of Muriel and other friends, at the Hay Literary Festival, from where we took off to lunch in the hills. England comes up more often than its detractors like to admit with days so perfect you have to forgive it on the spot for its extremes of gloom and dark. The country around Hay is, when the sun shines, paradisiacal. Birds, flowers, trees in blossom, brooks babbling and streams sparkling. On a sandy spit in the middle of the Wye, that treacherous stream which can flood in an instant, two swans sat on their eggs with the sun shining on their backs. A delicious day. Such days cannot be planned for. They happen.

NOTE

Doris Lessing, "Now You See Her, Now You Don't," originally appeared in *Time Bites: Views and Reviews* (London: Fourth Estate, 2004). Copyright © 2004 by Doris Lessing. Reprinted by kind permission of Jonathan Clowes Ltd., London, on behalf of Doris Lessing.

WORKS CITED

Spark, Muriel. *Aiding and Abetting*. London: Viking, 2000.
———. *Territorial Rights*. London: Macmillan, 1979.

# CHAPTER FOURTEEN

# The Culture of an Anarchist

An Interview with Muriel Spark

JOHN MORTIMER

"Have I ever been happy? Not for long. It's always been on, off, on, off. I mean, I sometimes think that happiness is boring. Look at happy marriages, for instance. And I don't want to go to heaven if it means sitting looking at the Virgin Mary standing on a cloud for ever and ever. I may not have been happy but I've been very amused."

"Have you been happy writing?"

"Writing? I had to write because it's the only thing I've ever been able to do well."

We were in the modern dining room of the Hotel Continentale in Arezzo. It was the holiday of the Epiphany and around us huge Italian families were celebrating with huge Italian lunches. Children dived under the tables and young girls looked forward to happy marriages and to an eternity of watching the Virgin on a cloud. Muriel Spark, small, girlish and beautiful when she smiles, a writer who can run rings round all of us, peered inquisitively through large spectacles at the menu. She spoke with a trace of Edinburgh accent, so that she "sometaimes" thought that happiness was boring.

"My father was Jewish, a Scottish engineer, and my mother was born in England. Did I get on with them? Of course. They were my first audience. I wrote things for them. I tried to improve 'The Pied Piper of Hamelin' by giving it a happy ending. Every day after school I was in the public library, reading everything. I was certainly taught by Miss Jean Brodie, or she was a sort of mixture of my mistresses. I did Latin and Greek." Muriel Spark's *Collected Poems* contains translations of Horace and Catullus. "Where did I get my style? Well, my mother was a great hypocrite. I used to watch her say, 'Goodbye, my dear. Such a wonderful treat to see you,' and when the door was shut she'd say, 'Silly old bitch.' In a way I disapproved of that because we're always meant to be sincere in Edinburgh. But it gave me a satirical attitude and I think that showed in my style. I was married when I was nineteen, to a schoolmaster who took me out to Rhodesia. Better not say too much about that. I was absolutely inexperienced. You are quite a different person when you're nineteen. You change entirely, don't you think?"

"Do you think so? I'm sure that if that little twelve-year-old girl who went to the public library every day after school were sitting here, you'd feel quite like her."

"Oh yes," Muriel Spark agreed with one of her sudden, youthful smiles. "I'd recognise *her* all right. The love of literature doesn't change."

"What about Rhodesia?"

"Well I won a poetry prize there, but that wasn't much. Anyone could win a poetry prize in Rhodesia. I thought the whole place was rather shabby and I didn't like the people at all. The black or the white. Oh, I met an occasional chemist or priest or oddball I could talk to, but on the whole the white people were frightful. The black people weren't very nice either and I didn't blame them for that. I much preferred the birds, the beasts, and the flowers. Then I got divorced and went to Cape Town to wait for a boat back to England. I had to wait for a long time because the war was on. I liked the Dutch people there, the 'Boers' they called them. They were crude in many ways, but they were real people who'd been there hundreds of years. Not like the English in Rhodesia, who came from nothing and showed off about having five servants."

Life appears in her novels to be full of brilliant, comic and outrageous surprises. One of those was now in store for Mrs. Spark. Arrived in England she went to the Labour Exchange, as girls of her age were compelled to do, to seek useful employment. She waited, deep in a novel by Ivy Compton Burnett, and, seeing what she was reading, the woman in charge decided that no ordinary job would do for her and sent her to work for British Intelligence at Woburn Abbey, broadcasting misleading news items to the Germans. One of those false bulletins, concocted by the brilliant journalist Sefton Delmer, informed the German people that Hitler had had his trousers burned off in the attempt on his life. This potent mixture of history and fiction seemed an admirable training for a novelist.

"I never wanted to be a novelist, which I thought to be a lazy way of writing. I wanted to be a playwright or a poet. I like Auden, Spencer and MacNeice, Chaucer, Shakespeare and Marlowe. Milton's impossible. I can never get to the end of his sentences."

There were four of us at lunch. I was with my sixteen-year-old daughter, and Mrs. Spark had been driven over by her friend and helper Penelope Jardine, a sculptress who lives in a converted church near Arezzo. We ordered another bottle of Chianti and agreed on the interminable nature of Milton's sentences.

"What about novelists apart from Ivy Compton-Burnett? Virginia Woolf, for instance?"

"A spoiled brat." The judgement might have come from Miss Jean Brodie at her most severe. "All right, she committed suicide but she didn't have to take the dog with her."

"But Muriel," Penelope Jardine intervened, as counsel for the defense, "how do you *know* Virginia Woolf killed the dog?"

Muriel Spark smiled charmingly, and Virginia Woolf followed Milton into the shadows of the afternoon.

"After the war I lived in Camberwell and I had a wonderful landlady called Milly. Milly's husband was an organist at the Odeon. He sat at an organ which came up out of the ground all lit up, so Milly understood the life of an artist. I won an *Observer* short story competition. Two hundred and fifty pounds, an enormous sum in those days, so I took three months off and read Proust and Max Beerbohm and Cardinal Newman."

When she had finished reading these authors, Mrs. Spark became secretary of the Poetry Society, worked for publishers and entered the strange literary half-world she describes in her stunning new novel *A Far Cry from Kensington.* And like the central character of that book, she wanted to be thin. "I took slimming pills and I began to have hallucinations. I'd get the letters of words all mixed up. If I saw 'lived,' I'd read it as 'devil.' So I wrote a book about a girl who heard strange voices and Evelyn Waugh reviewed it in the *Spectator* or somewhere. He was such a generous man. He said it was better than *The Ordeal of Gilbert Pinfold,* which he was writing then." Evelyn Waugh was not the only writer to help ignite the young Spark. "I had a friend—well all right, I had an affair with him—and he took a great interest in me until I became more successful, when he started to write things about me which weren't exactly true. He told Graham Greene that what I needed was a patron and Graham Greene asked if he could apply for the job. So he paid me twenty pounds a month. Well, I could live on that."

"Did you meet Graham Greene?"

"No. He said he didn't want to meet me. And, above all, he said he didn't want me to pray for him."

We had spent the morning wandering in Arezzo. We had stood in the church and looked at the Piero della Francescas which trace the progress of the Cross from a tree in the Garden of Eden to the dreams of the Emperor Constantine. We sat in the pale January sunshine on the steps of the law courts in the Piazza Grande, which looks unchanged since Petrarch lived there, and where horsemen armed with lances still gallop at a pivoting quintain every year on the first Sunday in September.

"Although Graham Greene didn't want you to pray for him, you are a Catholic convert," I said. "How did that happen?"

"I was always a believer. When I asked my Jewish father what I believed in he said, 'the Blessed Almighty,' and went back to his racing paper. Then I joined the Church of England but I soon saw through *that*: it was so bounded by the British Empire. Then I became an Anglo-Catholic and went to a church in Queensgate all tricked out fit to dazzle the Pope. The vicar there preached this ridiculous sermon in which he said, 'I am the Catholic authority in Queensgate!'

I couldn't take that so I rang up a priest in Ealing. I go to church now but I leave before the sermon. I regard it as mortal sin to listen to sermons."

"Does being a Catholic give you framework for your books?" The best English novelists in my lifetime, Evelyn Waugh, Graham Greene and Muriel Spark, have all had the same religion.

"It's a help because it gives you a point of departure. But I wouldn't recommend anyone to take up religion as an aid to writing."

"How do you reconcile yourself to a God who allowed the slaughter of seven million Jews, for instance?"

"I noticed you asked the two aunties, Runcie and Basil Hume, about the Holocaust. It's a very good question. Basil Hume should have said that it means God is: a) good, or b) evil, or c) indifferent. But he didn't say that."

"Which do you think He is?"

"I think He's a mystery. I suppose the answer sometimes filters through the Sermon on the Mount. There's a passage by a mystic usually printed at the end of *The Cloud of Unknowing* which says that God is nothing that you think He is."

"What do you think He is?"

"Sometimes I feel like agreeing with Dylan Thomas."

"What did he say?"

"Oh, God thou art a bloody cad."

"Do you believe in hell?"

"I think hell is empty and all the devils are here. That's what it says in *The Tempest*. I believe the Holy Ghost has been seriously underestimated. You know Penelope's an unbeliever but she drives me to church rather as people used to drive their servants. Well, one day I did listen to a sermon and the priest was telling the Italian peasants to avoid being Protestant. What nonsense! They had no intention of being Protestants. He also told them lies about the English persecuting Catholics. That man should have paid more attention to the Holy Ghost."

[At the end of the 1960s, disturbed by the attention she was getting with the success of *The Prime of Miss Jean Brodie*, Muriel Spark came to live in Italy and bought the apartment she still keeps in Rome.]

"Did it sometimes seem a long way from Edinburgh?"

"Edinburgh to me means rationalism. Believing in a strong difference between right and wrong. Honesty of thought. The work ethic. All that sort of thing. I went through all that. There was a time when I produced two books a year. It nearly killed me. I don't think you should work hard when you're young, do you?" She looked at my daughter. "The young should sleep a lot and look beautiful. Edinburgh has always been a European city: its ties are with Europe and not with England. So when I'm in Italy and English people say, 'What are you doing out there?,' I say 'What are you doing out on the fringe of things?' Rome was the religious centre, the centre of antiquity. And of course I didn't want to do anything but write. I might have liked to have been happily married, but that wasn't for me. I mean, I might have made a good wife but not *very* good." Mrs. Spark gave one of her sweetest smiles. "I didn't have it in me to attract men for long."

"What about politics? Do they interest you?"

"Interest me, yes. But of course I'm an anarchist. I'm firmly persuaded that all politicians simply want to manipulate people; that, mixed with a marked tendency to kleptomania."

"Our local Mafia head just died," Penelope said. "And things have been a bit chaotic since then."

Now Muriel Spark spends most of her time writing on the top floor of Penelope Jardine's house. Miss Jardine helps her with her business affairs and, when the post arrives, shouts through the bathroom door, "You won't believe what those robbers are doing to you now!" They seem an undomesticated couple who eat out, most of the time, in local restaurants. "I was making a bed about ten years ago," Mrs. Spark said, "and I broke my ribs. I shan't do *that* again." She was taken to hospital. "I woke up and saw my maid sitting on the floor, eating a bun. In Italy all your family and friends come into hospital to chase away the bugs and find out what they're doing to you."

"What do you do in the evenings?"

"Watch Mexican soaps dubbed into Italian on the television. They are wonderful—full of illegitimacy and sudden death, like Elizabethan drama."

"Can I ask your age?"

"Seventy next month. It doesn't mean anything to me. It's just a number. And I must say, in the last twenty years I've found relationships with men have been much easier."

In an act of generosity which equals the conduct of Graham Greene and Evelyn Waugh, Muriel Spark has, in her latest book, told her readers how to write a novel. "Write privately, not publicly; without fear or timidity as if it were never going to be published. Before starting, rehearse in your mind what you are going to tell, something interesting, your story. But don't rehearse too much: the story will develop as you go along, especially if you write to a special friend, man or woman, to make them smile or laugh or cry. Remember not to think of the reading public. It will put you off."

It sounds easy but it is advice few can take. You have to have the knack of talking in your own voice, as freely on a printed page as over a bottle of Chianti on an Epiphany day lunch in a modern family hotel in Arezzo.

NOTE

John Mortimer, "The Culture of an Anarchist: An Interview with Muriel Spark," originally appeared in the *Telegraph Sunday Magazine*, March 20, 1988. Reprinted by permission of the *Sunday Telegraph*, The Telegraph Group Ltd., 1 Canada Square, Canary Wharf, London E14 5DT.

# CHAPTER FIFTEEN

# "Fascinated by Suspense"

## An Interview with Dame Muriel Spark

ROBERT E. HOSMER JR.

This interview with Dame Muriel Spark took place at her home in the village of San Giovanni d'Oliveto, off in the hidden hills of Tuscany, on an early spring day in March 2001, when fresh snow had dusted the olive trees surrounding the rambling fourteenth-century rectory that she and Penelope Jardine called home. In person, Dame Muriel belied her age, and recent bouts of ill health and surgery had left no mark: vivacious, stylishly coiffed and attired, she was very much a Jamesian figure of vivid intensity and probity, an Edinburgh enchanter of the first order. Her wit and charm, her grace and elegant, effortless courtesy revealed the woman who was long the sought-after dinner guest when Sir Harold Acton or Gore Vidal or cardinals at the highest reaches of the Vatican entertained.

INTERVIEWER: I'd like to begin by asking some questions about your life and the first volume of your autobiography, *Curriculum Vitae*, published in 1992. Your intention is clearly articulated at the opening of *Curriculum Vitae* when you state, "so many strange and erroneous accounts of parts of my life have been written since I became well known, that I felt it time to put the record straight": do you think that you succeeded?

SPARK: Partly, yes. I think I partly did, but people of course go on repeating what their first impression always was. There's nothing I can do about that, except that I think, generally speaking, the autobiography did stick in people's minds as my account, and it also helped. I've got a biographer, Martin Stannard, who did Evelyn Waugh's biography—a two-volume work—and he found it very useful just as indications of where to go. And then I found that my records and the people who were writing about my life were very much assisted by the fact that I lodged all my family papers with the National Library of Scotland. They've got my mother's voluminous letters and my son's letters and every time people get things wrong they can go there. There is a source at least of things. I thought it just as well to let the records speak for themselves. It does help me, because I can then get on with my work.

INTERVIEWER: There is a very definite sense that the truth will out in the end.

SPARK: I think it does, yes. I have nothing much to complain about, really, and it's just that small things mislead people very much into larger misconceptions.

INTERVIEWER: As the author of well-received biographies of Emily Brontë, Mary Shelley, and John Masefield, how would you compare the process of writing the life of another and writing your own?

SPARK: Very much the same. Very much the same. I really got out of myself and I really researched my own autobiography. It goes up to the point where I thought that my life spoke for itself in my books, my novels, when I started writing novels and first published in 1957. And then I haven't done more; I intend to finish my autobiography. But I thought I'd get that bit done. I treated it exactly as if it was somebody else's. I checked every fact. I think you can see that it looks researched. I decided not to put anything in from my memory, unless I could either have an eyewitness (mainly in my younger years my brother who is still alive and is a living witness to all I say) and documents or letters. And between the two supports, I didn't rely entirely on my memory.

INTERVIEWER: Roland Barthes once said that a biography is "a novel that does not speak its name." Do you think that this might be said of autobiography, yours in particular?

SPARK: "A novel that does not speak its name." I think I'm rather different because I didn't give it the shape of a novel; there is more of a string of chronological events. I think perhaps there is a shape in that in my very early years, because of my type of perceptions, you do see the later writer. So in that case it could be the story of a writer, if you want to look at it that way. Many autobiographies or biographies are novel-wise, I think. I'm not very keen on the ones that resemble novels. I get irritated by "Jane Austen went out into the garden and thought what a lovely day it was." How do we know?

INTERVIEWER: Some critics were not happy with *Curriculum Vitae*, calling it "maddeningly underwritten" (John Cornwell), "brilliantly anorexic" (Victoria Glendinning), even "something of a failure" (Stephen Schiff). Just what was their problem?

SPARK: I think perhaps it's not emotional enough, that's all, I think. If that's what they say. I haven't really seen all the reviews.

INTERVIEWER: I didn't mean to bring those complaints to your attention.

SPARK: No, no. I quite agree that people felt unsatisfied. . . . You know I have noticed in my life that a lot of the disasters have turned out to be quite lucky, quite good fortune, in the end. That I find is providential. It's a way of looking at things, perhaps. It is how I've found things to be.

INTERVIEWER: In important ways, Augustine's *Confessions* set the model for autobiography in the Western literary tradition; his brilliant and moving illumination of his conversion is a high point within a tradition that stretches before him and on after him, to Newman and to you. Though your own conversion to Roman Catholicism in 1954 is the central event of your life, too, you compress the narrative of that moment into a mere two hundred words, some of them Newman's, not your own. Why?

SPARK: Yes, I think there's a very, very different book to be written on my conversion. It took such a long time and it did cover the whole of my life in retrospect and that in fact the whole of my life would be a process towards conversion into. . . . so you would hardly call it conversion, it was just a moving into a place where I was destined for. It wasn't a blinding light or a revelation, so that I really didn't feel I could dramatize it, honestly. You know a great deal of my conversion resulted from a long process of elimination. I tried the Church of England, for example.

INTERVIEWER: That certainly makes sense, thinking of conversion as a sort of natural evolving, awakening, doesn't it, then?

SPARK: Yes, yes. I think it was one of Newman's favorite, very unorthodox early Fathers, Tertullian, who said the soul of man is naturally Christian, which would be Catholic in those days. The human being is made like that. This isn't, of course, a modern idea, where we have comparative religions, and all other religions are taken into account. He said, "The soul is naturally Christian," and I felt that. I felt it was a natural process. But let me say here that I spent many years in studying the different Christian theologians, so that my final choice was the result of a gradual elimination of all but the Roman Catholic faith. These theological studies have been a great help to me creatively. What people believe is their character and as such is of vital interest to a novelist.

INTERVIEWER: I certainly respect your reticence on the subject of your conversion; let me ask you not to tell more about that "moment," but to tell us how now, more than fifty years later, you view that conversion—in itself and in its impact upon your life and work.

SPARK: Well, it's had a terrific impact on my life and work. My faith has been strengthened to the extent that I could not not believe. It would be impossible for me to lose my faith. And I see that the Church, of course, has changed, the Catholic Church, and I think for the better. I think it's better that more freedom should be given to the individual conscience, I think it better that the Church should be open, that the Pope should speak to all people and not only to Catholics. I think that the whole opening of religion is very much a better thing, but to do that the twentieth century has had to suffer for it in many terms, that of the Holocaust, for one outstanding example. By the way, my father was a Jew so that I'm a half, although the orthodox Jews don't recognize that you can be a half-Jew, and as my mother was not a Jew, they don't reckon that I am anything. In fact, I have this culturally half Jewish heritage, although I wasn't brought up in any particular strict faith. My mother and father were very casual, very free about their religion; they believed in God, and there was no problem. As we were a poor family anything else would have been a luxury.

INTERVIEWER: An extraordinary process for you, isn't it, bringing you to where you are at this moment?

SPARK: Yes, yes.

INTERVIEWER: And you've always been very careful to make a distinction between the deposit of faith and the accidents that surround the everyday activity of the Church.

SPARK: Oh yes, I think so, because they vary geographically, culturally, and in every way.

INTERVIEWER: Near the end of *Curriculum Vitae*, you refer to your life after 1957, saying, "That will be the subject of another volume." How is the sequel progressing, and can it be that there will be only one more volume?

SPARK: No, I don't know, really. What I'm doing at the moment, if you'd like to know, is I'm writing a play and I'm writing a novel at the same time. I'm very busy with this novel, and it should be done this year. And right now I'm writing about animals for the newspaper because we've had an outbreak of poisoning in our area, of hunters poisoning our animals, so I've had a lot of that just immediately, so until Easter I'm pretty bogged down with commissioned work. Then I've got this novel which is half-way finished. The play only just beginning.

INTERVIEWER: So it's not fair to talk about it?

SPARK: I don't think so, no.

INTERVIEWER: If we can't talk about it . . .

SPARK: Well, I've got one character, if you want something, in the play, a man who can see out of his head, from behind, his eyes are virtually at the back of his head. That's all I'd really like to say.

INTERVIEWER: Perhaps, then, we could talk about your poetry?

SPARK: Yes.

INTERVIEWER: Some people may not realize that you edited the selected poems of Emily Brontë and did a biography of her, that you wrote a wonderful biography of John Masefield, and that you've published, I think, three collections of your own poetry.

SPARK: Yes. I've got another collection ready, or rather I've got, if you like, a number of poems ready to add to the collection, to extend it, enlarge it.

INTERVIEWER: And there are plans to publish that soon?

SPARK: I think I'll put it all together, together with my prose work, which has not been published, except in magazine forms, various essays throughout the years. There are hundreds of those. Penelope—my friend Penelope Jardine—is editing those at the moment, and she'll have to choose what to publish or not. They go back to the 1950s, or 40s even; and those are nonfictional, critical work. They come under the headings of "critical," "literary critical," "religion," and just "general observations." I forget. She's got a lot of headings. She'll tell you.

INTERVIEWER: I certainly hope that she includes that marvelous piece on Proust from the Church of England newspaper that I want to talk about later—it's spectacular.

SPARK: Thank you, yes, she has that, I expect.

INTERVIEWER: And that beautiful meditation on the Piero fresco that was in, of all places, *Vanity Fair*.

SPARK: You like it? . . . Yes. Well, it is a lovely picture. Have you been to see it? It's not far away from here. You don't have a car?

INTERVIEWER: Let's talk more about poetry for a few minutes.

SPARK: Yes, let's do that.

INTERVIEWER: When did you begin to write poetry?

SPARK: Well, I was about nine or ten and I never stopped. I never stopped till I started writing novels, really. It was my main thing and I never thought of myself ever as being anything but a poet, and when I started writing novels and began getting a name for novel-writing, I still thought of myself as a poet and I still do. I can't somehow think of myself as a novelist as such, because I have a poetic way of seeing things. I know that I have. It's different from not every novelist, but different from the novelists in the sense of, say, Trollope or a good novelist like Balzac. I know I'm different from that sort of writer, for better or worse.

INTERVIEWER: It has to do with your vision as much as anything, doesn't it?

SPARK: Yes, my vision is nearer to Flaubert or Proust or another French writer who has influenced me a great deal, called Robbe-Grillet, and the *nouveau roman* he wrote which was rather devoid of emotions; devoid of stated emotions, but not devoid of felt emotions that you read between the lines. And that to me was very much akin to another very good writer everyone knows, but I don't think he's had his due as a regular writer, and that is Simenon, and even in his non-detective, non-Maigret books, Simenon seems to me to write beautifully. I'm very influenced by French writers.

INTERVIEWER: Robbe-Grillet doesn't have the lyricism and humor that you like to put in your work, though, does he?

SPARK: No, he doesn't. All I have from him is a certain detachment. I think my best book, my favorite novel, is called *The Driver's Seat*. I don't know if you've read it. And that is very Robbe-Grillet, except I have more characters. He likes to have few characters. Clear the world of other people! But I like to have the passing scene.

INTERVIEWER: I like *The Driver's Seat* myself, very much, more each time I read it.

SPARK: I'm glad you like it. That's nice of you. I really do appreciate the interest you take in my work.

INTERVIEWER: I'm fascinated by all that you've written. So just to finish a bit on the poetry side, Allen Tate's comment that "a novel is a poem, or it is nothing," is on target, so far as you are concerned?

SPARK: Yes, very much.

INTERVIEWER: What poets do you read and return to?

SPARK: Do you know, I read American poets quite a lot. I read Crowe Ransom, Robert Frost, and Allen Tate. I read Auden. I think Auden was awfully good, very good. I'm not sure but that he wasn't even better than Eliot, although Eliot was very impressive. And now I read . . . oh dear, it's gone out of my mind. He's often published in *The New Yorker*. Yes, I know, Richard Wilbur.

INTERVIEWER: Wilbur was a distinguished member of the English faculty at Smith for years. Any Brodsky?

SPARK: I do like his work—no, there's another one. I like that Irish poet who won the Nobel Prize.

INTERVIEWER: Seamus Heaney.

SPARK: Yes, I think he's awfully good. Penelope will remind me of the names of other poets that I like. And then in England I think that Andrew Motion is a very, very fine writer, a poet. He is named for Poet Laureate now.

INTERVIEWER: A decided change after Ted Hughes, whose poetry I didn't much care for.

SPARK: It didn't move me at all. I think poetry should move you.

INTERVIEWER: Do you read our famous Emily Dickinson?

SPARK: Yes, yes, all of it. She's really good, sharp, marvelous. I used to read quite a lot of eighteenth-century poets, nineteenth-century poets, but mostly I like the metaphysicals—Marvell, Donne, all those.

INTERVIEWER: There's a greater intellectual challenge there.

SPARK: Oh, yes, and a greater charm of rhythm certainly. I wrote an article, a short article for the BBC recently, I read it on the BBC, on the difference between verse and poetry. I'm very interested in verse forms, different rhythms, different meters, different compositional types of verse, the formal ones, and different types of rhyme. I think if you master those, practice those, you can then write free verse, because you've got more to throw away. Art is essentially a throwaway activity.

INTERVIEWER: It's a matter of discipline, isn't it, learning the discipline?

SPARK: Yes, but a lot of poets have never heard of trochees, iambics, and things.

INTERVIEWER: Poetry figures in every single one of your novels, either overtly, as with Freddy Hamilton in *The Mandelbaum Gate* or with the Book of Job, that great poem which figures in one of your later novels, *The Only Problem*, or more subtly, in the rhythms, cadences, and images of your language in all your novels and stories.

SPARK: Yes [chuckles]. I can't keep away from it.

INTERVIEWER: It is about those stories I'd like to talk next. In 1951 you won the *Observer*'s short story contest with "The Seraph and the Zambesi." What drew you away from poetry towards the short story at that point?

SPARK: I was moving towards the narrative form, in my own narrative poems and my deep interest in Masefield. I wrote "The Seraph and the Zambesi" for a story competition in the *Observer*, and it won the prize. That was a milestone in my life.

INTERVIEWER: "The Seraph and the Zambesi," and several other stories—I think immediately of "The Curtain Blown by the Breeze," "Bang Bang You're Dead," and "The Pawnbroker's Wife"— have African settings, but not one novel. Why have you not written a novel set in Africa?

SPARK: I didn't feel that I lived enough there. I was in Africa enough actual years to write a novel, but I wasn't really taken much by the place. There is a great deal to be written about colonial life in Africa, but it is inevitably much too political for me. I don't work on those lines. The minute you mention Rhodesia, you're into politics, or Africa, or black and white. It's a political situation. The better novels of Doris Lessing can achieve that; I think she's very good at it. It's not my thing.

INTERVIEWER: Please correct me if I am mistaken, but I think that only three of your novels—*Robinson, Loitering with Intent, A Far Cry from Kensington*—are cast in the first person; however, a number of your short stories are in the first person. I haven't counted, but I wonder if more are in the first person than the third. Is this an important difference?

SPARK: Yes, I think so. Oh yes, I think short stories are quite different from novels in that they deal in the first place with one theme and only one, with maybe some trimmings. But a novel can ramify through incidents and works out to one composition. I think that a short story, also, is designed to gain immediate sympathy. And nothing gains sympathy better than the first person. It's very difficult writing in the first person because you can't be everywhere as you can in a third-person novel, in which you could be a fly on the wall, you could be everything, you can see everything, you can describe everything, you can enter people's minds. With a first person you can only see what one person can see and hear. But it attracts sympathy.

INTERVIEWER: A little more on the stories (and some novels): Why don't children figure more in your work? I think that "The First Year of My Life" is a simply brilliant use of an infant's point of view for reinventing the Neoplatonic/Wordsworthian notion that children are born with preternatural powers of perception that gradually atrophy in the world we live in. But no more children?

SPARK: Well, I have one in *Robinson*, I have two horror children in a short story called "The Twins." No, I don't have many children. I think it's because they're not ready yet. You can't size them up, you can't make them the center. I don't like devoting, putting onto children, ideas and thoughts they couldn't possibly have. There is not much of a story to be made out of children's perceptions. They feel very, very keenly, but it's not articulated. And it is difficult for an author to articulate for them. I think, of course, of "The Turn of the Screw." But are they children as you mean the word? I don't really like children in literature. I can't think of any that I like very much, least of all Ivy Compton-Burnett, her children seem to me to be absolutely far too old for their years. And I don't like Dickens's children at all. I'm sorry for them, it's awful, but it's too heart-wrenching for words, too much of a tract. I don't know—I don't like children undifferentiated to challenge me as a writer. They are differentiated, I know, like animals, no two are alike. They tend to be clumped together. I suppose children's points of view are memorable, individually. I did it in my own *Curriculum Vitae*, and that's as far as I can go.

INTERVIEWER: In an interview for the *Paris Review* some time ago, William Trevor called the short story "the art of the glimpse," elaborating, "if the novel is like an intricate Renaissance painting, the short story is an Impressionist painting." What is your definition of a short story?

SPARK: Yes, I think that's very good, "impressionist." But I wouldn't say always "impressionist"; it could be a detail in a bigger picture, from which you gather what the big picture is like. There are all sorts of short stories, of course. Quite a lot of very good short stories are not about anything. They just don't add up and they're good. It's because they have atmosphere, they have characters. Personally, though, I like a story that is round, that has a sharp point. I wouldn't say it's necessarily an impressionist painting. I would say it's more of a detail.

INTERVIEWER: What short story writers offer you stories that fit what you've just described?

SPARK: Well, de Maupassant. I think that Somerset Maugham is really wonderful. I know that he's not considered a highbrow. I don't care what he's considered. He really is very, very good at observing, especially in the East, observing things. Graham Greene is very good as a writer, and Evelyn Waugh as a writer of short stories. Graham Greene has atmosphere; and Evelyn Waugh had point, he always had some quite sharp and revealing point.

INTERVIEWER: I'm wondering about Edna O'Brien, but I shouldn't suggest a name to you.

SPARK: I think she's such a good writer. She's very fresh. Whatever she writes seems to me freshly written, as if she was quite a young person. I think she's very good. I like to read her. I don't think it adds up to much, but I like to read her work. It gives me pleasure.

INTERVIEWER: Few people likely know that you have written three enchanting stories for children: "The Very Fine Clock," "The French Window," and "The Small Telephone." What drew you to write stories for children, and why have you written so few of them?

SPARK: Well, really, I don't know. I was in a hotel, I was waiting for a visa to go to the United States and I had my usual pens and papers around me to write a novel or something. So I just took a notebook and wrote those three short stories one morning. I thought it would be nice for children and grown-ups to read this, just for a change. And I had a secretary then. She was a Miss Stirling from Stirling Castle, Stirling and I thought it would amuse her, too. She was so tired of doing nothing, I thought I'd give her something funny to type out.

INTERVIEWER: But no more than those three?

SPARK: Oh, no—I got my visa.

INTERVIEWER: Could we talk about character and shift our attention to your novels now?

SPARK: Yes.

INTERVIEWER: I think your first novel, *The Comforters*, is a terribly complicated and complex exercise deliberately designed to be so, isn't it?

SPARK: Yes.

INTERVIEWER: And really it seems to be a kind of Shakespearean overture to all of your novels, a kind of act I, scene 1 for all that follows.

SPARK: I think so. I'm glad to hear you say so, because I've always felt it was something like that. I was setting the tone that I wanted to set. I had had an experience, a visual experience of—I'm not sure if it's what they call dyslexia—words jumping together. I rather foolishly took Dexedrine, which had this effect on my mind, that the words got jumbled up on the page. Well, I got better, I stopped taking barbiturates. It's not a habit-forming drug, so I stopped taking it. And I wasn't well for a while, but I got better, and the words stopped jumping about. Well, I wanted to write about this experience in a way, because it came at a sort of special moment in my life, when things were changing rapidly for me. I was becoming a writer and various things like that; I became a Catholic. And I wanted to write, but you can't really write about a visual thing like that—it's technically quite impossible, so I changed into voices. The funny thing was that somebody sent it to Evelyn Waugh, and he was in the middle of *The Ordeal of Gilbert Pinfold*, and he said himself he couldn't see how he could end his book. When he saw mine, he saw how he could end it by making this the book within the book. But he was very, very generous. He reviewed my book and said that it was like a book he was doing, but I had done it better, which really was very generous. And for a young writer, I was very impressed by all this and naturally it helped the book and it helped me to be established. So I was very grateful to Evelyn Waugh. And he had been having some other sort of pills just at the same time I was, which had made him really hear voices. I was very interested in his experience and his book about it.

INTERVIEWER: But he couldn't figure out the significance of the title, *The Comforters*, could he?

SPARK: No. I had various titles. One was called *Holiday of Obligation*. Then I thought, it's rather like Job's comforters, all the people around this young girl and so I called it *The Comforters*. It's a good title, but it's not a very meaningful title. I tried many, many titles, but the publishers didn't like them and we left it at that.

INTERVIEWER: Would you change it today?

SPARK: I would, but I don't know what I'd change it to. I really can't think of a title. I will offer a $500 prize for a better title if you will be the judge.

INTERVIEWER: I accept the honor and eagerly await entries. *The Comforters* introduces one of the great themes of your work: suffering. You have had a longstanding interest in the problem of human suffering; your citing Newman's remark about suffering ("Let them be to the trouble I have been to") in discussing your own conversion in *Curriculum Vitae* is amplified by your preoccupation with the Book of Job: you wrote about it for the Church of England newspaper, and began a book on it in 1953, I think.

SPARK: Yes.

INTERVIEWER: And though suffering figures in every novel you've written, you returned to that theme in a larger and more explicit way in *The Only Problem* (1984). Exactly what fascination does the Book of Job cast for you?

SPARK: Well, first of all, it is the most beautiful poem, it really is the most beautiful thing in the Bible, to my mind, and one of the best pieces of literature out of antiquity: the reality of Job, the way it describes his reaction. And then I thought, oh, these different characters: I must see where they differ, and it suddenly struck me they don't differ. One comes in after the other and they say the same thing, and they were just like modern interrogators coming in, going over the whole thing, trying to get a confession out of a man, going over and over again, each one a different person. The technique of third-degree interrogation was there and Job was saying, "No, I didn't do it, I'm innocent," and they kept saying, "but Job you must have done something," and he keeps saying to the last, "I haven't done anything." Then comes God out of the whirlwind, saying, "I did this, I did that . . ." which takes Job's mind off his sufferings. It's the most beautiful poem, really, and psychologically sound.

INTERVIEWER: And it's a moving paradigm for the inexplicability of human suffering.

SPARK: Oh it is, absolutely. It is.

INTERVIEWER: And the foolishness of trying to answer the question.

SPARK: Yes. We know before and after, we know that time is an invention but that . . . that we somehow have agreed to suffer for a very good cause, it could be. Suffering as punishment for past sins is simply not logical, it's not rational; it simply doesn't stand to any reason that children should suffer—it's mad, that theory.

INTERVIEWER: Considering a topic like that really radically underscores the insufficiency of the human intellect, doesn't it?

SPARK: Yes. It's exactly what we can't see, can't grasp; and without mystery, there's no point to faith. That's what faith is. If we understood everything, there would be no point in faith.

INTERVIEWER: I like what you say in *The Only Problem* about the Book of Job: "it's a poem, it's not meant to come clear."

SPARK: Oh no, it is a poem, it's not a tract.

INTERVIEWER: And the difficulty of living, especially now, with what cannot be explained.

SPARK: Yes, that's true. That's what I know.

INTERVIEWER: People don't want to live with mystery.

SPARK: No, but they have to, because life is a mystery, ultimately. The more we know, the more we don't know. And that is the truth.

INTERVIEWER: In reviewing the run of your novels, something of a departure occurs with *The Mandelbaum Gate*, which is a longer, more capacious creation; and more markedly afterwards with *The Public Image, The Driver's Seat, Not to Disturb, The Hothouse by the East River*: it is not just that these novels seem written under the spell of the *nouveau roman* but that the transcendent plot has disappeared. Is that a fair assessment?

SPARK: I think perhaps yes. I think so. The plots aren't quite so tight. There is a plot and many subplots in *Memento Mori. The Mandelbaum Gate* was an experimental novel; it doesn't look like an experiment. As an experiment, every chapter is from somebody else's point of view, that's the focus, the ego of the novel: not the I but the ego, the kind of narrator and focus is from different characters—the point of view of Freddy, then the Arab boy, then the girl. Every chapter is from a different point of view. And then I published part of the novel as short stories in *The New Yorker*, two or three of those chapters. I rather enjoyed doing that. It took me two years. It was much longer than I'd taken over anything else.

INTERVIEWER: The critical reception was curious. There were some critics who were rather disappointed, although not so disappointed as they'd been in the past. They thought it was a realistic novel and the touches of realism pleased them.

SPARK: Yes. At the Israeli universities it was well received but among the Israeli public, they didn't like it, because . . . I don't quite know why. They go along with a great deal of propaganda build-up which they believe in themselves. They don't like anything that breaks down their propaganda and with the Israeli readers having suffered greatly, they obviously looked for a great deal of that suffering to be—as with the Holocaust—to be emphasized. However I didn't emphasize the Eichmann trial. I gave what I experienced.

INTERVIEWER: That's someone else's novel, not yours, that some of the critics were looking for.

SPARK: Yes, I felt so.

INTERVIEWER: Another fascination of yours is violence: in your novels some horrible things take place—Georgina Hogg's drowning in *The Comforters*, a young woman murdered by nine strokes with a corkscrew in *The Ballad of Peckham Rye*, the fatal bludgeoning of Dame Lettie in *Memento Mori*, the brutal rape-murder of Lise in *The Driver's Seat*. Why so much violence in the works of a "Catholic novelist"?

SPARK: But there is violence in the world. I felt that even when I was writing Miss Brodie; there's this girl who dies in a fire, first she's in the lab and afraid of fire. I just feel life is cruel. You take that away, it's like taking away something very vital: these touches of violence are really vital to the story. If you can imagine the story without them. And it seemed to me in the case of Dame Lettie that the horror spoke for itself. It was a case that one might read of in the papers any day. You know that Newman wrote somewhere that it is impossible to write a novel without the factor of evil. He was right.

INTERVIEWER: Bernard Bergonzi has claimed that with Proust's *À la recherche du temps perdu* and Joyce's *Ulysses* "the minute investigation of human behaviour in all its aspects—physical, psychological, and moral—is taken as far as it can go while still remaining within the bounds of coherence." It seems to me that the canon of your work argues effectively against Bergonzi's contention. Am I mistaken?

SPARK: I feel Bernard Bergonzi was referring to human nature up to the first half of this century, maybe starting about the Renaissance. Certainly I believe that human nature changes and differs according to historical and geographical environments. Society has changed since Proust's time and literature has changed accordingly. For one thing, we have read and absorbed and applied Proust, which Proust could not do. Joyce could not "know" Joyce as we continue to do. But of course these two masters of human observation are incomparable as to their methods of penetration into the strange promptings of human behavior.

INTERVIEWER: Could I just follow up a bit on Proust? He is one of several writers you acknowledge as a considerable influence on your own fiction. You wrote a fine essay on him for the Church of England newspaper in 1953. Newman and Beerbohm are the other two, and one can readily appreciate their influence—but that of Proust is a little trickier, given his pagan aesthetic. How does this writer figure in your own thought and work?

SPARK: Proust, on the page, does not come out, to me, as an aesthetic pagan. What and how he writes is not in keeping with his personal claims. He seems to be informed by an advanced Judeo-Christian spirituality. The values arising from *À la recherche* are distinct from those arising, for instance, from Greek tragedy. Proust has a real grasp of the "reversal of circumstances" of Aristotle, whereas the Greeks could not portray Proust's lingering sorrow in such circumstances. Proust also differed spiritually from the sentimentalists who preceded him in France, England, and Germany. Yes, I believe my thought was greatly influenced by Proust, and my sense of construction in the novel was greatly assisted by his examples. In the matter of construction take, for instance, the chapter of *À la recherche* where Swann ends by deciding Odette was not, after all, his style. Next page, new chapter: Swann has already been married to Odette for some years. That is a great constructional stroke.

INTERVIEWER: Agreed. But I suppose you have been drawn to the subgenre of the detective story for very different reasons. Time and again the detective story makes its appearance—in a number of forms and ways—in your work. *The Comforters, Robinson,* and *Memento*

*Mori* come to mind immediately, though they are by no means the only examples. What is the particular appeal of the detective story for you? Is it in any way connected, somehow, with the detective story's flourishing in the late nineteenth century, during an age of declining religious faith?

SPARK: Yes, I admire good detective stories, their lack of frills and nonsense. I am also fascinated by suspense, on which many detective stories lean. I think suspense is often heightened if the author "gives away" the plot from the very beginning. The reader is then all the more anxious to find out how the conclusion came about. I adopted this method (from a chance remark of Trollope) in my book *The Driver's Seat*.

INTERVIEWER: With the publication of *The Mandelbaum Gate* in 1965, a number of critics who'd not warmed to your earlier work brightened. They thought they'd detected more realism, though they were upset that contemporary Middle Eastern politics, particularly the Eichmann trial, had only a minor role. Yet succeeding novels set them off again—why?

SPARK: I'm not sure that I saw these criticisms because I don't actually remember them. I was moving from New York, where I was working, to Italy at that time and I really didn't see what was written about me, but I do know that I got a lot of new readers, a whole class of new readers, through that book because it was more realistic, more like a regular novel and I think people were hoping I would continue on that line, but it was only a form and I wanted to try. I haven't ever repeated a form of the novel in any way. I like to vary with each novel, each theme, the religious theme of *The Mandelbaum Gate* called for a special type of form.

INTERVIEWER: Do you believe that the pursuit of absolute truth, to which you are committed, and the realistic tradition are incompatible?

SPARK: I don't know that I'm committed to absolute truth. I know that that is a doctrinal fact but I wouldn't be too sure that advanced Catholic thought is not becoming more relative in its attitude to truth. You can see already the Church's attitude to comparative religions and even to no faiths, to people of no religion, that the Church is moving towards—rather belatedly—towards a more relative stand-point. I don't know that it is in conflict with realism. As a matter of fact I find that realistic novels are more committed to dogmatic and absolute truth. I would say that the novels of George Eliot are extremely realistic and rather dogmatic, and more absolute in their tone.

INTERVIEWER: In the late 1960s your novels become more condensed and economical. Some said that you'd simply fallen under the spell of Robbe-Grillet and the *nouveau roman*, but there's more to it than that, isn't there?

SPARK: I don't know. I was very much impressed by Robbe-Grillet, not by the effect of what he did. I wasn't carried away by his novels, but I was very, very interested in his methods. He got away from the novel of descriptions of people's feelings: "he felt," "he thought," and "he said." "He said" is a fact, actually an outward fact, but "he felt" and "he thought" are interpolations by the author. I was very interested in this. I wrote one book without any expressed feelings and thoughts, that was *The Ballad of Peckham Rye*, although nobody has noticed that because feelings and thoughts are very much implied and understood. Feelings and thoughts are even more emphasized when you don't mention them. I like the construction, the first-person construction, of Robbe-Grillet's novels. The actual novels themselves were rather too flimsy for this very impressive body of effort. It didn't carry the weight of the new technique.

INTERVIEWER: Your novels of the late '60s—*The Public Image* (1968), *The Driver's Seat* (1970), *Not to Disturb* (1971)—Malcolm Bradbury called "all novels of ending," but isn't every novel you've written eschatologically driven?

SPARK: Yes, they are.

INTERVIEWER: Some of your later novels are indeed more difficult; I think particularly of *The Only Problem* (1984) and *Symposium* (1990). The clues to a resolution, if there be one, are minimal, perhaps even absent. Isn't that a compliment to the reader?

SPARK: In a sense, yes. In *Not to Disturb* I really have explored the question of whether causality and chronology are identical, and I think not. I think both the future and the past can influence the present—the future as much as the past; and I tried to write a novel to that effect.

INTERVIEWER: Your novel *Symposium* seems to me far more important than most have realized or admitted, and very much of a piece with all your work: how do you see it?

SPARK: Well, I'm glad you see it that way. I've got very little idea of how different people see my novels because the year they come out the critics tend to think one thing, and then when it comes out in paperback it comes up again for criticism and they [think] another thing. And then it is published in, say, France or Germany and there's a totally different reaction, and so I never know at any one time what critics are thinking of my work. But as for my intentions, I did intend *Symposium* to be taken as an essay on the mystery of life, I would say, such as would have been discussed by the Greeks at a dinner party.

INTERVIEWER: A little more about your reader, theoretically: At the end of *Loitering with Intent*, Fleur Talbot writes, "I always hope the readers of my novels are of good quality. I wouldn't like to think of anyone cheap reading my books." Do you think about your reader while you are writing? Do you hold for some sort of contractual, even adversarial relationship with your reader?

SPARK: No. I don't think of a reader as such, but I do have a very strong critical faculty. I did a lot of literary criticism before I wrote novels, and that seems to work simultaneously with my writing. I'm aware of how it sounds as I'm writing the novel.

INTERVIEWER: About the reader, practically: Your readership really spans the globe, with your works translated into twenty-six or so languages. Where is your work most popular? Are particular novels popular in certain countries?

SPARK: I'm not sure of that. I think that my novel *Memento Mori*, which is about death and old age, is popular in Germany. They tend to like what one might roughly call pessimistic novels. In France my best appreciated works are my short stories. The French like them very much, as do the Americans. I mean North Americans. In England their favorite book is *The Prime of Miss Jean Brodie* because it really is very much belonging to home. They love it in Scotland, too.

INTERVIEWER: You once wrote of Newman, "if there is one comprehensive thing that can be said about Newman's writing, it is that he has a 'voice,' it is his and no one else's." Same can be said of you. Is voice something only the reader hears? Do you hear your own voice in what you write? Do you seek to create distinctive voices for particular works?

SPARK: I am aware of my own voice, always, because I speak with my own voice and nobody else's. I could never write with my own voice in the same way that Newman did because he had one subject which was theology, largely. Even his wonderful autobiography was theology and his voice is discernible through it all. With a novel you have to adopt various other voices. For instance, I wrote a short story called "You Should Have Seen the Mess" in which the "I" of the story, the first person, is quite a horror, a girl who is a compulsive cleaner, clean-compulsive, and there, although it's my voice which is pronouncing the story, it really is the voice of this girl, and it is quite a different prose from what I would use if I was speaking in some other character's voice. In my novel, *A Far Cry from Kensington*, I have a voice which isn't really that of myself, it's a character called Mrs. Hawkins and she has phrases and ideas that aren't mine, phrases which I wouldn't use, so that I think if I have a voice it's probably only in the descriptive and narrative parts.

INTERVIEWER: One of the particular characteristics of your narrative procedure is a fondness for the early giveaway—early on in *The Prime of Miss Jean Brodie* we know that it is Sandy who has betrayed Miss Brodie; by page 7 in *The Girls of Slender Means*, we know Nicholas' fate; by page 25 in *The Driver's Seat* we know that Lise will be found murdered; more recently, we know early on in *Symposium* that Hilda Damien will be found dead in her son's flat. Is this device simply to direct the reader's attention elsewhere, away from plot?

SPARK: Well I think it does two things: that device is quite deliberate. To give the show away in a strange way, strange manner, creates suspense more than the withholding of information does. Secondly, I think that it has an eschatological function, as you indicate—mentioned—before.

INTERVIEWER: Often your handling of time throws your readers for a loop. In *The Girls of Slender Means*, the fireman who comes on near novel's end says, "It's just a question of time." Is it?

SPARK: In *The Girls of Slender Means* everything is very finely attuned to timing and to actual measurements and sizes, and certainly a question of time does come into it. I do not like to (as I did in my novel, *Not to Disturb*) play around with time because it is a very important ingredient of the novel, especially the modern novel.

INTERVIEWER: One of the things that has been overlooked about your work is the influence of Greek tragedy upon your fiction, an impact on style, construction, and theme—the paradox, perhaps, of pagan influence? Throughout your work one can detect elements like the frequent use of choral element/commentator; highly stylized/dramatic dialogue; the themes of suffering and wisdom. It came as no surprise that in *Symposium* you drew upon classical precedent for more than epigraphs. Is it fair—truthful—to think about Greek tragedy and your work?

SPARK: Oh very much so because I was very influenced by Aristotle's *Poetics*. I believe I was very, very attracted by the idea of peripeteia—that means the reversal of circumstances—and I also, especially in *The Driver's Seat*, which I think is the nearest I have to Greek tragedy, I also have that feeling for fear and pity, which Aristotle claims is the essence of tragedy.

INTERVIEWER: And because you look straight on at the world, evil figures prominently in your novels as well. Indeed, every one of your novels and a good many, if not all, of your stories deal with the reality of evil. Are we talking about the traditional notion of the Devil, wandering the world seeking the ruin of souls, or something quite other?

SPARK: No. We are talking about Evil. I am not sure about the Devil as a personification. But the Devil is a very useful personification of what we really do see in the world. Evil exists. Evil is in the world and we know it because we are born with a knowledge of good and evil.

INTERVIEWER: And the power of evil can be hypnotic, can't it?

SPARK: I suppose it can. I hadn't thought of that.

INTERVIEWER: If I read what I think of as the single most striking passage in *The Prime of Miss Jean Brodie* correctly—I refer to that moment near the end of the novel when we are told that it had taken Sandy Stranger, now Sister Helena of the Transfiguration, twenty-five years to recover from the creeping vision of disorder perpetrated by

Jean Brodie—and about the dynamic contrast between someone like Nancy Hawkins who cannot help doing good and Margaret Murchie Damien who cannot help doing evil, confrontation and struggle between the forces of good and evil is the heart of your fiction, isn't it?

SPARK: Well, if you put it like that I am sure it's true. I hadn't thought of it that way. I think that's a very interesting summing up. The thing about Miss Brodie in a person like Sandy—I don't put Sandy as the wise woman of the novel, I put Miss Brodie as the wiser—the thing about Miss Brodie is that she has no restraining influence whatsoever, whereas Sandy did. In the case of *Symposium* Margaret Murchie is a kind of carrier, just as some people carry a disease although they don't necessarily suffer from it themselves, but they carry it.

INTERVIEWER: And though you have employed a number of literary genres and forms, parable and medieval morality play seem closest to you.

SPARK: I really wouldn't know about that. I used to read morality plays. I suppose they sank in like a lot of my early reading of literature and had an effect. But I am really not aware of it.

INTERVIEWER: And so, given your not shrinking from the presentation of such themes and concerns, might you agree with Flannery O'Connor who noted that "to look at the worst will be for him [the writer] no more than an act of trust in God"?

SPARK: Oh yes, I do agree with that.

INTERVIEWER: In *Loitering with Intent*, Fleur Talbot notes, "When people say that nothing happens in their lives, I believe them. But you must understand that everything happens to an artist; time is always redeemed, nothing is lost, and wonders never cease." What moves you to write?

SPARK: What moves me to write is pure instinct. As soon as I could hold a pencil in my hand. I have always wanted to express my thoughts.

INTERVIEWER: Where and when do you like to write?

SPARK: I like to write at home in the morning and after lunch. About 4 o'clock in the afternoon. At home at my desk.

INTERVIEWER: Do you write in longhand or on a computer?

SPARK: I write in longhand.

INTERVIEWER: Do you keep a journal or notebook to record what you see and hear?

SPARK: I have notes, but I don't keep a journal.

INTERVIEWER: Do novels spring from overheard conversation, as Fleur Talbot claims in *Loitering with Intent*?

SPARK: They can do. They can spring from anything; if one is on the wavelength of a novel, I would say, all sorts of messages come unbidden.

INTERVIEWER: Although I know that you recast *The Hothouse by the East River* all in the present tense and that you redid the trial scene in *The Bachelors*, I also know that it is said that revision is not a part of the writing process for you. Frank Kermode once said that you showed him a draft of *The Mandelbaum Gate* and there wasn't a single revision on it. Does revision really play so minor a role in your work?

SPARK: Yes, it is very rare that I have to recast anything. As far as construction is concerned, I never touch it and it is only for factual reasons that I did do the trial scene in *The Bachelors* over again. What I do is generally go through the typescript, the first, and change it here and there for words and commas and other punctuations. I don't do very much revision but I do a lot of thinking before I write to make up for it.

INTERVIEWER: Edna O'Brien has said that "when a writer, or an artist, has the feeling that he can't do it anymore, he descends into hell. So you must keep in mind that although it may stop, it can come back." Have you known times like these, between projects? How have you coped?

SPARK: Well, rather in the middle of projects. I just cope by writing about something and I don't have a great deal of trouble with writer's blocks, so far. My greatest struggle comes from interruptions of an everyday nature.

INTERVIEWER: When you reflect on your life as a writer, what has been the greatest obstacle to your success? Has being a woman been a drawback in making your way in the literary world and in life?

SPARK: I don't think so. I don't think being a woman has. I think my greatest obstacle might have been the family problems and problems with insensitive publishers, of which I've had my share. Especially to begin with, and in some respects I've had to research every book that I write because I'm very careful about that. That takes a lot of time. That is an obstacle. And the only other obstacle would be limitations of talent about which I can't pronounce.

INTERVIEWER: How do you respond to being labeled a "woman writer"?

SPARK: I don't like it because I know myself to be just a writer. For my first short story, which won a prize in the *Observer*, we had to put a pseudonym and our own name in an envelope when we submitted the story, and I did this and they were quite sure that the author was a man. I don't know why they thought it was. They were quite amazed that it was a woman who had written the story. But I quite like to think that my writing belongs to no particular sex.

INTERVIEWER: What do you think of this feminist endeavor to teach courses about literature by women exclusively, or to publish anthologies with the work of women only?

SPARK: I think it's a mess. I think for commercial purposes it might be a very good idea. People buy, women buy, women's books, I suppose, but for no other literary purpose. It's not intrinsically a good idea.

INTERVIEWER: What about Harold Bloom's notion of the anxiety of influence? How do your perceive your relationship to great writers of the past?

SPARK: Well, I think if I was writing for anybody, although I don't, as I've already said, have a particular person in mind, or a reader in mind, I would be quite happy to write for the great past, for the great dead.

INTERVIEWER: What about Virginia Woolf? The only place I know where you mention Virginia Woolf is in your marvelous story, "The First Year of My Life."

SPARK: I enjoy reading Virginia Woolf, but I find her rather tiresome at times, indulged and tiresome. That's all I can say.

INTERVIEWER: An American critic and a British novelist appeared on television to lament the passing of Iris Murdoch; they agreed that she was "the greatest English [*sic*] woman writer of the twentieth century." What do you think about that judgment?

SPARK: Well, I don't know yet. It's too near. I think Iris was a very considerable writer and I wouldn't say she was the greatest woman writer of the twentieth century. But I do think that she shouldn't be judged as a woman writer at all. Just as a writer. I think she's among the best of the twentieth-century writers.

INTERVIEWER: What writers—male or female—do you read now with more than passing interest?

SPARK: Heinrich Boll, Marquez. I still read Newman with great delight for his wonderful prose and his clarity of mind. Simenon and Proust. Henry James.

INTERVIEWER: One the Russian formalists, Shklovsky, said that "art helps us to recover the sensation of life." Do you agree?

SPARK: Oh, I do. It renews one, one is renewed by it. If I go to a very good show, you know in an art gallery, I feel completely renewed, as if I were young again.

INTERVIEWER: What makes an artist? Was Joyce correct when he isolated silence, cunning, and exile?

SPARK: What makes an artist is really a genetic question. It's a mixture of aspirations and genes, and opportunity.

INTERVIEWER: Does the artist have a moral responsibility? The words of Nancy Hawkins in *A Far Cry from Kensington* come to mind: "It is enough for me to discriminate mentally and leave the rest to God." Is discriminating mentally enough for you?

SPARK: Discriminating mentally? No, you have to actually act on your convictions.

INTERVIEWER: You once described the artist as "a changer of actuality into something else." What is that "something else"?

SPARK: Art is that something else. Art is an illusion which contains truth.

INTERVIEWER: Among other things, your fiction is distinguished by its often satiric edge. Despite a long and rich tradition in Western literature, a tradition you know well as translator of Horace and Juvenal, satire and ridicule seem misunderstood today—misunderstood by writer and reader alike? Why?

SPARK: That is a matter of education. Satire and ridicule will always be understood by a more sophisticated mind and it is—I can only say that it is a matter of education.

INTERVIEWER: In *The Bachelors*, Ronald Bridges says, "being Catholic is part of my human existence." How do you react to those who persist in calling you a "Catholic novelist"? Does such a term have any meaning?

SPARK: It has a meaning, yes, but only like saying that I write in the English language. It's only a fact. I'm a Catholic and a novelist, but there's no such thing as a Catholic novel, unless it's a piece of propaganda.

INTERVIEWER: Your conversion coincided with your finding your voice as a novelist. Flannery O'Connor once said that when the subject of "the Catholic novelist and his problems" came up, she always thought of the story of St Francis and the Wolf of Gubbio: after his conversion, the wolf remained a wolf. For her, the Catholic writer who fought his nature as a writer would be like that wolf walking on his hind legs." Is that a valid and meaningful way of describing conversion and identity, so far as you are concerned?

SPARK: Yes, it is. It's the first time I've heard it and I think it is most amusing and very valid.

INTERVIEWER: So you would agree with O'Connor who said, "when people have told me that because I am a Catholic, I cannot be an artist, I have had to reply, ruefully, that because I am a Catholic, I cannot afford to be less than artist"?

SPARK: Yes, I think there's plenty in that, too, but . . . it is true that if someone who is destined to be a Catholic—in an artist who is destined to be a Catholic—they had better become a Catholic or they will never be an artist. We must follow our "daemon," our inward voice as Socrates taught.

INTERVIEWER: Incumbent upon you, then, amongst other responsibilities, is the duty to banish sentimentality, de-emphasize what O'Connor called "an early arrival at a mock state of innocence," and look at everything before describing truthfully what you see?

SPARK: I'm not very conscious of that process, of any process like that to tell the truth. I'm not very conscious of any process that goes along with my writing, my work. What I'm conscious of is the technique I adopt, methods that I adopt. Let me tell you I enjoy my writing.

INTERVIEWER: You are not propagandizing, proselytizing, or evangelizing for Roman Catholicism in your novels; indeed, you've created some of the nastiest Catholics in fiction, and you are often at pains to point out that the burden of living the faith in the modern world is great. What spiritual impact would you like your fiction to have? I wonder if Flannery O'Connor's comment that "Job was left with a renewed sense of mystery" might describe the impact you'd like a reader to feel after having read one of your novels?

SPARK: Yes, I would like people to feel that I have opened windows and doors in the mind.

INTERVIEWER: And one last excerpt from O'Connor: "The fiction writer presents mystery through manners, grace through nature, but when he finishes there always has to be left over that sense of Mystery which cannot be accounted for any human formula."

SPARK: Yes, I think that's true, but I do think that what this mystery must convey is a certain plausibility. There is no use having just mystery if people don't believe it. I approached that problem in my first short story, "The Seraph and the Zambesi," because I had a seraph which was giving out heat and it was gliding and skimming the surface of the river, so I made it give out heat, give out spray, heat, steam from its own seraph-like heat to make it a part of natural history. And that is a kind on microcosm of what I have always done.

INTERVIEWER: Frank Kermode once said that, "the devil as the father of lies, is the patron of novelists." How can this be, especially for someone with your vision and commitment?

SPARK: I think it's quite a profound statement and it really needs Frank Kermode to answer that question himself, but certainly the novel is not truth. It is lies, officially. Fiction is not truth. But through these lies some truth emerges. I don't know if the Devil is the patron of the novel. I haven't thought of that. Maybe Frank Kermode will enlighten us one day.

INTERVIEWER: Did *Aiding and Abetting* with its controversial subject matter—the case of the infamous "Lucky" Lucan—prompt a different response from the usual?

SPARK: Yes, it involved a great many new readers who had read about the Lucan case in the newspapers or heard of the Lucan case through the media. The response was very intelligent, too.

INTERVIEWER: How about from the family of the missing peer?

SPARK: Before publication the wife was afraid I was going to libel her, but in fact I didn't touch on the family apart from the known facts. But I suppose they are quite used to being discussed.

INTERVIEWER: *Aiding and Abetting* reads like a screenplay on its own—has anyone approached you about acquiring the rights for television or film? Do you have any ideas about casting?

SPARK: Yes. Film rights are always being discussed and there are discussions going on right now. I don't know what will become of them as I have an agent to handle all dramatic developments of my work. About casting: Anthony Hopkins would be a very good Lucan. It is an ideal part for an actor, as he would have to play two men at the same time.

INTERVIEWER: Some people might not know that you have written poetry from an early age and that you have continued to do so, with frequent publication in *The New Yorker*. What is it about writing poetry that continues to hold you?

SPARK: Poetry is, to me, the expression of an idea that I conceive in passing. I suppose it is like catching a butterfly. If I have an idea that is suitable for poetry, and has some lyrical feeling, I write a short poem. My poems are to be published shortly by New Directions and a selection by La Table Ronde in both French and English in the same volume.

INTERVIEWER: Can you give us some sense of the scope and contents of the New Directions volume?

SPARK: The contents are all poems that I want to keep, dating from 1947 to the present day. If there is a constant thread running through them all, I would say it is lyrical thought.

INTERVIEWER: Grand prizes have come your way in the course of your career, most recently the Boccaccio Europa Prize for European Literature. How do you feel about the whole business of prizes and awards? Does one mean more than the others?

SPARK: I greatly approve of prizes for outstanding work and literary effort. I think that prizes, precisely like the Boccaccio Europa Prize, are to be cherished more than the commercial literary prizes for novels, but of course one always needs money to buy a new automobile, etc. I don't think prizes should be split between separate authors, such as recently happened in England when the David Cohen British Literature Award was divided between Beryl Bainbridge and Thom Gunn. I know they both deserved the prize, but they should have had the full prize at different times.

INTERVIEWER: Now that *The Finishing School* has been published, what projects will occupy your attention, both in the near term and later? A second volume of your autobiography? Another novel or play? More poetry?

SPARK: I hope to write more poetry and I also have in mind writing a collection of biographical vignettes. I am at an age now when I don't enjoy the prospect of any massive enterprise.

INTERVIEWER: Is there any question I've not asked, that you would like to ask and answer?

SPARK: Well. Let's think. Yes, I would like to know what physiologists and psychologists make of the fact of inspiration. I haven't heard that anyone has come up with a scientific definition or answer.

INTERVIEWER: Thank you, Dame Muriel.

NOTE

Robert E. Hosmer Jr., "'Fascinated by Suspense': An Interview with Muriel Spark," originally appeared in a slightly different version in *Salmagundi* (Spring–Summer 2005). Copyright © Robert E. Hosmer Jr.

# CHAPTER SIXTEEN

# "Now I Know They Want Me Back-Stage"

BARBARA EPLER

## THE VERY FAMOUS AUTHORS NEVER ARRIVE ALONE

The very famous authors never arrive alone: even at our small publishing house there's always a boyfriend, a wife, an agent, a translator, a journalist in tow. Walking into the office in 1993, Muriel Spark—dressed in floor-length couture, coiffed to perfection, radiantly smiling—*is* alone for exactly half a second. I round the corner, alerted by the doorbell, and there she is, pretty as her picture (and authors are never that, either), what I can see of her in the swarm of excited New Directions' employees. I see a glimpse of a scarf trailing to her shoes, I see she's a beauty, and the curled top of her auburn hair, and a truly great smile. I see a bejeweled hand and a cane. She enjoys all the admiration that way a cat enjoys cream.

In our office for a half-minute, and already the affair is mutual. It is *love*. I've never seen anything like it. All restraint (which we'd all been schooled in: Do Not Touch the Authors) was gone: "You look like a million bucks" "I am so *thrilled* to meet you!" "Would you sign my book?" "I love your books—" There was no getting my colleagues away from her. Especially as she had no desire to be separated: "You are all so marvelous, really . . . You are too kind . . ."

I don't know how but I finally moved her out onto the little balcony, where I had the idea I'd be alone with this adored writer; and, yes, I had her all to myself as she stepped onto the little terrace looking over downtown: "What a wonderful view! I do love Manhattan—" she exclaimed to me—and to Griselda my boss, Declan a fellow editor, Laurie the publicity director, and Dan the art director: all, hopelessly besotted, had crowded onto the tiny balcony. The peach tree and cherry tree were admired by Muriel; Muriel was admired by all. I couldn't help myself either: "Is that a Schlumberger?" I asked about her fabulous brooch in a fish shape on her gorgeous gown at the shoulder. "Oh yes it is! Do you like it?" Oh yes we were on sure ground: we could talk jewelry for hours but then we were off the terrace again. The mob carried her off. She was like a solo Beatle. I was embarrassed, and I was in the thick of the pack. Muriel relished the tour, the long hallway studded with author photos: "Oh yes, Dylan Thomas, poor Caitlin, but what a lovely muff. Oh and Tennessee Williams: what a handsome portrait . . . and Pound, well I never cared for Pound you know . . ." She admired the Cocteau drawing, the old editions in the library: everything was worth a good look.

At last, at long last, I had narrowed the party down to Griselda and Declan and we were off to lunch, just the four of us. On the street, we meet Muriel's incredibly handsome driver in aviator sunglasses. Muriel, smiling happily, exclaimed, "Oh Manuel, how lovely, please meet my publishers—this is Griselda, Declan and Barbara—and I think we will walk—it is very nearby isn't it?" She waved her cane like a long-necked flower. We told Manuel the address, and he replied, "I will be directly at the entrance, Mrs. Spark."

At the restaurant I am happy at last, seated at Muriel's left hand, eyeing her brooch like a hungry raccoon. The two of us thick in jewelry talk, she confides she would like an Order of the Golden Fleece collar, with her bright eye on my own products. (Griselda lent over her menu to kindly point out: "Look, Muriel, she made the rings, the earrings *and* the bracelet!") All were pulled off and admired with real generosity and even zeal: she liked it that I was a craftsperson. She acted as if it were a distinction—rather than a distraction from publishing—and as if it made me more agreeable to contemplate. She mentioned that each time she finished a novel she bought herself a piece of jewelry: "This," she explained about the Schlumberger brooch, "I gave myself for *The Only Problem.*" She gave herself a lot. She gave herself to us and she gave herself the sheer pleasure of being present and of being Muriel Spark.

"Muriel, last night—" Griselda began, cackling, happy to let a cat out of the bag, "last night . . ." (We'd all been at her triumphant sold-out 92nd Street Y reading in honor of *Curriculum Vitae*: the limo and the reading were both arranged by Houghton-Mifflin, her uptown publisher. We'd been thrilled that she read some of our *Public Image* at the Y.) "Last night you know how they asked the audience to write questions for the author down on little scraps of paper? Barbara's question was too strange for the moderator, but it really is a marvelous question: Would you like to hear it, Muriel?"

"Oh *yes*, of course," Muriel smiles back at Griselda: they are like two bright-eyed very old children.

"Well," I began . . . and faltered: "Well—"

"Muriel, she asked," Griselda plowed, delighted, on: "she asked if you had ever met the Devil!"

Muriel is instantly serious. Looking down at the tablecloth, she replies: "No I have not. My view is that the Devil per se does not exist, does not exist as a *person*, but rather like the Holy Spirit, is an entity, an ineffable being, but not, no, not a person. And I myself have never met the Devil though I do believe like the Holy Spirit he can influence people." This was delivered steadily with a fraction of a smile.

"But you have written about the Devil, so I just wondered—"

"I have never," Muriel said kindly, "written about the Devil."

"But Dougal Douglas, or Douglas Dougal, and—"

"Dougal Douglas is not the Devil," Muriel corrects.

"He has *horns!*"

"Bony protrusions," Muriel smiles at me, indicating the spots on her own forehead, and turns away. "And Declan now tell me, what do you do at New Directions . . ."

And after lunch, Muriel insists that we all climb into her limo and be driven the half a block back: the pleasure of her pleasure at the absurdity of the ride, and the two-handed long handshake of farewell. Then she waves farewell like a queen; and the three of us, tumbled out on 14th Street, grin and wave, the thrilled Americans.

## NEVER STAY WITH AN AUTHOR

After a wild ride from Bologna (and a little behind schedule), Claudia and I find the Arezzo exit, we find the right tiny road, we find San Giovanni di Oliveto: success! We drive up the beautiful road between olive groves, grey green over dry stone walls: and there's the house. The beautiful fourteenth-century church with its ancient rectory and its happy red door. We park, we knock, a dog goes wild but does not appear.

We knock again. Silence. We knock again, louder, setting off the dog again, and at last, a very deep fake pirate voice, calls through the door, demanding: "FRIEND OR FOE?"

"Friends!" we squeak. The door, which must be three inches thick, opens, and a friendly laughing Penelope is there: pretty, grey-haired, in work-a-day clothing. We have never met but in her amused and tony British way she waves us in, "Muriel is languishing for you, we thought we'd lost you to the bad men . . . We were sure you had been gobbled up by the Italians . . ."

The stone entryway is dim; the house is massive and crazily layered. Muriel is resting and Penelope is charming, showing us our rooms, with windows set into walls two and a half feet thick: one leans in to see the olive groves, the rolling hills, the tower far away . . . all green and grey under a beautiful watery sun. "So, what would you like to do after your long drive? A nap? A walk?"

We'd love a walk . . .

"Well, you will have to watch out for the boars—and for the Bad Men—oh, and look, Barbara, here is a brand-new story—Muriel wanted you to see it . . ." I am happy and sad at the same time: we had just published *Open to the Public,* billed as ALL the stories of Muriel Spark.

As we exit, Penelope warns us: "Oh the awful hunters—the Bad Men—you be careful; they love to kill the song birds. Only in Italy do people kill song birds, they cook them up, or actually down, to the size of a piece of popcorn. When I was first here the hills sang, now you'll see, the birds are gone. The awful people: they shoot the song-birds and they poison the cats. Muriel has their back up—she has written about them, the nasty poisoners, she's been on the radio and TV and they all hate her, it's been marvelous. Now do be careful, you can walk down to the village or, maybe nicer—though do watch out for the bad men—the road that way is beautiful," she says, unbolting a myriad of locks, and letting us out the huge heavy door: "Knock loud when you come back," she chides, pulling back the door, glee-fully adding, "*If* you come back . . ."

Claudia and I march along like children, burbling about our host-esses, the seen and the unseen, and just the pleasure of arrival . . . That sense of being in your own two shoes, complete, parked, luggage-free, welcome and welcomed. After rambling a while, we spot a shady grove, a perfect place to lie down, where the light falls in through the olive trees, broken up like light falling through water. The air is deli-cious and smells like a just-snapped dry twig.

I listen for boars. I listen for Bad Men. I lie down. The birds *are* there and they are singing. After a while, Claudia begins to read aloud "The Snobs." She lets each page fall. In about twenty minutes, she is through. I am sitting bolt upright, and then we look at one another. The story concerns an author just finishing a novel at her best friend's chateau, and it is all going very well until the awful, really hideous *"guests" from Hell* arrive one day on a tour bus. They then refuse to leave. *The snobs will not leave. . . . The hideous guests . . .* I can see the white around Claudia's eyes. It is clear that we are both tempted to bolt. But then we laugh, hearing the snap of the little trap, set happily by Muriel, ensconced in the castle, wearing a cat smile.

NEVER BE TOO SURE

And then, back after our walk and the alarm of "The Snobs," we are greeted so happily by Muriel, in high style; we sit down to cham-pagne and lasagna. We enjoy the dinner under a beautiful portrait of

Muriel reading. In Penelope's painting she is a small, young, slender figure in a garden chair; in the forefront is a large crouched cat, admiring Muriel, perhaps as it would a bird. (Later, I read in a BBC interview: "*You've described yourself as a writer in action, and you've said you pause and you think, and then you strike like a cat.*" "Yes, that's it. I strike. I'm absolutely aware of striking.")

I had a plan: "Party favors!" I cried and laid on each of the three ladies' plates a little bamboo woven box with something pearly and sparkly inside. The perfect ice breaker. And Muriel, delighted with her ring, hooting at Penelope: "Mine's nicer! Oh you shan't have it! No, no! *It's mine!*"

Beaming at me, twirling her hand to catch the light, admiring the chatoyancy of the spectralites, words she also twirled—"Oh *spectralites*! Oh, *chatoyancy*!" to me, and "No, you shan't have it!" to Penelope.

In her glee, she promises to show me all her jewels the next day ("well, the really good stuff is in the bank, but there are some lovely little things here, too").

The next morning we pad after Muriel into her inner sanctum. She lifts a small painting off the wall, revealing a neat little safe, and begins some expert twirling. She adopts a mock-professional safe-cracking air, gets it on the first try and, smiling, pulls the door open. It is stuffed to the gills with little velvet pouches, little suede boxes, larger gold-trimmed leather boxes, modern Roman bright leather boxes, old red velvet ring boxes, in every size. We take handfuls, and following Muriel, lay them all on her bed: quite a heap.

An Austro-Hungarian emerald and pearl necklace; a very 1960s abstract gold and diamond brooch; a plant-like emerald and gold modern brooch; a huge sunburst gold ring; a pair of old sapphire and pearl earrings: each has a story. Many are gifts to herself from herself. There we are: they hardly know us—pawing emeralds on our first visit.

NEVER FORGET

If you are Muriel Spark, cats like being rubbed with your elbow. Going to mass can be dangerously germy. Her movie star glasses, her joy in her new reading machine, manipulating its magnification powers.

How she threw a party! The caterers in tall white hats, the open fire pits, the endless champagne, the wickedly glamorous lighting: one tipsy lady walked off in the wrong direction, into the dark, in search of her car, only to return a little battered with runs in her stockings and her hair awry a while later to gamely plop right back in her chair for more wine.

It was a strange thing over the years of publishing Muriel's books to watch one thing after another happen as if predicted, as if foreseen by Muriel: the rigors of health in old age (so brilliantly described in *Memento Mori*); the death by lightning (like a zipper) in *Not to Disturb*, decades before a lightning ball flashed thorough their house in a terrible storm; all the robberies in her novels and their own dreadful burglary (everything taken: all the paintings, including the one with Muriel reading, watched by a giant cat).

Somehow one day the topic of organ donation came up on a visit to the ladies. "Oh, *no thank you*," Muriel remarked. "Reminds me of our two friends: they were always going on and on about how important it is to be an organ donor, about our having to have it marked on our driver's licenses—that they can harvest our poor organs, and you know what happened to them?" Muriel leans in. "An awful accident. They'd pulled their little car over on the autostrada and an enormous lorry just smashed them, just obliterated the car." Penelope concurs: "Terrible, just a smear." And Muriel concludes, "Nothing left to donate."

In Florence in the late 1990s for Muriel's hip operation, Penelope reports that the hospital is located right across the road from the English Cemetery. Muriel's doctor jokingly remarked: "How convenient."

When I mentioned Eugene Walter's memoir about life in the heyday of Rome in the 1950s, I comment: "Muriel, you're in it!"

"*Oh no!* He couldn't tell the truth *if his life depended on it!*"

"But still, you're pretty delightful in it, in your grand salon, all empty and airy and you giving magic carpet rides to your cats: dragging a cat around on a rug behind you as you run all through the apartment, whooping—"

"I never swooped around like that in my life! He is the one, that awful Eugene Walter, you remember Penny, he's the one who pawned the poor Princess's silver: she never did get it back, no, never saw it again . . ."

Jealousy: Another famous woman writer accused Muriel of being jealous of her. "But," Muriel explained, "when someone says you are jealous of them, you know what *that* means don't you?" And leaning in, gleeful: "That they're jealous of *you*!"

America is sex-obsessed. Sitting on Muriel's bed as she marvels over CNN's endless coverage of the Clinton impeachment. She waves derisively at the fat pink face of Ken Starr: "Well they can't very well accuse the president of that, of adultery *and* lying!" "Well, I guess they can . . ." I begin. "Oh no!" Muriel states: "lying *is part* of adultery!"

On our last visit, Muriel and Penelope take us to the most marvelous restaurant in a castle up in the hills; they serve many courses and the castle has its own vineyard—there are ghosts on the wine labels. It is the most beautiful time; next we're taken to see the Piero della Francescas, and they seem as perfect as our visit.


NEVER BEGIN AT THE BEGINNING

First things last: the day when I was about twenty years old and standing in Paragon, on the second floor of that wonderful (now gone) 12th Street bookstore, browsing in the mustiness. My hand fell on *Muriel Spark: Trio*. Or was it *Three by Spark*? I remember the contents, *The Comforters, The Ballad of Peckham Rye, Memento Mori*. The old clothbound edition was inscribed "Howard Moss." "Muriel Spark" sounded somehow familiar. I read the first page of *The Comforters*, and then the second and third and bought the book. I knew I had encountered a wizard. Never could a first novel be so magisterial. (What was wrong with Mr. Moss?)


NEVER END EITHER

Muriel's way of regarding you with such keen interest, like a child opening a present: but she makes you feel that you, her visitor, are the gift. And Muriel actually being the gift: the incredible and amazing books. And in her being the radiance: the pleasure she allowed in giving and taking pleasure, the circularity a rondelle like one of her poems.

I recently had a dream of setting up chairs for a New Directions' reading: it wasn't important in the dream that I was not sure which author might be reading; I was arranging the seats and handing out drinks. And out of the blue, Muriel walks up beaming. I am so thrilled: we hug, and she *is* there as large as life and happy. I wonder, "But didn't you pass away?" Yet, hugging her, we are all so happy, and I think, *Apparently not!* "Oh it is so wonderful to see you all again," Muriel smiles at us: "It is so wonderful to see you all again—my favorite publishers!" (She would say that sometimes, to give us a thrill.) "Now I know they want me back-stage." And she is off, caning along between eager fans, smiling all around, happy, rejoicing. "You'll come and see me right afterwards, won't you?"

## NOVELS

*The Comforters.* London: Macmillan, 1957.
*Robinson.* London: Macmillan, 1958.
*Memento Mori.* London: Macmillan, 1959.
*The Bachelors.* London: Macmillan, 1960.
*The Ballad of Peckham Rye.* London: Macmillan, 1960.
*The Prime of Miss Jean Brodie.* London: Macmillan, 1961.
*The Girls of Slender Means.* London: Macmillan, 1963.
*The Mandelbaum Gate.* London: Macmillan, 1965.
*The Public Image.* London: Macmillan, 1968.
*The Driver's Seat.* London: Macmillan, 1970.
*Not to Disturb.* London: Macmillan, 1971.
*The Hothouse by the East River.* London: Macmillan, 1973.
*The Abbess of Crewe.* London: Macmillan, 1974.
*The Takeover.* London: Macmillan, 1976.
*Territorial Rights.* London: Macmillan, 1979.
*Loitering with Intent.* London: Macmillan, 1981.
*The Only Problem.* London: Bodley Head, 1984.
*A Far Cry from Kensington.* London: Macmillan, 1988.
*Symposium.* London: Macmillan, 1990.
*Reality and Dreams.* London: Constable, 1996.
*Aiding and Abetting.* London: Constable, 2000.
*The Finishing School.* London: Constable, 2004.

## AUTOBIOGRAPHY

*Curriculum Vitae.* London: Constable, 1992.

## DRAMA

*Voices at Play.* London: Macmillan, 1961.
*Doctors of Philosophy.* London: Macmillan, 1963.


## STORIES

*The Go-Away Bird and Other Stories.* London: Macmillan, 1958.
*Voices at Play.* London: Macmillan, 1961.
*Collected Stories I.* London: Macmillan, 1967.
*The Stories of Muriel Spark.* London: Macmillan, 1987.
*Bang-Bang You're Dead and Other Stories.* St. Albans: Granada, 1987.
*Collected Short Stories.* London: Macmillan, 1995.
*Madam X.* London: Colophon Press, 1996.
*Harper and Wilton.* London: Colophon Press, 1996.
*Open to the Public: New and Collected Stories.* London: New Directions Books, 1997.
*The Quest for Lavishes Ghast.* London: Cuckoo Press, 1998.
*The Young Man Who Discovered the Secret of Life and Other Stories.* London: Travelman Publishing, 1999.
*All the Stories of Muriel Spark.* New York: New Directions, 2001.


## UNANTHOLOGIZED STORIES

"The End of Summer Time." *London Mystery Selection* 37 (June 1958): 65–69.


## CHILDREN'S BOOKS

*The Very Fine Clock.* London: Macmillan, 1968.
*The Small Telephone.* London: Colophon Press, 1983.
*The French Window.* London: Colophon Press, 1993.


## POETRY COLLECTIONS

*The Fanfarlo and Other Verse.* Adlington: Hand and Flower Press, 1952.
*Collected Poems I.* London: Macmillan, 1967.
*Going Up to Sotheby's.* St. Albans: Granada, 1982.
*All the Poems of Muriel Spark.* New York: New Directions, 2004.

OTHER PUBLISHED POETRY

"Snowflakes." *Gillespie's School Magazine* (July 1929): 31.

"Starshine," "Other Worlds," and "The Door of Youth." *Gillespie's School Magazine* (July 1932): 37–38, 50–51.

"Pan's Pipes" and "Says Beetle." *Gillespie's School Magazine* (July 1932): 22–23.

"Shell Tales," "A Dog-Day Dream in School," "Out of a Book," and "Seagulls in the Links." *Gillespie's School Magazine* (July 1933): 28–29, 36–37, 44.

"Dust." *Gillespie's School Magazine* (July 1934): 16.

"The Idiot." *School: The Annual of the Rhodesia Teachers' Association* 2.1 (1941): 39.

"On Seeing the Picasso-Matisse Exhibition, London, December, 1945." *Poetry Review* 37.2 (April–May 1946): 165–66.

"The Victoria Falls." *Poetry Review* 37.4 (August–September 1946): 285.

"Frantic a Child Ran" and "Three Thoughts in Africa." *Poetry of To-Day* 1.72 (1946): 80–82.

"Poem for a Pianist," "They Sigh for Old Dreams," and "I Have a Lovely Meadow Land." *Poetry of To-Day* 3.74 (1946): 10–12.

"The Well." *Poetry Review* 38.1 (January–February 1947): 82–86.

"Leaning Over an Old Wall" and "Autumn." *Poetry Review* 38.2 (March–April 1947): 106, 155–56.

"The Robe and the Song." *Poetry Review* 38.4 (May–June 1947): 192–93.

"Birthday." *Poetry Review* 38.4 (July–August 1947): 270.

"The Bells at Bray" and "Cadmus." *Poetry Review* 38.5 (September–October 1947): 359, 379.

"Omega." *Poetry Review* 38.6 (December 1947): 519.

"Song." *Outposts* 9 (Winter 1947): 10.

"You, Dreamer." *Canadian Poetry Magazine* 11.3 (March 1948): 23.

"Invocation to a Child." *Poetry Quarterly* 10.1 (Spring 1948): 22.

"Poem." *Prospect* 2.10 (Summer 1948): 5.

"Song of the Divided Lover." *Poetry Commonwealth* 1 (Summer 1948): 5.

"Standing in Dusk." *Variegation* 3.3 (Summer 1948): 3.

"Lost Lover." *Outposts* 11 (Autumn 1948): 3.

"Anniversary." *Variegation* 3.4 (Autumn 1948): 17.

"A Letter to Howard." *Poetry Quarterly* 10.3 (Autumn 1948): 152.

"Tracing the Landscape." *Poetry Commonwealth* 1 (Summer 1948): 5.

"Sin." *Punch* 215 (27 October 1948): 395.

"She Wore His Luck on Her Breast." *Outposts* 12 (Winter 1948): 10, 19–20.

Spark, Muriel, and Howard Sergeant. *Reassessment: Poetry Pamphlet No. 1*. London: G. Nicholls, 1948.

"Reassessment." *Women's Review* 4 (January 1949): 18–19.

"Magdalen." *Gemini* 1 (May 1949): 3.

"The Beads." *Poetry Quarterly* 11.3 (Autumn 1949): 144–45, 162–68.

"Indian Feathers." *Variegation* 4.4 (Autumn 1949): 4.

"This Plato." *Arena* 21 (1949): 12–13.

"The Voice of One Lost Sings Its Gain." *Poetry Quarterly* 11.4 (Winter 1949–50): 221.

"Invocation in a Churchyard on All Hallow's Eve." *Gemini* 3 (January 1950).

"The Dancers." *World Review* (12 February 1950): 3.

"Elegy in a Kensington Churchyard." *Fortnightly* 174 (September 1950): 191.

"Kindness or Weakness?" *Public Opinion* 4643 (17 November 1950): 24.

Spark, Muriel, and Derek Stanford. Translation of "Poem XVII" from *Shadows of My Love*. Guillaume Apollinaire. *Poetry Quarterly* 12.3 (Autumn 1950): 149.

"Snowfall." *Public Opinion* (16 March 1951): 688.

"No Need for Shouting." *Poetry Quarterly* 13.1 (Spring 1951): 24.

"A Sleep of Prisoners." *Spectator* 6413 (25 May 1951): 688.

"Birthday Acrostic." *Poetry Quarterly* 13.2 (Summer 1951): 68.

"Portrait." *Recurrence* 2.2 (Autumn 1951): 7.

"Conundrum" and "The Miners." *Chanticleer* 1.1 (Autumn 1952): 10.

"A Letter at Christmas." *Outposts* 20 (1952): 5–6.

"The Pearl-Miners." *Poetry* (Chicago) (September 1953): 318–20.

"Domestic Dawn." *Saturday Review* 40 (13 April 1957): 30.

"Faith and Works." *Aylesford Review* 2.2 (Winter 1957–58): 37.

"On the Lack of Sleep." *New Yorker* 7 December 1963: 58.

"The Card Party." *New Yorker* 28 December 1963: 30.

"Canaan." *New Yorker* 16 April 1966: 48.

"The She-Wolf." *New Yorker* 4 February 1967: 44.

"The Messengers." *New Yorker* 16 September 1967: 44.

"Created and Abandoned." *New Yorker* 12 November 1979: 60.

"Conversation Piece." *New Yorker* 23 November 1981: 54.

"Abroad." *New York Times Magazine* 10 March 1984: SW134.

"The Lonely Shoe Lying on the Road." *New Yorker* 20 September 1993: 82.

"The Dark Music of the Rue du Cherche-Midi." *New Yorker* 21 February 1994: 104.

"Mungo Bays the Moon." *New Yorker* 25 November 1996: 66.

"The Empty Space." *New Yorker* 4 February 2002: 30.

"What?" *Times Literary Supplement* 5 July 2002: 10.

"Holidays." *New Yorker* 16 December 2002: 86.

"That Bad Cold." *New Yorker* 10 March 2003: 44.

"Facts." *Times Literary Supplement* 21 March 2003: 17.

"Hospital." *Times Literary Supplement* 21 March 2003: 17.

"The Creative Writing Class," "Letters," and "Hats." *World Literature Today* 78.3/4 (September–December 2004): 5, 6.

"Nothing to Do" and "Is This the Place?" *Spectator* 296 (18 December 2004): 90, 91.


CRITICISM AND BIOGRAPHY

Spark, Muriel, and Derek Stanford, eds. *Tribute to Wordsworth*. London: Windgate, 1950.

*Child of Light: A Reassessment of Mary Wollstonecraft Shelley*. Hadleigh, Essex: Tower Bridge Publications, 1951.

Spark, Muriel, and Derek Stanford. *Mary Shelley*. Essex: Tower Bridge Publications Limited, 1951.

*A Selection of Poems by Emily Brontë*. London: Grey Walls Press, 1952.

Spark, Muriel, and Derek Stanford, eds. *My Best Mary: Selected Letters of Mary Shelley*. London: Wingate, 1953.

*John Masefield*. London: Peter Nevill, 1953 (republished with new introduction, London: Hutchinson, 1991; Pimlico, 1992).

Spark, Muriel, and Derek Stanford, eds. *Emily Brontë: Her Life and Work*. London: Peter Owen, 1953.

*The Brontë Letters: A Compilation with Essays*. London: Peter Nevill, 1954; Norman, OK: University of Oklahoma Press, 1954.

Spark, Muriel, and Derek Stanford. *Letters of John Henry Newman*. London: Peter Owen, 1957.

*The Plain Sermons of Cardinal Newman*. Ed. Vincent Blehl. Foreword by Muriel Spark. New York: Herder and Herder, 1964.

*Mary Shelley*. 2nd ed. London: Penguin, 1987.

*The Essence of the Brontës*. London: Peter Owen, 1993.


ESSAY COLLECTIONS

*The Golden Fleece: Essays*. Ed. Penelope Jardine. Manchester, UK: Carcanet, 2014.

*The Informed Air: Essays*. [U.S. edition of above.] Ed. Penelope Jardine. New York: New Directions, 2014.


CRITICAL ESSAYS AND JOURNALISM

"The Catholic View." *Poetry Review* 38.6 (December 1947): 402–5.

"Criticism, Effects and Morals." *Poetry Review* 39.1 (February 1948): 3–6.

"Reassessment." *Poetry Review* 39.2 (April–May 1948): 103–4.

"Reassessment—II." *Poetry Review* 39.3 (August–September 1948): 234.

"A Pamphlet from the U.S." *Poetry Review* 39.4 (October–November 1948): 318.

"Poetry and Politics." *Parliamentary Affairs* 1.4 (Autumn 1948): 12–23.

"Review Article." *Outposts* 12 (Winter 1948): 10, 19–20.

"Poetry and the Other Arts." *Poetry Review* 39.5 (December 1948–January 1949): 390.

"The Dramatic Works of T. S. Eliot." *Women's Review* 5 (March–April 1949): 2–4.

"African Handouts." *New English Weekly* 26 May 1949.

"The Poetry of Anne Brontë." *New English Weekly* 26 May 1949: 79.

Review of *Beyond the Terminus of the Stars*, by Hugo Manning. *Poetry Quarterly* 11.2 (Summer 1949): 122–23.

"Introduction." *Forum* 1.1 (Summer 1949): 1.

"The Poet in Mr. Eliot's Ideal State." *Outposts* 14 (Summer 1949): 26–28.

"Cecil Day Lewis." *Poetry Quarterly* 11.3 (Autumn 1949): 162–68.

"Poetry and the American Government." *Parliamentary Affairs* 3.1 (Winter 1949): 260–72.

"Three Vintages." *Poetry Quarterly* 11.3 (Winter 1949): 252–56.

"Mary Shelley: A Prophetic Novelist." *Listener* 22 February 1951: 305–6.

"*Passionate Humbugs*, Book Review." *Public Opinion* 23 February 1951: 20.

"*The Complete Frost*, Book Review." *Public Opinion* 30 March 1951: 21–22.

"Two-Way." *Church of England Newspaper* 25 May 1951: 12.

"In Defense of the Highbrow." *Public Opinion* 8 June 1951: 28.

"The Stricken Deer" [Review of *William Cowper* by Norman Nicholson]. *Poetry Quarterly* 13.2 (Summer 1951): 89–90.

"The Apple and the Spectroscope" [Review of *The Apple and the Spectroscope* by T. R. Henn]. *Poetry Quarterly* 13.2 (Autumn 1951): 139–44.

"A Post Romantic" [Review of *The Poems of Arthur Hugh Clough*]. *Poetry Quarterly* 14.2 (Summer 1952): 59–60.

"Does Celibacy Affect Judgement?" *Church of England Newspaper* 16 November 1951: 10.

"Civilised Humor." *Journal of the Scottish Secondary Teachers' Association* 7.1 (October 1952): 30, 32.

"Ex-pagan Reader." *Church of England Newspaper* 19 December 1952: 10.

"Reflections on Mr Tate's Article." *World Review* (January 1953): 2–3.

"All Laugh Together?" *English Speaking World* 35.2 (March 1953): 32–36.

"R. E. Williams, 'Punch Replies.'" *English Speaking World* 35.3 (May 1953): 24–28.

"If I Were Punch." *English Speaking World* 35.4 (June 1953): 23–25.

"Eyes and Noses." *Observer* (18 July 1953): 8.

"Edinburgh Festival Diary: A Prophet's Married Life." *Church of England Newspaper* 4 September 1953: 5.

"Edinburgh Festival Diary: The Wisdom of T. S. Eliot." *Church of England Newspaper* 11 September 1953: 5.

"The Religion of an Agnostic: A Sacramental View of the World in the Writings of Proust." *Church of England Newspaper* 27 November 1953: 1.

"Review of John Masefield." *Journal of the Scottish Secondary Teachers' Association* 8.2 (February 1954): 58.

"Aylesford Priory." *Tablet* 12 February 1955: 154.

"The Mystery of Job's Suffering: Jung's New Interpretation Examined." *Church of England Newspaper* 15 April 1955: 7.

"St. Monica." *Canadian Messenger of the Sacred Heart* 67.5 (May 1957): 318–25.

Review of *Ronald Knox* by Evelyn Waugh. *Twentieth Century* 167 (January 1960): 83–85.

"How I Became a Novelist." *John O'London's Magazine* 1 December 1960: 683.

"Minor Victorians." *Observer* 19 February 1961: 29.

"The Poet's House." *Critic* 19.4 (February–March 1961): 15–16.

"My Conversion." *Twentieth Century* 170 (Autumn 1961): 58–63.

"Edinburgh Born." *New Statesman* 10 August 1962: 180.

"Poetry and Politics." *Parliamentary Affairs* 16 (Autumn 1963): 445–54.

"The Sermons of Newman." *Critic* 22.6 (June–July 1964): 531–34.

"The Quest for Lavishes Ghast." *Esquire* (December 1964): 216, 218.

"Memento Mori for Bluebell." *Book Week* (27 December 1964): 11.

"The Brontës as Teachers." *New Yorker* 22 January 1966: 30–33.

"Exotic Departures." *New Yorker* 28 January 1967: 31–32.

"What Images Return." *Memoirs of a Modern Scotland*. Ed. Karl Miller. London: Faber and Faber, 1970. 151–53.

"The Desegregation of Art." *The Annual Blashfield Foundation Address, Proceedings of the American Academy of Arts and Letters and the National Institute of Arts and Letters.* 2nd ser., 21. New York: Spiral Press, 1971. 21–27.

"When Israel Went to the Vatican." *Tablet* 24 March 1973: 277–78.

"A Pardon for the Guy." *Observer* 6 November 1977: 13.

"Heinrich Boll." *New York Times Book Review* 4 December 1977: 66–70.

"The Books That Made Writers." *New York Times Book Review* 25 November 1979: 7.

"Venice in Fall and Winter." *New York Times* October 25, 1981: sec. 10, 8.

"I Would Like to Have Written." *New York Times Book Review* 6 December 1981: 7.

"My Most Obnoxious Writer." *New York Times Book Review* 29 August 1982: 7.

"The Pleasures of Rereading." *New York Times Book Review* 12 June 1983: 14.

"Breaking Up With Jake" [Review of *Pitch Dark* by Renata Adler]. *New York Times Book Review* 18 December 1983: 1, 24.

"My Rome." *New York Times Magazine* 13 March 1983: 36, 39, 70–72.

"Side Roads of Tuscany." *New York Times Magazine* 7 October 1984: 28–29, 72–79.

"Spirit and Substance." *Vanity Fair* 12.47 (December 1984): 102–3.

"On Love." *Partisan Review* 51.4 (1984/1985): 780–83.

"Footnote to a Poet's House." *Architectural Digest* 42.11 (November 1985): 38, 44, 48.

"Echoes of Shelley in Italy." *Architectural Digest* 43.6 (June 1986): 262, 266.

"Ravenna's Jewelled Churches." *New York Times Magazine* 4 October 1987: 50–51, 68–71.

"Plotting an Alpine Cliffhanger: The Baggatti-Valsecchi Villa above Lake Como." *Architectural Digest* 44.2 (February 1987): 124–29, 156.

"A Winterson Tale: Review of Jeanette Winterson's *The Passion*." *Vanity Fair* (May 1988): 57–58.

"Manzu Giacomo: Triumphs of Matter and Spirit in Bronze." *Architectural Digest* 45.5 (May 1988): 40, 46, 52.

"The Sensation That Is Venice." *London Times* 13 May 1988: 32.

"Tranquil Tuscany." *World Press Review* 35.7 (July 1988): 61.

"Shelley's Last House." *Independent Magazine* 29 July 1989: 42–43.

"Whose Europe Is It Anyway?" *New Statesman and Society* 22 June 1990: 16.

"Home Thoughts: Muriel Spark on How to Write a Letter." *Independent Magazine* 18 August 1990: 16.

"The Ravenna Mosaics." *Antique and New Art* (Winter 1990): 122–25.

"The School on the Links." *New Yorker* 25 March 1991: 75–85.

"Visiting the Laureate." *New Yorker* 26 August 1991: 63.

"Venture into Africa." *New Yorker* 2 March 1992: 73.

"Living With Culture." *Chronicles of Culture* (April 1993): 18–19.

"Highland Flings." *Sunday Times* 23 June 1996: sec. 7, 1.

"My Watch, a True Story." *New Yorker* 2 June 1997: 63.

"My Madeleine." *New Yorker* 25 December 2000–1 January 2001: 105.

## INTERVIEWS WITH MURIEL SPARK *(BY INTERVIEWER)*

Barber, Lynn, "The Elusive Magician." *Independent on Sunday* 23 September 1990: 8, 10.

Blume, Mary. "Muriel Spark: The Infinitely Mysterious." *International Herald Tribune* 29 May 1989: 16.

Booker, James, and Margaritta Estevez. "Interview with Dame Muriel Spark." *Women's Studies* 33.8 (December 2004): 1035–46.

Brockes, Emma. "The Guardian Profile: Muriel Spark, the Genteel Assassin." *Guardian* 27 May 2000: 6.

Brown, Allan. "Will the Read Muriel Spark Please Stand Up?" *Sunday Times* [London] 5 April 1998: 6.

Close, Ajay. "Nothing Like a Grand Dame." *Scotsman* 6 March 2004: sec. 2, 1.

Conti, Samantha. "Murder, She Wrote." *W Magazine* (March 2001): 214, 216.

Cornwell, John. "Published and Be Damned: An Interview with Muriel Spark." *Sunday Times* [London] 15 May 1994: 19–25.

Daspin, Eileen. "A Spark of Evil." *W Magazine* 21–28 January 1991: 14.

Emerson, Joyce. "The Mental Squint of Muriel Spark." *Sunday Times* [London] 30 September 1962: 14.

Frankel, S. "An Interview with Muriel Spark." *Partisan Review* 54.3 (1987): 443–57.

Franks, Allan. "Igniting the Spark." *Times Magazine* [London] 13 June 1998: 18–22.

Galloway, Janice. "The Vital Spark." *Sunday Herald Magazine* [Scotland] 11 July 1999: 6.

Gillham, Ian. "Keeping It Short: Muriel Spark Talks about Her Books." *Listener* 24 September 1970: 411–14.

Glendenning, Victoria. "Talk with Muriel Spark." *New York Times Book Review* 20 May 1979: 47–48.

Greig, Geordie. "The Dame's Fortunes." *Sunday Times* [London] 22 September 1996: sec. 7, 8–9.

Grove, Valerie. "Interview: The People Watcher." *Times Magazine* [London] 19 September 2001: 8.

Hamilton, Alex. "Alex Hamilton Interviews Muriel Spark." *Guardian* 8 November 1974: 10.

Holland, Mary. "The Prime of Muriel Spark." *Observer Colour Supplement* 17 October 1965: 8–10.

Hosmer, Robert E., Jr. "An Interview with Dame Muriel Spark." *Salmagundi* (Spring–Summer 2005): 127–58.

Hosmer, Robert E., Jr. "A Certain Plausibility: An Interview with Dame Muriel Spark." *London Magazine* (August/September 2005): 22–48.

Howard, Elizabeth Jane. "Writers in the Present Tense." *Queen* (August 1961): 136–46.

Ivry, Benjamin. "Knowing at Second Hand." *Newsweek* 24 August 1992: 56.

Jenkins, Allan. "Beneath a Stylish Surface." *Sunday Times* [London] 13 March 1988: G8–9.

Jury, Louise. "The Homecoming of Dame Muriel Spark." *Independent* [London] 23 August 2004: 5.

Kermode, Frank. "The House of Fiction: Interviews with Seven English Novelists." *Partisan Review* (Spring 1963): 79–82.

Koenig, Rhoda. "Bella Donna Muriel Spark." *British Vogue* (September 1990): 368, 430.

Lord, Graham. "The Love Letters that Muriel Spark Refused to Buy." *Sunday Express* 4 March 1973: 6.

Massie, Allan. "Spark of Inspiration." *Times* [London] 1 August 1987: 18.

McQuillan, Martin. "'The Same Informed Air': An Interview with Muriel Spark." *Theorizing Muriel Spark: Gender, Race, Deconstruction.* Ed. Martin McQuillan. New York: Palgrave, 2002. 210–29.

Merritt, Stephanie. "Men Can't Cope with Women Who Are Successful." *Observer Review* 10 September 2000: 15.

Mortimer, John. "The Culture of an Anarchist: An Interview with Muriel Spark." *Sunday Telegraph* 20 March 1988: 16–20.

Mullan, John. "Lightning, Lord Lucan and Living Forever: Dame Muriel Spark Interviewed." *Sunday Herald* [Scotland] 17 September 2000: 7.

Riding, Alan. "Mythmaker Confident in Her Memories." *New York Times* 3 November 2004: C1, 7.

Robson, David. "Spark Still Burning Bright." *Toronto Globe* 7 October 2000: D8, D9.

Ross, Deborah. "The Deborah Ross Interview: The Brightest of Sparks (And Still In Her Prime." *Independent* [London] 17 September 2001: 1, 7.

Sage, Lorna. "The Prime of Muriel Spark." *Observer* 30 May 1976: 11.

Saunders, Kate. "An Elegant Withdrawal from Literary Fuss." *Independent* 2 August 1989: 17.

Schiff, Stephen. "Muriel Spark Between the Lines." *New Yorker* 24 May 1993: 36–43.

Shakespeare, Nicholas. "Suffering and the Vital Spark." *Times* [London] 21 November 1983: 8.

Shenker, Israel. "Portrait of a Woman Reading." *Washington Post Book World* 29 September 1968: 2.

Theroux, Paul. "The Prime of Dame Muriel Spark." *Talk* (February 2001): 118–19.

REGINA BARRECA is professor of English at the University of Connecticut and author of several books, including *They Used to Call Me Snow White But I Drifted* (Penguin, 1991; UPNE, 2013); *Untamed and Unabashed: Essays on Women and Humor in British Literature* (Wayne State University Press, 1993); *Perfect Husbands and Other Fairy Tales* (Harmony/Anchor, 1993); *I'm with Stupid* (written with Gene Weingarten, Simon and Schuster, 2004); *It's Not That I'm Bitter* (St. Martin's, 2009); and *Babes in Boyland: A Personal History of Coeducation in the Ivy League* (UPNE, 2005). She is also the editor of sixteen collections and anthologies and founding editor of the scholarly journal *LIT: Literature Interpretation Theory.*

GERARD CARRUTHERS holds a personal chair in Scottish literature since 1700 at the University of Glasgow. He is general editor of the new multivolume Oxford University Press edition of the works of Robert Burns. His books include *Scottish Literature, A Critical Guide* (EUP, 2009), *Robert Burns* (Northcote, 2006); as editor, *The Devil to Stage: Five Plays by James Bridie* (ASLS, 2007), *Beyond Scotland: New Contexts for 20th-Century Scottish Literature* (Rodopi, 2004); and as co-editor, *The Cambridge Companion to Scottish Literature* (Cambridge, 2012).

BARBARA EPLER, the publisher of New Directions Press, grew up in Evanston, Illinois, and started to work for New Directions immediately after graduating from Harvard in 1984. At that point she was already a confirmed Muriel Spark devotee, but it was only in 1993 that

New Directions began its program of republishing out-of-print Spark novels, beginning with *The Public Image*. New Directions now has nineteen books by Muriel Spark on its list, including *All the Stories of Muriel Spark* and *All the Poems of Muriel Spark*, both original volumes, as well as her essay collection, *The Informed Air*, edited and with a preface by Penelope Jardine.

JOHN GLAVIN is professor of English at Georgetown University, where he also serves as director of the Office of Fellowships, Awards, and Research for Undergraduates. Originally a playwright, he has focused his scholarly work on issues of adaptation. Most recently he has authored *After Dickens: Reading, Performance and Adaptation* (Cambridge, 1999, reissued 2006) and edited *Dickens on Screen* (Cambridge, 2003) and *Dickens Adapted* (Ashgate, 2012). He has recently completed "With Shakespeare in Italy," a memoir of teaching Shakespeare's Italian plays while living in Tuscany. He was fortunate to meet Dame Muriel in the spring of 1987 in Tuscany and was able to enjoy almost two decades of personal and scholarly correspondence with her.

DAN GUNN is professor of comparative literature and English at the American University of Paris (AUP), where he is also director of the Center for Writers and Translators. He is the author of *Psychoanalysis and Fiction: An Exploration of Literary and Psychoanalytic Borders* (1988), *Wool-Gathering or How I Ended Analysis* (2002), and the novels *Almost You* (1994), *Body Language* (2002), and *The Emperor of Ice-Cream* (2014). He is co-editor of and contributor to the four-volume *The Letters of Samuel Beckett* (2009–) and is series editor of the chapbooks collectively entitled the Cahiers Series, in which no. 2 is *Walking on Air* by Muriel Spark (2007).

ROBERT E. HOSMER JR. is senior lecturer in the Department of English Language and Literature at Smith College, where he has taught courses in Western classics, British women writers, fiction, and advanced essay writing since 1989. He has written about a number of modern and contemporary authors, including Somerset Maugham,

Elizabeth Taylor, Edna O'Brien, Anita Brookner, Molly Keane, and Penelope Fitzgerald. His publications include *Contemporary British Women Writers: Texts and Strategies* (London: Macmillan, 1993) as well as reviews, essays, and interviews for the *Chicago Tribune, America,* the *Boston Globe,* and the *Paris Review.* "A Certain Plausibility: Robert Hosmer Interviews Muriel Spark" appeared in *London Magazine* (August/September 2005) and *Salmagundi* (Spring/Summer 2005). Recent publications include "Muriel Spark" in the *Cambridge Companion to Scottish Literature* (2013) and "Muriel Spark: Landscape of Life and Letters" in *London Magazine* (2013).

JOSEPH HYNES is professor emeritus of English at the University of Oregon, where his special interests are modern British fiction and drama as well as Henry James. His publications include *The Art of the Real: Muriel Spark's Novels* (1988) and articles on Dickens, James, Greene, Waugh, Stoppard, Pinter, Shaw, J. F. Powers, Henry Green, Doris Lessing, and Heinrich Boll. He edited *Critical Essays on Muriel Spark* (1992).

GABRIEL JOSIPOVICI is a writer of international reputation who retired from the faculty of the University of Sussex in 1998. He is the author of sixteen novels, short stories, plays (a dozen for stage and radio), a memoir, and a substantial body of criticism. He is a frequent reviewer for the *Times Literary Supplement.*

FRANK KERMODE, dean of English literary critics, held distinguished academic appointments at major universities in Britain and the United States, most prominently at the University of Cambridge, where he was King Edward VII Professor of English (1974–1982), and at Harvard University, where he was Charles Eliot Norton Professor (1977–1978). His numerous publications include *The Sense of an Ending* (1967); *The Art of Telling* (1983); *Forms of Attention* (1985); *Shakespeare's Language* (2000); and *The Age of Shakespeare* (2004). A prolific essayist and reviewer, he wrote regularly for the *Times Literary Supplement,* the *London Review of Books,* and the *New York Review of Books.* "Unrivalled Deftness: Four Novels by Muriel Spark" first appeared as the introduction to *Muriel Spark: The Prime of Miss Jean Brodie, The Girls of Slender Means, The Driver's Seat, The Only Problem* (Everyman, 2004).

JOHN LANCHESTER, journalist, book editor, and former restaurant reviewer, is the author of three novels, *The Debt to Pleasure* (1996); *Mr Phillips* (2000); and *Fragrant Harbor* (2002), the last shortlisted for the James Tait Black Memorial Prize for Fiction. Formerly deputy editor of the *London Review of Books*, where he now serves on the editorial board, he writes essays and criticism for the *New Yorker*, *Granta*, the *New York Times Magazine*, and the *New York Review of Books*, where "In Sparkworld" was first published.

DORIS LESSING, novelist, short story writer, essayist, and critic, long occupied a place at the forefront of English letters. Her groundbreaking novel, *The Golden Notebook* (1962), is a cornerstone of the feminist literary enterprise, and her subsequent writings dealt with humanitarian issues and causes in a number of places, including Zimbabwe, Afghanistan, and Iraq. In a distinguished literary career, with more than fifty books to her credit, several stand out: the *Canopus in Argos* series (1979–1983); *The Good Terrorist* (1985); *African Laughter: Four Visits to Zimbabwe* (1992); and *The Grandmothers* (2003). She was awarded the Nobel Prize for Literature in 2007. Though, as "Now You See Her, Now You Don't" makes clear, Doris Lessing and Muriel Spark never knew each other in Africa, in later years they became good friends and occasional literary collaborators.

DAVID MALCOLM is professor of English literature at the University of Gdansk, Poland. He is co-author (with Cheryl Alexander Malcolm) of *Jean Rhys: A Study of the Short Fiction* (Twayne, 1996) and author of *Understanding Ian McEwan* (2002), *Understanding Graham Swift* (2003), and *Understanding John McGahern* (2007, all University of South Carolina Press). He is co-editor of *The British and Irish Short Story, 1945–2000*, volume 319 of the *Dictionary of Literary Biography* (Thomson-Gale, 2006), and *The Blackwell Companion to the British and Irish Short Story* (with Cheryl Alexander Malcolm, 2008). His study *The British and Irish Short Story Handbook* was published by Wiley-Blackwell in February 2012. His translations of Polish and German prose and poetry have been published in the United Kingdom, the United States, Austria, and Poland.

JOHN MORTIMER was one of Britain's most prolific writers with dozens of novels, short stories, and plays as well as a best-selling three-part autobiography to his credit. His professional writing career spanned seven decades: his first novel, *Charade*, appeared in 1948, his last, *The Antisocial Behaviour of Horace Rumpole*, in 2007. His Rumpole books featured a distinctive and memorable character inspired by Mortimer's own career as a barrister. In addition, Sir John wrote for film (*Tea with Mussolini*, with Franco Zeffirelli) and television, adapting a number of his own Rumpole stories and Waugh's *Brideshead Revisited*. Perhaps less well-known are his interviews—with actors, writers, clergymen, and criminals—published as *In Character* (1983) and *Character Parts* (1988).

ALAN TAYLOR is a Scottish writer and journalist who is associate editor of the *Sunday Herald* and the editor of the *Scottish Review of Books*. He has contributed to numerous publications and, with his wife, Irene, co-edited two anthologies: *The Assassin's Cloak: An Anthology of the World's Greatest Diarists* and *The Secret Annexe: An Anthology of War Diarists*. He is also the editor of *The Country Diaries* and is writing a memoir of Muriel Spark.

JOHN UPDIKE, distinguished American poet, critic, short story writer, and novelist, published more than fifty books in a career that covered as many years and earned him several major literary awards and prizes, including the Pulitzer Prize, the National Book Award, and the National Book Critics' Circle Award. His five-part series of novels about Harry "Rabbit" Angstrom (*Rabbit Run*, 1960; *Rabbit Redux*, 1971; *Rabbit Is Rich*, 1981; *Rabbit at Rest*, 1990; and *Rabbit Remembered*, 2000) is an American classic. Updike's *Collected Poems* appeared in 1993, and much of his art criticism was published in *Just Looking* (1989). Updike was one of Muriel Spark's most devoted readers. He frequently reviewed her work, particularly for the *New Yorker*, where "Stonewalling Toffs" first appeared.

Robert E. Hosmer Jr.
is senior lecturer in the Department of English Language
and Literature at Smith College.